20-Minute

Learning

Connection

by Douglas B. Reeves, Ph.D.

Simon & Schuster
New York - London - Singapore - Sydney - Toronto

Kaplan Publishing
Published by Simon & Schuster, Inc.
1230 Avenue of the Americas
New York, NY 10020

For bulk sales to schools, colleges, and universities, please contact:
Order Department, Simon & Schuster, Inc.,
100 Front Street, Riverside, NJ 08075
Phone: (800) 223-2336 Fax: (800) 943-9831.

Kaplan® is a registered trademark of Kaplan, Inc.

Designed by Richard Oriolo

Manufactured in the United States of America

September 2001
10 9 8 7 6 5 4 3 2 1

Library of Congress Cataloging-in Publication-Data

ISBN: 0-7432-1171-5
ISSN:

Contents

Acknowledgements

In my discipline of statistics, we learn about *a priori* and *a posteriori* probabilities. There is a lesson in such study. My *a priori* obligations include a debt of thanks to the grandfather I never knew, Sherman Vester Reeves, but whose 1906 teaching license I found in my father's office. Teachers in Green Forest, Arkansas at the dawn of the 20th century had their test scores on their teaching licenses. If one were to search for the genesis of high academic standards, the search might profitably begin in Carroll County. My grandmother, Laura Anderson Johnson, was a teacher and superintendent of schools. My mother, Julie Reeves, taught as a volunteer for decades, with her only compensation being the love and admiration of her students. My father, J.B. Reeves, devoted his last years of his life to the professorate, but those who knew him would argue that from his time as a field artilleryman in World War II until his last breath, he was a teacher to generations.

My *a posteriori* obligations are to my children, whose enthusiasm, love, and kind words are the lights of my life. Having said those nice things, I offer this plea: If you see four children laughing uproariously in the education section of your local bookstore as they point at this book, their names are Brooks, Alexander, Julia, and James. Please tell them to behave themselves and return to the self-improvement aisle where they belong.

Between the past and future lies the present, in which I wrote this volume. Maureen McMahon of Simon & Schuster is walking evidence of Stephen King's maxim that, "to write is human; to edit, divine." Rudy Robles provided encyclopedic knowledge of state standards and synthesized his knowledge in a manner so clear and concise that he will never find employment in Washington, D.C. Lori Duggan Gold provided a steady stream of connections to reporters and policy analysts who helped me distinguish the rhetorical chaff from the intellectual wheat. Abby Remer's creative and thoughtful voice preserved an emphasis on art, music, beauty, and enjoyment in a world in which standards are stereotyped as sterile and dull.

Special thanks are due to the hundreds of parents, teachers, and school leaders who took the time to participate in focus groups and personal interviews as part of my research for this book. I am particularly indebted to Charles Sodergren, a retired principal and teacher, whose extensive comments and perspectives as a parent, grandparent, and career educator were very helpful.

For reassurance at just the right time, challenge when I needed it, and love when I least deserved it, I am always indebted to Shelley Sackett. This mother, lawyer, teacher, and wonderful spouse makes books worth writing and life worth living.

dr
Swampscott, Massachusetts

How to Get the Most Out of This Book

Here is the most important test question you will ever have:

A parent's best strategy to promote school success is to:

a) *Terrorize* children by threatening them with failure and loss of promotion to the next grade.

b) *Humiliate* children by comparing them to other kids with better scores.

c) *Exhaust* children by engaging in frantic last-minute test preparation.

d) *Build, nurture, and empower* children by giving them the skills to be confident and capable learners.

If the last choice appeals to you more than the first three alternatives, then this book is written for you. You will learn not only how to help your child meet academic standards and succeed on tests, but more importantly, you will learn how to help your child become a confident, capable, and empowered learner.

a busy parent

How Can You Make a Difference in Just 20 Minutes a Day?

Although we have not met, I believe I have a good idea of who you are and why you selected this book. You are a busy parent. Whether you work at home, at an office, or on the road, you manage multiple priorities and face many demands on your time. You want to be more involved in your children's education, but some days it seems as if the time required by your other responsibilities leaves little time for a focus on your child's schoolwork. You read the report cards and newsletters and often look at your child's schoolwork, some of which may be on your refrigerator door. You attend parent meetings and school events whenever you can. You read with your child, though not as much as you did during the preschool years. You have heard about academic standards and know that some of the tests required by the state and school district are very important, and you have a nagging feeling that your child should be better prepared. But at the end of a long day, you really don't feel like adding the role of substitute teacher to your long and growing list of duties. Am I getting close to your reality?

Practical Advice for Busy Parents

Your busy lifestyle is the norm, not the exception. Less than a third of children attending school today come from a home of the 1950s' television stereotype with a stay-at-home mother whose principal role is the management of family and nurturing of children. Far more typical is a case in which both parents are working outside the home or there is only one parent in the household, and that person must work to support the family. Even the parents who have chosen to stay at home and make the raising of children their primary goal have a far different routine than Donna Reed and her television counterparts. The caricature of the stay-at-home parent has given way to parents who are active in political, cultural, and social causes and for whom school activities are one of many other pursuits. The fact that these parents earn no money outside the home does not indicate that they are not working. These parents are subject to the same exhaustion, burn-out, and frustration as parents who rise at 5:30 every morning, get children ready for school, work a full day and more, and return home in the evening to potentially overwhelming demands for help from their children.

Here is the good news: If you can devote 20 minutes each day to helping your children succeed in school, you can make a profound difference in the intellectual development and emotional growth of your child. If you like the ideas put forth here, you may find that the amount of time you spend building confident, capable, and empowered children will be worth more than 20 minutes a day. But make no mistake: Twenty minutes a day, focused on the right questions and the most effective activities, can make a huge difference in the lives of your children and their success in school. We are not talking about aimless discussions and unproductive questions such as the exchange known to every parent:

"What did you do in school today?"
"Nothing."

Rather, we offer practical advice for kids and parents. Throughout this book you will find checklists, activities, even letters to school officials that have been written for you. While no one, least of all authors, can take the place of parents, we can save you some time and make your role in supporting school success somewhat less stressful and time consuming.

The path to student success is not without some challenges. Therefore, we will address the requirements for making some reasonable trade-offs and minor changes in family routine. Fair warning: This will involve a little less television and a little more reading. It will involve moving a few chairs and creating the space and time for an effective home learning environment. But our goal is joyful learning, not joyless boot camp. Even as an exceptionally busy parent, you can make twenty minutes into a powerful learning experience if you will commit to three principles:

First, be yourself. Find activities that you genuinely enjoy and with which you can model the creative energy that comes from intellectual engagement with your child. This book contains a wonderful variety of activities that directly support essential knowledge and skills for your child. Although the activities are arranged in the same order as the state standards, you need not go through them in that sequence. Find activities that are engaging, exciting, interesting, and fun for both you and your child.

The second principle that will make your 20 minutes most valuable is that you are supportive. Remember the last time you learned a new skill? Perhaps it was a computer program, a foreign language, or a musical instrument. No matter how talented and brilliant you are, learning new things takes some time and patience. No matter how motivated you are, learning requires some perseverance and emotional resilience. Some of the academic requirements for children in school today are as challenging for them as they were for you when you were struggling with and eventually acquiring complex skills. If you can recall the need for patience, understanding, and clarity during your own difficult learning experiences, then assume that those needs apply in exponentially large proportions for your child. An important part of your support is the clarity of your expectations. Two of the most important intellectual skills you will build with your child are reflection and self-evaluation. You will build those skills by regularly asking your child to revise and improve work, whether it is a letter to a relative or a recipe for dinner. Performing these activities will be most valuable if you encourage your child to take a moment to reflect and ask, "What did I learn and how can I do this better next time?"

Third, it is important that you are consistent. Find a regular time, perhaps immediately before or after your evening meal, for your 20-Minute Learning Connection. During this time, the television is off and the telephone answering machine is on. You are giving your children the gift that they need, indeed crave, more than anything else in the world: your undivided attention. The focus that you provide during these 20-minute activities will model the concentration and diligence that you associate with learning.

What Are Standards and Will They Last?

Academic standards have been the single most important movement in education in the last fifty years. Standards—simple statements of what students should know and be able to do—will continue long after every other contemporary educational fad has expired. While teachers and parents are weary of the "flavor of the month" educational reforms that come and go with the phases of the moon, standards have two qualities that guarantee their success: fairness and effectiveness.

Because so many educational movements have come and gone, it is reasonable to wonder whether standards will follow "new math" into oblivion. The enduring nature of standards rests with the fact that standards are the key to fairness, and fairness is a value that is timeless. Lots of trends come and go in education, but the simple requirement—that teachers, students, and parents should understand what students are expected to know and be able to do—is an enduring element of education both in the U.S. and abroad. Every state, and virtually every industrialized nation in the world, has some form of academic standards. The actual content of the standards varies, with some sets of standards emphasizing certain academic areas more than others. But the central idea of standards is consistent from Peoria to Paris, from Florida to Florence, from Los Angeles to London: School should not be an impenetrable mystery, and students have a right to know what is expected of them. Fairness will not go out of style.

Rather than exposing children to a demoralizing environment in which lucky students understand what makes the teacher happy and the unlucky just "don't get it," standards-based schools offer a clear set of expectations. With standards, students, teachers, and parents have the opportunity to know and understand what is expected of every student. Children have an innate sense of fairness. They understand that clarity is better than ambiguity and that consistency is superior to uncertainty.

The second essential quality of standards is that they are effective. When they are properly implemented, school standards have an impact on test designers, curriculum creators, teachers, and school leaders, as well as students. Far from transforming schools into joyless boot camps, effective school leaders use academic standards to make connections to the arts, extracurricular activities, and every other element of school life.

Thus standards are related not only to academic success but also to the emotional and intellectual welfare of children. Our desire is to help build confident, capable, and empowered learners. This means much more than drilling students in math and spelling facts (though that is still not a bad idea), and more than asking children to read aloud after dinner (though that is a wonderful family practice). Children become confident, capable, and empowered not only when they know the right answer on a test, but when they have the emotional resilience to persist in learning difficult concepts and when they persevere in the face of challenging, ambiguous, or seemingly impossible test items. Real student empowerment rests not in the futile effort to memorize the answer to every conceivable test question, but on the realistic prospect of developing strategies that can be used on every test in school, in college, and in the world of work and life beyond school.

empowered learners

Connections: Music, Art, Physical Education, and More

Although this book focuses on the most commonly tested academic standards—mathematics, language arts, social studies, and science—it is important to note that other areas of the school curriculum remain vitally important for your child's intellectual growth and development. Evidence from a number of research studies is consistent: Students who participate in the arts, physical education, and extracurricular activities consistently demonstrate superior academic and social skills. Thus, our focus on academic standards is not intended to diminish other athletic, artistic, and extracurricular activities that enrich the lives of children. In fact, many of the activities in this book combine academic and artistic, or academic and athletic skills.

Stress and Anxiety

Perhaps the most important message for parents is this: Stress and anxiety are communicable diseases. Children are not born with stress about school, homework, and tests; they *learn* that debilitating stress and anxiety are a part of school. Perhaps these destructive lessons are learned from schoolmates and teachers, but it is far more likely that such lessons are learned at home. No parent intentionally creates anxiety and stress for a child, but our conversations about school—particularly our discussions of tests—can have such an effect. This is very likely a reflection of the parents' own attitude toward school and testing. Take a few minutes to think about your own experiences and the stress and anxiety you experienced as a student. Most parents can objectively recognize that their school experiences had some good and bad elements. We are far more likely, however, to recall and transmit the parts of school that had the strongest emotional impact, and strong emotional impact in school is quite likely to be negative. The embarrassment over a failed exam, the humiliation as other students laughed, the feeling of despair and rejection when a teacher expressed disappointment—these memories linger far more than a hundred "smiley faces" that we routinely received on schoolwork. Thus, it is the parent, and no one but the parent, who adds balance and clarity to the school experience. The two essential ways in which effective parents add this balance include constructive and accurate discussions about school and the creation of learning opportunities that occur outside of school. The activities in this book are designed to support schoolwork and they will also develop students who are confident and capable. These activities have value not only because they are related to educational standards, but also because they will help to create a learning environment in your home. They will help you model the love of learning that every child must have and which every parent can nurture.

only a parent

The Most Important Teacher: You

The enormity of the task ahead can be daunting. After all, a parent might ask, "Shouldn't schools be doing this?" It's a fair question. In some cases, the schools can and should do more. But there is one thing that even the best schools with unlimited resources and brilliant teachers cannot do: They cannot be parents. The parents are the most important teachers any child can ever have. This doesn't mean that parents must be experts in every subject or masters of teaching techniques. But only a parent can give a child the ability to say words such as:

"I know that my mom and dad are proud of me."

"I mess up sometimes, but it's okay, because I know I can learn from my mistakes."

"I didn't do as well as I wanted to, but I know how to get better next time."

Only a parent can provide the emotional security and strength of character that build a child who is confident, capable, and empowered. Unfortunately, some parents substitute their own academic expertise for emotional resilience. Every time there is the "nuclear-powered science fair project" obviously done by a parent, the emotional consequence is not pride, but the absolute conviction by the child that "I'm not good enough to do this on my own." The activities in this book will show you how to create a learning environment in which you and your child learn together, make mistakes together, laugh together, and maintain a love of learning amidst all the chaos of daily life, as your child develops independence and confidence.

If You Don't Have Time for the Whole Book

A few readers are thinking, "I can't read the whole book—where do I start?" Although every page is here for a purpose, we recognize the limits of time and the need to focus on the essentials. Therefore, if your time is limited and you want the maximum value in the minimum time, we suggest that you focus on three areas. Start with Chapter 2 for the "why" of standards, then proceed to Chapter 5 for the "how" of standards. Then find an activity from the section starting on page 139 that you and your child will enjoy. Finish with a review of the appendices, where you can find additional resources that are directly relevant to your particular needs. Not every reader will be interested in the sections for students with special needs nor will everyone find the chapter on home schooling essential. We include those chapters because they represent significant and growing areas in education.

Learning Activities

At the end of this book you will find a variety of learning activities. You will find that these ideas have value, not only because they are directly related to the academic standards of your state, but also because they help to build the necessary thinking, reasoning, and communication skills your child needs in any school in any state. These activities will help you make family learning time a regular part of your routine.

A Special Note for Parents of Children with Special Needs

More than ten percent of students in school have a disability that influences their success in school. These disabilities range from differences in the way that they process information to profound physical and neurological challenges. These students are protected by a variety of federal and state statutes, the Individuals with Disabilities Education Act (IDEA) being the most significant legislation in this area. Parents of these students are often alarmed when a school official states that academic standards must apply to "all" students, sometimes adding sarcastically, "What is it about the word 'all' you don't understand?" Chapter 9 is devoted entirely to students with special needs. The bottom line, however, is the clear legal mandate that the individual needs of students must be taken into consideration in all matters involving standards, testing, and curriculum. Standards have great merit for schools, but there is danger in linking legitimate educational standards to the "standardization" of policies for students for whom the law clearly requires attention to individual needs.

It has been said that education is the "new civil right." This is true for students with special needs as well as disadvantaged families. The individualization of standards and testing requirements for students with special needs is not merely a nice thing to do; it is a legal requirement. Chapter 9 and the appendices provide sample letters and checklists for parents of students with special needs to ensure that you are empowered to protect the rights of your child and serve as an advocate on his behalf.

What about Changes in Standards and Tests?

Finally, the subject of standards and testing is changing on a daily basis. As this book goes to press, legislatures throughout the nation are being challenged to change tests and reformulate standards. The only thing that is certain is that tests and standards will continue to change. To help you keep up to date on the latest changes in standards and assessment for your state, we have created an Internet website with current information on the latest changes in standards and tests for your state. Just go to www.kaptest.com/crusadeintheclassroom or www.edaccountability.org and click on the name of your state for the latest updates on standards and assessment in your area. You will also find links to the state education department for your state where you can find the latest information on policy and procedures for education in your state.

The prospect of changes in standards, however, must not obscure this essential fact: While individual standards and particular testing policies may change, the fundamentals of standards are here to stay. Standards will endure because they are the most fair and effective way to educate children. While change may be a certainty in our world, it is also certain that the educational system will not retreat to the age of mystery in which a "standard" was whatever captured the interest of a teacher and "proficiency" varied from one classroom to another. Fads may come and go, but the imperatives of fairness and effectiveness will never vanish from the educational landscape.

communication

A Dose of Reality

My children are in public schools, including elementary, middle, and high school. My travels to schools throughout the world place me in contact with teachers, school leaders, and parents, hundreds of whom contributed ideas for this book. Each year I speak and listen to more than a hundred audiences, and thus far have worked in 49 states as well as Africa, Asia, and Europe. Whether these conversations take place in the United States or abroad, whether in an economically advantaged setting or a financially depressed area, there are remarkably common themes that I hear from parents, teachers, and school leaders. The number one issue is always communication. Parents want to hear more specific and more frequent information from the school; teachers want to have more immediate feedback from parents. Parents want to be welcomed into the classroom and insist that the individual needs and characteristics of their children be taken into account; educators and school leaders want parents to understand that today's schools are different from the classrooms of three decades ago. Most of all, parents do not wish to guess about the educational needs of their children. They want to know more than a list of subjects accompanied by a list of grades on a report card and demand to know what the expectations are and how their children can improve. This clarity and specificity is the essence of effective educational standards. I am also the beneficiary of a regular dose of blunt advice from Brooks, Alex, Julia, and James, children whose patience, love, and insight into educational matters are an unending source of inspiration and understanding. Thus, the following pages are not theoretical musings, but the result of daily contact with the real world of the reader.

Special Note to Academic and Professional Readers

Some teachers, school leaders, researchers, and professors may read the following pages and ask, "Where are the footnotes?" It is a fair question and it deserves a straight answer. This book is directed to a lay audience. In the interest of clarity, I have not provided the citations and footnotes that would normally accompany every allusion to research and each assertion of fact. For readers interested in my most recent writings directed toward a professional audience where the research is clearly cited, please consult the articles and book chapters that can be downloaded free of charge at www.edaccountability.org.

Chapter 1

Making the 20-Minute Learning Connection Work for You

The Power of 20 Minutes a Day

As important as the role of parent is, many parents have multiple roles, including spouse, worker, employer, neighbor, volunteer, and parent to other children. When asked to find 20 minutes a day for educational activities in an already crowded schedule, an exhausted parent might respond, "I've been up since 5:30 this morning and have four phone calls to make, dinner to cook, and after that comes Cub Scouts and choir practice. And you want me to do more to enrich my child's education? That's the school's responsibility. I'm doing the best I can!"

Both the fatigue and frustration are understandable, and the recommendations we offer to parents are not a retreat to the 1950s or an appeal only to parents with unlimited reserves of time and energy. There is great power in 20 minutes a day. This is not merely a convenient figure taken out of the air, but rather an amount of time that is both validated by research and supported by the practicalities of the busy lives of families. In one study of student achievement, those children who completed 20 minutes a day of independent reading outside of school were 60 percentile points higher than their counterparts who did no such reading. While reading an hour or more a day is wonderful, the greatest gain in achievement occurred from just 20 minutes a day.

What can you do in 20 minutes? This book is full of activities that are directly related to the academic standards of your state. But consider the routines that any family can create in just 20 minutes a day.

In 20 minutes you and your child can . . .

- **Read aloud for 15 minutes, and then describe what the story or news article was about for another five minutes.**

- **Write a letter to a grandparent, friend, or relative.**

- **Measure the ingredients for dinner.**

- **Explore the factors affecting recent weather patterns and predict tomorrow's weather.**

- **Draft and revise step-by-step instructions for the use of adult-defying devices such as VCRs and electronic games.**

- **Use the sports section of your newspaper to practice math ("How many more three-point shots did the Knicks need to make to beat the Heat?" "How much faster did the second-place marathoner need to run to tie the winner?").**

This chapter considers the practical details of creating the place and the time for your 20-minute learning connection. The habits you develop and the time you invest in making a learning connection with your child can fundamentally change the way you talk about school and, more importantly, the way your child thinks about learning. You can move away from conversations that are unproductive and threatening to discussions that are focused on interesting and engaging activities. You can move away from an inspection of the backpack and the dreary march through the daily homework toward learning for the sheer joy of spending time together, developing new skills, and contemplating new ideas. Of course, the 20-Minute Learning Connection does not replace homework any more than it will avoid death and taxes. But these moments will give your child the skills, enthusiasm, and knowledge to make homework and other academic challenges more accessible.

opportunity for reflection

"What Did You Do in School Today?"

Most parents have had the following unproductive conversation:

"What did you do in school today?" Nothin.

"Why did you get that grade?" I dunno.

The antidote to this conversational dead-end is not browbeating the child until, after parental cross-examination, the child confesses some activity during the school day. Rather, we must re-frame the conversation about school. Let us begin by asking different questions. Here are some conversation starters that are quite different from "What did you do in school today?"

"What did you learn in school today?"

"What happened in school today that was scary?"

"What happened today that made you happy?"

"What happened today that made you sad?"

"What happened today that made you feel great?"

By shifting the conversation from a narrative of news events to a focus on the child's own feelings, there is the opportunity for reflection and personal engagement. Without asking these sorts of emotionally relevant questions, parents risk waiting until they read a bad report card or receive an alarming call from school before learning about significant problems.

The Power of Expectations

In a famous series of experiments in the early 1960s, two different groups of teachers were given students who were similar with regard to prior learning and demographic characteristics. One group, however, was described to their teachers as the "smart" group, while the other was described as "slow." A year later, both groups of students were measured on a variety of academic and intelligence tests. Despite the similarity of these two groups, the teachers and their widely varying expectations had an enormous impact on student performance, with the students living up to—and down to—the expectations of their teachers. Parental expectations are even more profound in their influence on student achievement. There is a fine line between parental pressure and expectations, and the difference is not always clear. We all know of the parents who "expect" their child to become a doctor or lawyer, and any professional or educational decision short of the mark leaves the child feeling like a failure in the eyes of the parent. Far more common, however, is the reluctance of parents to articulate clear expectations of academic success. While most parents are quite clear in their expectations of behavior and integrity, the same parents are less clear about the "house rules" regarding reading, homework, and learning.

The older children get, the more ambiguous the academic expectations of parents become. While every kindergartner has a world of potential ahead, the impulse to rate, rank, sort, and label children is in full flower by late elementary school. The child with brilliant potential in first grade has, by the sixth grade, been determined to be someone who "just isn't a reader" or "just isn't very good at math." While every second grader can express ambitions to be a jet pilot, opera singer, astronaut, or brain surgeon, parents none too subtly scoff at such ambitions just a few years later. The skepticism is not always obvious, but the message is clear. Even the well-intentioned, "If that's what you want to do, then you will have to do a lot better in school" becomes "You've got to be kidding! You—a brain surgeon? Forget it." This destructive disapproval is a long emotional distance from the cheering parent on the sidelines at a basketball game assuring the six-year-old who makes one basket out of 50, "I know you can do it!"

How do parents express their expectations for student success? Here are some positive practices you may wish to consider. Parents who expect their children to do well in school and in life value learning and model that value, just as parents who expect their children to have integrity and compassion model those values. In order to model a love of learning, parents should consider the following steps toward the creation of learning time and learning space in their home.

learning together

Time and Space for Your 20-Minute Learning Connection

Set aside a "learning time" of 20 minutes every day. Many families devote the time after dinner to this purpose. Among my fondest memories of childhood are the times after dinner when someone would ask a question, and the family would discuss the idea, read about it, and learn something new. These were not extended multi-hour discussions, but they were clearly opportunities to learn that were not related to the school day. The discussions, readings, and questions were the result of a love of learning and a passion for inquiry. There is another critical element to such discussions: They provide adults with an opportunity to take the views of children seriously. A child's day is full of reminders of the impotence of children compared to the power of adults. When a parent or other significant adult takes the time to listen, question, and learn together with a child, there is more than merely the acquisition of new information taking place. There is the development of a sense of value, the ability of children to take themselves seriously, and in time, to expect others to take them seriously as well. The time consistently devoted to learning and exploration should be appropriate to your family's lifestyle and it should be consistent. Many families identify one night a week in which other activities are not allowed to intrude and they play games, read, discuss, and enjoy one another's company. Other families take just 20 minutes after dinner. Still other families carve out time first thing in the morning before the busy day begins. Whatever time you establish, consistency will be important. It is important that you not allow the ideal to be the enemy of progress. In other words, even if ideally you would like to have a two-hour after-dinner discussion that is free of interruptions and unfettered by the activities of children and parents, such a vision should not stop you from making the best use of 20 minutes any time during the day.

Every home should have some "learning space" that is the family equivalent of a library. This space need not be a room devoted only to learning, for few family homes have libraries or studies. Rather, the learning space is instantly created by the way it is

5

used. Your learning space might be the dinner table, a desk in the basement, or any place set aside that meets three conditions. First, it is relatively free of distractions. This means that when the learning space is being used, the television is turned off and a sibling is not practicing the trombone in the same area. Second, there is abundant light. Third, it is easily accessible. If the table in the kitchen or dining room is to be used as the learning place, then it becomes the learning place as soon as someone sits down and opens a book, begins to write, or otherwise starts learning. If it requires 15 minutes of clearing and setting up before learning can begin, then it is not sufficiently accessible. The learning place need not be formal or expensive, but it does need to be quiet, well lit, and easy to use.

Parents' Checklist:

❏ Create a "learning space" in your home that is quiet, well lit, and easily accessible.

❏ Identify 20 minutes of "learning time" for your family to stop their other activities and learn together. This might involve reading alone or aloud, asking questions, or investigating a puzzling problem. To start your journey, we have suggested a number of learning activities that are specifically linked to the academic standards of your state. You will find the list of standards and activities starting on page 139.

---

a learning space

Chapter 2

What Are Academic Standards and Why Do We Have Them?

Academic standards give every parent essential information about what children are expected to know and be able to do in school. Parents need not guess or speculate about the idiosyncratic preferences of teachers. More importantly, children need not worry about what it takes to succeed in school. With the proper implementation of academic standards, guesswork is replaced with clarity.

The Importance of Knowing the Rules

Any parent who has observed children playing games in the park or on the playground knows the following scenario well. Children are playing a game and a new child joins the fun. Within minutes, however, it is clear that something is wrong. Cries of "That's not fair!" fill the air. The sounds of playground glee are replaced by tears, anger, and the indignant wail, "I'm never playing this game again!" When the mess is sorted out, there are no villains, no cheaters, no schemers determined to deny the aggrieved party his due. Rather, the tears, anger, and resolution to play no more all stem from ambiguity about the rules. All parties to the dispute thought that they knew how the game was played, and all had strikingly different understandings of what the rules of the game were supposed to be. Our children know that it is impossible to play any game without knowing the rules. Without clear rules, our determined efforts are reduced to random guessing, and the errors that we make do not provide useful feedback to improve our performance, but only greater frustration, more anger, and a river of tears. Whether the game is a seemingly inconsequential contest in the park or a high-stakes test with important consequences for a child's future, it is impossible to play the game without knowing the rules.

clear rules

Standards: The Rules of the Game

Any discussion of games in the context of education invites cynicism. The careless use of this analogy might indicate that education, standards, and testing are nothing more than trivial games where strategy is elevated above moral, ethical, and educational issues. Nothing could be further from the truth. In fact, there are a number of elements of games that reflect not merely strategic considerations, but fundamental values, such as fairness. Thus, my reference to games in the context of educational standards is designed to force us to confront the fact that, while clarity and fairness are routine requirements in games ranging from the playground to professional sports, the necessity for clarity and fairness applies no less to every important endeavor, including education. While these values may have trivial implications in a game, they are at the very heart of understanding why standards are so essential. Standards provide students with clear, unambiguous statements of what is required of them. In other words, standards are the rules of the game in school.

As I stated before, academic standards are statements of what students should know and be able to do. Although there are, to be sure, numerous examples of standards that are poorly worded, vague, over-reaching, unrealistic, and otherwise unhelpful, we must consider the alternative. Without standards, what would students have? They would be left with the mystery, guesswork, and ambiguity that prevail in the absence of rules.

Whenever I ask grandparents and experienced parents to tell me about the lessons they have learned about effective parenting, I find a theme in their advice. "You have to be consistent," they counsel. "Don't confuse sympathy and understanding with weakness. You have to be clear." For added emphasis, they warn, "You won't always make the right decisions, but children must know that they can count on you, and that requires consistency and dependability." There is wisdom in the words of these elders. Because perfection in parenting is not an option available to most of us, we are left with making the best of our imperfection. One way to reduce the risk of the mistakes that we inevitably make is clarity and consistency. This certainly does not guarantee the popularity or even the rectitude of our decisions about parental discipline, but clarity and consistency certainly will increase the probability that our children perceive us as fair, predictable, and dependable.

In contexts as diverse as child discipline and playground games, the role of standards is clear. Rules are necessary for motivation and fairness. Why is the role of standards so controversial in education? The value of clarity, consistency, and fairness is clear in the context of discipline and games. When the third-grade soccer championship or the sixth-grade music competition is on the line, few people doubt the necessity of standards, for the rules are the guarantor of fairness. Why does a football field always have 100 yards or a chessboard always have 64 squares? The answer is obvious: Without such clear and consistent rules, few people would be willing to play the game. Clarity and consistency are essential if people of any age are to be motivated sufficiently to engage in an activity. These standards are necessary in order for contests of any type, from the trivial to the most serious, to be regarded as fair. The fundamental rationale for educational standards is the same: a commitment to fairness.

The Old Way: Grading "On the Curve"

There are some people who are very upset with the standards movement and who have led angry demands for the abandonment of educational standards. They see standards as a device by which schools are rendered joyless boot camps and the needs of children are sacrificed to the needs of corporate employers. We should, therefore, consider where classrooms and schools would be if we had no standards. Recent history (and, unfortunately, many present-day schools) provides the answer. Without standards, we have the bell curve. You know that your child's school does not have a commitment to standards when you overhear the following conversation among children:

"How did you do on that assignment?"

"I didn't get the question right, but I was better than Steve!"

It is untrue that this school lacks standards. The standard is Steve, or any other child to whom another student can be favorably compared. No one knows what is really expected, because no one knows what Steve can do from one day to the next. But they do know this: If they can just beat Steve, then the teacher will have someone else on whom negative attention can be focused. Am I overstating the case? Consider the following authentic conversation from teachers in the schools I routinely visit:

"How do you evaluate students?"

"The best paper gets an A, the worst paper gets an F."

"How do you know what student work is acceptable?"

"I can't really tell you, but I know it when I see it."

Astonishingly, some parents embrace grading on the curve because it appears to foster the competitive spirit. After all, they reason, the cream rises to the top. It's a tough world out there, so my kids must get used to the competition. Ironically, grading on the curve does not produce the superior results and competitive spirit desired by parents. Rather, it creates the worst of both worlds because it discourages the competent student and fosters complacency in the incompetent student. The

"Steve Standard" provides justification to students who produce schoolwork that is incomplete, inaccurate, and disorganized but that is not quite as wretched as Steve's scrawl. With equally bad logic, the "Steve Standard" demoralizes the student who worked exceptionally hard to complete a wonderful assignment, but despite its exemplary quality, it was one footnote shy of the work submitted by Steve. Whether Steve is a wonderful student or a terrible student, the "Steve Standard" represents the shifting standards of grading on the curve. It is an inherently unfair and inaccurate way to evaluate students.

Some parents have a ready rejoinder: "But I don't want my child to be just 'good enough,' I want her to be the best. Only by comparing my child to other children can I be sure that she is meeting high standards." The subtext of this reasoning is the unrelenting counsel of successful business leaders of the past few decades who have insisted that business managers must be graded on the curve. This logic receives reinforcement from the sports world where there can be, after all, only a single champion. Because grading on the curve has proponents in business and athletics, it might be useful to use terminology that more accurately distinguishes a standards-based system from the alternative. Rather than call the competitive system "grading on the curve," we shall label it more accurately: mystery grading.

The Worst Evaluation System: Mystery Grading

Imagine two children playing in the park. Lois challenges Robert to a ball game. With pleasure, Robert accepts the challenge, confident that he has played ball games successfully in the past. Lois then takes the ball and runs past an imaginary line and exclaims, "That's one point for me—I'm ahead!" Robert catches on quickly, takes the ball, and runs past the line happily. "You ran the wrong way!" Lois shouts. "That's another point for me—it's two to zero, my favor." Robert starts to pick up the ball, but Lois provides a quick elbow to his solar plexus, takes the ball, and runs past the line. "Three to zero," she says with a smile. Robert is upset, but under control. Confident that he now understands the game a bit better, he delivers a retaliatory blow to Lois and takes the ball, crossing the line with a smile of victory. "Foul!" Lois cries. "That's an automatic point for me—it's four to zero!" Robert is a bright child. How long do you think he will continue to play this game? It is a testimony to Robert's good grace and self-control that he has not been dispatched to the principal's office after having let his aggravation with Lois get the better of him. But despite his chivalry, this much is certain: Robert will not play this game again.

When the awarding of points is a mystery and when the rules of the game appear to shift with the winds, then children will not continue to play the game. When victory involves guessing and no amount of skill or prior information is of any value, then the game becomes an idle pursuit and not a purposeful enterprise.

Is this analogy exaggerated? Ask students why they received the grade they did. Sometimes you will receive a well-reasoned and clear answer. One student might say,

"The requirements of the assignment were this, but I actually did that. Therefore, I failed to meet the requirements and received a low grade. Having received this valuable feedback and recognizing the error of my ways, I shall return to my desk forthwith, revise this assignment and resubmit it to my teacher."

If your child provides such a response, please return this book for a refund, proceed to the nearest radio station, and host a call-in show for perfect parents with perfect children in perfect schools. For most of us and for our children, grading remains mysterious. Even teachers who take the time to create clear and precise grading systems find that precision is an illusion, far clearer to the designer of the system than to the students who must perform under its mandates.

For the vast majority of students, grading remains a mystery dominated by the largely unknown personal preferences of the teacher. The student is placed in the role of the sorcerer's apprentice, weakly emulating the acts of the master, hoping that some of the magic will rub off. Systematic learning is impossible because teaching comes only from the inscrutable wisdom of the master teacher, and learning is a matter of fortunate insight rather than diligent work. It is no wonder that such a system is discouraging to the student who finds luck more important than skill. There is a better way. We can replace mystery with clarity. Students can replace guesswork with hard work. Parents can replace aimless searching with careful direction. In brief, we can have standards.

The Best Way: Know the Rules Before You Play the Game

The game played by Lois and Robert was unfair. The failure of fairness was not a result of the scheming of Lois, but rather the absence of rules. The fundamental requirement of fairness is the existence of clear and consistent rules—standards, if you will—that let the participants know what conduct is acceptable and what is not. We can only play the game when we know the rules.

This is hardly an alien notion to schools. During the first few hours of the first day of classes in most schools in the country, teachers discuss the importance of behavior, respect, and decorum in the classroom. Teachers do not display elaborate posters on classroom walls that contain the precise words of the Board of Education's disciplinary policy or the state criminal statutes. Rather, each teacher has a single piece of paper labelled "class rules," which lays out in simple and clear language the requirements of conduct for students. "Respect yourself and others," the rules typically begin. "Do not talk while others are speaking." "Raise your hand before speaking." "Be kind and help others." There is a long tradition of identifying the standards of behavior in classrooms with clarity and precision. These same qualities must be the goal of those desiring academic excellence.

clarity

What Standards Mean for Students

While the word "standards" conveys to some parents a threat of failure and an association with difficult academic tests, the actual implications of school standards are quite positive. In a standards-based school, students know what is expected and they routinely receive constructive feedback on how to improve their performance. The typical parent-child conversation after report cards are issued in a school without standards begins with the question, "How did you get that grade?" followed by the plaintive response, "I don't know." With standards, this unproductive conversation is replaced by these confident statements:

"I know what the teacher wants me to do."

"I know when I'm successful and when I am not."

"I know how to get better and I can do so tomorrow."

"I know what it takes to win and I know that I can be a winner."

"I can help someone else and still be a winner—I don't have to beat Steve to be a great student."

real achievement

What Standards Mean for Parents

It is stunning for me to hear some parents bemoan the standards movement as a new educational fad when the requirement for fair and reasonable relationships among teaching, learning, curriculum, and assessment are as old as Socrates. Although our children may think their parents went to school in the Lyceum, we need not recall ancient Greece to consider our own examples of standards. Think of your favorite teacher or coach. Did that person patronize you with constant pats on the head or make your success a matter of mystery and luck? Or did that favorite coach or teacher let you know that whatever else had happened in your life, you would be a success if only you worked hard, followed the rules, and met the standards that the teacher clearly identified? These favorite teachers did not make learning easy, nor did they make learning impossible. Rather, our favorite teachers and coaches made learning challenging, fair, reasonable, and rewarding. This is the essence of standards-based teaching and learning.

Now that they are vividly called to mind, these influential teachers and coaches offer another interesting quality. Your success was not accomplished when you simply defeated another student, but when you met the standard articulated by the coach. Chances are, that standard included not only personal excellence, but also a willingness to help your teammates. While rivalries within teams are natural, the team that is beset by constant competition within the team is seldom able to deal with competition against other teams. In fact, your success was elevated by your willingness to help your colleagues. When you helped other students, you discovered an important truth: Not only did their performance improve, but your understanding of the same subject soared when you had the opportunity to help others master the subject. You found that helping other students was not an entirely altruistic act, but rather was the result of a collaborative process in which you both gave and received valuable lessons.

Academic standards imply a very different environment in school than many parents may have experienced. If your educational experience involved grading on the curve, frantic efforts to please a teacher, and a certain degree of mystery about the nature of your performance, then it is only natural that you might expect your own children to have a similar experience in school. If you have been successful in school and in life, you might initially prefer that your children attend a school that closely matches your own experiences when you were a student. Nevertheless, the case we have made for standards is based not upon personal history or popularity, but upon the fact that standards are fair and effective. Even if a standards-based approach to student achievement is not what you experienced as a child, please give it a chance. Your children will thrive in an environment in which the rules of the game are clear and their performance is rewarded based on real achievement rather than merely on a victory over a classmate.

What Standards Mean for Teachers and Schools

Standards offer clarity, fairness, and effectiveness, so teachers should universally rave about the use of academic standards. After all, if the case for standards is so overwhelming, why would any educational professional object? In fact, the reaction to standards by teachers and school administrators has been varied. Some teachers enthusiastically endorse the idea of standards and emphasize that it is hardly new. "What you call standards," they remark, "is what I have called 'good teaching' for about 25 years now."

But many other educators are wary. They have seen a number of educational fads come and go, and they reasonably wonder if this is just one more trend that will evaporate when something more popular comes along. In addition, some teachers resent the fact that standards were oversold when they were first introduced. Some proponents of standards let their enthusiasm surpass their judgment when they gushed, "Standards will make teaching easy!" Of course, nothing makes the difficult and complex job of teaching easy. Most of the objections to standards come from the failure of those who wrote the initial drafts of state standards to express their expectations with precision. Many standards swing from one extreme to the other, either describing curriculum content in excessive detail, or describing expectations of student performance in such broad generalities that teachers are left with little constructive guidance. Some teachers object that the standards are too difficult and too numerous. Considering all the other subjects that traditionally have been in the school curriculum, the additional layers of academic content seem to be too burdensome given the limited amount of time students spend in school. Finally, there are teachers who sincerely object to any outside interference in their classroom. Their rejoinder to standards or other intrusions is, "Just leave me alone and let me teach!" In their judgment, standards easily could become standardization, and such an approach to teaching fails to recognize the unique qualities of each individual student. Only the teacher, they argue, can make the subtle judgments required to identify what is appropriate for each child, and standards designed at the state or school district level fail to take into account the individual needs that are known only to the teacher.

Many parents have heard these arguments, and have interpreted them as arguments against all academic standards. Every argument but the last one, however, is actually a persuasive case against poor standards, and the logical response is not the abandonment of standards, but the continuous improvement of them. Those people who make the final argument characterized as, "Just leave me alone and let me teach," will object to any standard. Improvements would not be sufficient, for even the most clear and constructive standard would represent an intrusion into their classroom and their curriculum.

Parents naturally appreciate a teacher who wishes to take into account the individual needs of their children. Moreover, most parents would object to any policy that appears to "standardize" their unique children. A balanced approach to standards might look something like this: The freedom and discretion of teachers are honored, respected, and encouraged, provided that this discretion takes place within a framework. That framework is one of academic excellence and equity in which all students have clear and fair guidelines and expectations. Educators have broad discretion to consider alternative strategies for teaching reading to a student who appears to be slow to catch on to phonics; the teacher does not have the discretion to say, "Considering his difficult upbringing and poor neighborhood, we really can't expect him to learn to read this year." Teachers can be creative and have wide latitude to collaborate with their colleagues to determine the best ways to improve mathematics skills, but they do not have the discretion to say (as I have actually heard a teacher and administrator claim), "Well, those kids don't need algebra anyway." In a balanced approach to standards, there is neither micromanagement by school administrators, nor aimless anarchy among teachers. Standards need not dictate the day-to-day, minute-to-minute agenda for the classroom, but standards do establish the expectations of what all students should know and be able to do. When teachers have creative supplementary strategies to help students meet those expectations, that creativity is respected and rewarded. When, however, teachers make decisions that take students outside of the framework at the expense of meeting standards, then they have supplanted the needs of the child with the personal preferences of the teacher. That, in a school committed to excellence and equity, is not acceptable.

an effective classroom

What Standards Mean for Daily Life in School

The best way for students and teachers to succeed in school and to meet academic standards is a consistent emphasis on the thinking, reasoning, analysis, communication, and love of learning that characterizes any effective classroom. The frequent claim that the path to meeting standards lies in mindless drills, rather than analysis and thinking, is wrong. In extensive research from organizations as diverse as the Education Trust, the Center for Performance Assessment, and the National Science Foundation, the evidence is clear: Higher test scores on standards-based assessments are more likely to occur when students and teachers engage in critical thinking, extensive analysis, and frequent writing. The appropriate application of academic standards encourages an increase in thinking, reasoning, and communication by students.

To be sure, standards are the cause of some changes in schools, and those changes can be uncomfortable for the critics of standards. There are elementary classes that devote many hours of prime reading time to craft projects and preparation for performances, few of which are related to the improvement of student achievement. Some secondary teachers announce that next quarter will be devoted to current events "rather than standards," as if the possibility of relating contemporary political events to the study of history and government is impossible. There are many traditional projects that consume large chunks of time and the only thing that sustains these activities is their popularity, not their contribution to student learning. What is lost by the establishment of standards? Surely not thinking, reasoning, or even the fun of interactive and engaging activities in the classroom. What must be abandoned or modified, however, are the projects that have persisted year after year based only on the personal preference of the teacher and popularity with students and parents. Perhaps the least attractive feature of the standards movement is that it displaces popularity with effectiveness.

Does this mean that the kids can no longer carve pumpkins in October or dress up like Pilgrims in November? Certainly not. We know that hands-on activities and dramatic reenactments are splendid ways for students to learn. But some of these activities require close reexamination and detailed modification. If pumpkins are to be the theme for a few days, then much more than carving and candy must be the order of the day. There are wonderful classrooms in which students read about pumpkins, write about them, measure them, weigh them, compare them, and explore them. The traditional Thanksgiving drama, in which two students speak and many others look on in silence, can be replaced by an activity in which many students participate in writing the play based on their own reading and research. The speaking parts can be widely shared among all students, and the predominant feature of the activity is student learning rather than parent entertainment.

reasonable preparation

Won't Standards Result in Teaching to the Test?

Some teachers and parents have linked standards and testing to the point that any suggestion that standards are the basis of classroom instruction leads to the allegation that schools are "teaching to the test." It is true that there are examples around the nation in which some misguided administrators have encouraged a regimen of test drills and memorization rather than deep study, analysis, and reflection. It is also true that there are some schools that have curtailed traditional classroom activities and field trips, and a few people have blamed standards as the culprit that turned their schools into grim, academic factories.

The very phrase "teaching to the test," implies something unethical, as if teachers had sneaked into the State Department of Testing, secretly copied the test, and then conducted drills in class in which students memorized the answers by chanting,

"Number 1 is C, number 2 is A, number 3 is B..." In fact, what most teachers have done is to use the freely available models of the practice tests to let students look at sample items in order to become more familiar with the format of the test. Moreover, thoughtful teachers also have reviewed their own curriculum and made appropriate revisions. "If my students need to know about graphs and tables for a test in March, and I was not going to address those skills until April, then it would be much more fair to my students if I changed my schedule to give them those skills before they take the test."

The contention that ethical teaching requires that testing must be a mystery must be challenged as absurd and unfair. Can you imagine students in a musical performance sitting down to discover that the music before them is completely unfamiliar? Can you imagine the football coach who refuses to use a football in practice or take students near an actual football field because practicing under such conditions would be "teaching to the test?"

The most appropriate way to discuss the relationship of classroom teaching to the tests students take is not "teaching to the test," but "teaching to the standard." Teachers cannot anticipate every single item on the test, but they can provide students with a fair opportunity to do well on any test. The opportunity for fairness is best provided when students have received curriculum and instruction based on the standards, and when the test designers have used those same standards as the basis for creating the tests. When the context is driving, music, or football, this would be called common sense. When the context is academic performance, it is not only common sense, but also fair and effective.

The Most Important Teacher Your Child Will Ever Have

When I was discussing this book with a teacher and grandparent in a border community where Spanish was the predominant language, she suggested a title for the Spanish-language edition of the book. "There's no doubt about it," she said. "Your title must be *Los Primeros Maestros*." This is a play on words, indicating that parents are not only the first teachers, but also the most important teachers that children will ever have. Her insight speaks volumes to parents of every culture, because we are all the first and most important teachers for our children.

Parents teach children so many things that they will never learn in school, including integrity, values, and respect for oneself and others. Parents also teach children about their interest in learning. This is not the same as their interest in school. Our children see through the ruse of the parent who berates a child over a poor grade in reading but never picks up a book for pleasure. Our children notice our inconsistency when we exclaim our disappointment in their writing abilities, but fail ever to take pen in hand ourselves to write a letter. The most important lessons we teach are those with our actions and values, not our lectures.

Parents' Checklist:

❑ Read the standards appropriate to your child's grade.

❑ Find one activity that you can complete in 20 minutes that will help your child achieve standards.

❑ Talk with your child's teacher about standards. If the teacher's attitude is negative, ask if the problem is the specific wording of the standards, or if the problem is any effort by the state to influence classroom activities. It is important for you to understand the teacher's commitment or aversion to standards.

❑ Find the exact dates of state tests for your child. Mark them on the calendar so that you can limit distractions and interruptions during that week.

❑ Ask your child about standards. "What do you think you have to do this year to be a great student?" Then listen carefully for the response. Standards only have meaning when children understand them. The response you receive will be your guide to future activities and discussions with teachers, school leaders, and your child.

ask your child

Chapter 3

What Tests Tell You—and What They Don't

Tests are part of life. Babies take the Apgar test within moments of birth in the delivery room, and the results of that test can lead to essential and immediate medical intervention for the newborn child. Before formal schooling has begun, children routinely explore the world around them by experimenting with language and behavior. They "test" the world dominated by adults and older children and make instant observations about effective and ineffective strategies to meet their needs. When the young child is the one doing the testing and when the results of the test are immediately used to benefit the child, it is a remarkably effective way to learn about the world. In a few short years, however, the word "test" gains a very different meaning. It is no longer a way of learning and exploring, no longer a mechanism for gaining new knowledge and meeting the child's needs. Tests are soon associated with anxiety, demands for performance, and the prospect of failure. Three-year-old children take admissions tests for preschool and their older siblings are subjected to tests that will determine their acceptance or rejection by special programs in kindergarten. Within the minutes or hours that it takes to administer these tests, the path is set. Perhaps the child will bear the label of "gifted and talented" or "special needs" or, heaven forbid, "normal."

Because the tests purport to have scientific properties, the labels bestowed on children are rarely challenged. The purpose of this chapter is to confront the common acceptance of these labels by providing some background on what tests can and cannot tell parents about their children. Once you know that tests are merely snapshots of knowledge rather than definitive pronouncements about student ability, both you and your child can examine test results for what they are—a momentary record of achievement, not a certain prediction of future failure or success. Whether the test in question affects the labeling of a child, the acceptance into or rejection from a special program, or simply the awarding of a grade on a report card, the way that parents talk with children about tests reflects a philosophy that can be either discouraging or encouraging. Only through a deliberate effort to change the talk between parents and children into learning conversations will we make the transition away from test terror.

conquering anxiety

From Test Terror to Testing for Learning

Parents who have witnessed the transformation of testing from innocent exploration to childhood terror may express their dismay at how much inappropriate pressure is placed on children, not knowing that their own comments have already signaled the parents' anxieties to their children about the importance of tests. There are few more powerful psychological forces than the fear of disappointing a parent. Perhaps you can recall a time in which you would have preferred physical punishment to that look of dissatisfaction from a parent who sent the message, "I am disappointed in you." Few spankings could have been as painful. While no parent ever intends to send debilitating and terrorizing messages to children, we sometimes cannot help it. The stress and anxiety of every examination we have ever taken can subtly and unintentionally become the test terror we transmit to our children.

Constructive Skepticism for Tests

Fortunately, history is not destiny. Parents can fundamentally change their children's perceptions of testing. This cannot be accomplished by casually dismissing tests as unimportant. Our children see through that ruse, knowing that tests are indeed important, but that we are seeking to protect them. As surely as children know if they won or lost the soccer match in the supposedly "fun and scoreless" games that masquerade as noncompetitive exercises, children also know when tests are important, but their parents don't want to talk about them. If we are to liberate our children from test terror, we will do so not with patronizing tales about the irrelevance of tests, but with a philosophy toward testing that can best be described as "constructive skepticism."

Perhaps the best way to understand constructive skepticism for tests is to consider the opposite. Rather than engaging in rational analysis of the test, some students fall prey to analytical paralysis, when the test taker is convinced that failure, inadequacy, and stupidity are the inescapable diagnoses from an unsuccessful test attempt. "After all," these children reason, "either you know it or you don't, and I guess I just don't know it." The results of such analytical paralysis are predictable: anger, fear, and the studied avoidance of test taking opportunities in the future.

Constructive skepticism for tests is strikingly different. The child with constructive skepticism understands that every test is a game. Most of the rules of the game are clear, but the moves of the other side are not always obvious. Therefore, some strategy, some knowledge, and yes, some luck is involved in the successful completion of the game. Supplied with constructive skepticism for tests, children know that their success on a test is not necessarily the mark of genius, but of capable gamesmanship. When confronted with a test question that is unclear and ambiguous, the child with constructive skepticism does not conclude, "I'm a failure and I can't do this." Rather, this empowered test taker says, "I'm as smart as the person who wrote this test, but the right answer isn't very clear. Now I know that "B" is dumb and "D" is impossible, so I guess it's "A" or "C." I'm going to make a smart guess and move on, because this game is just about over..."

Constructive skepticism does not involve anger or the presumption of failure as the inescapable result when the right answer is not immediately clear. Rather, constructive skepticism provides students with the emotional resilience to persist even in the face of ambiguity and uncertainty. It is not just the intellectual ability to narrow the range of possible answers to a test question; it is the emotional ability to remain engaged in the game of test taking long after other students have given up on that test question and perhaps on the entire test. When students feel a sense of failure, they tend to generalize it: "I'm not only a failure on the soccer team; I can't do *anything* right! I can't read, I can't do math, and I can't kick the darn ball into the darn goal..." By contrast, the child with healthy skepticism for the test at hand possesses the emotional resilience to say, "Okay, so I can't remember what a rhombus is. Big deal. This question is asking about sides of a polygon, so that means that the answer has to have sides. So it can't be a circle and it can't be an ellipse—it must be either a trapezoid or a rhombus. I'll guess that it's a rhombus and move on to the next question."

At this point, the student with constructive skepticism is still in the game, engaged in the next question, convinced that thinking, reasoning, and skill are the keys to success. The student without this sort of resilience has given up, with pencil held limply in hand while the head rests on the desk waiting for the torture of this test to end. Whatever tests the future holds for your child, among the many valuable gifts you can provide is the gift of resilience—the ability for your child to remain engaged in a test or other difficult challenge, even when the questions are ambiguous and the answers are elusive.

Some readers may be uncomfortable referring to tests as games, especially when discussing tests with their children. "This is serious," they reason, "and references to gamesmanship trivialize tests, school, and education in general." This is a legitimate concern and it deserves a serious answer. The references to games in this chapter have three purposes, none of which trivializes tests or education. First, references to games help children recall experiences that have been successful and enjoyable. This is a more constructive basis for a conversation between parents and children than a stern lecture about the life-changing importance of a test and the associated risk of parental disappointment should the child not score sufficiently well. Feelings of trust, confidence, competence, and fun are the foundations of happy children and successful students, and parents do better when they nurture those feelings. Second, references to games involve strategy that both children and parents understand. Because tests are never perfect and answers are not always free of ambiguity, knowledge alone is insufficient. Strategy—thinking about the point of view of the test writer, eliminating wrong answers, and dealing with the uncertainty and ambiguity present in every test—is not only a great thinking skill for children, it is also the key to emotional resilience. Strategy—gamesmanship, if you will—is the bridge from "I don't know the answer so

I must be stupid" to "The right answer may not be obvious, but if I work on this I think I can figure it out." Third, I have observed that parents (with the exception of the stereotype of the abusive "Little League Dad") usually approach the performance of their children in games in a constructive and encouraging manner that builds confidence, success, and emotional resilience. When children play games, parents applaud, encourage, laugh, and console—all qualities sadly lacking in many discussions between parents and children when the subject is testing, homework, and school. In the final analysis, the references in this book to games have one central theme: Our children are more than the sum of their test scores, and the role of parents is not to cram every conceivable answer into the heads of their children, but to build healthy, happy, confident, capable, and empowered kids who know that they are loved and accepted by their parents.

emotional resilience

Tests Are Important, But . . .

It is national sport to ridicule school tests. After all, many people believe it is common knowledge that children are over-tested, that tests are irrelevant, that tests are political tools misused by critics of public education, and that tests fail to tell the complete and accurate story of student achievement. While each of these allegations may contain an element of truth, a fundamental fact remains: tests are an important and continuing part of life both during the early years of school and continuing into college, technical education, and the world of work. Moreover, students who have the intellectual and emotional ability to perform well on tests will find more open doors for educational and professional success. No doubt about it: Tests are important.

Success in test taking involves not only knowing the material, but also understanding the emotional foundations for successful test performance. Many readers can recall an instance in which they were intellectually prepared for a test and, as soon as the test administrator uttered the words "you may begin," their minds went blank. Terror replaced confidence and mystery replaced the clear organization of facts and concepts that the student possessed only moments before the test began. To make matters worse, we knew of students who had scarcely prepared for the same test, but who appeared to breeze through the examination. Our recollections of the power of panic make a profound case in favor of recognizing the importance of emotions in test success.

encouragement

While the prevalence of emotions over intellect may be perplexing to students, it is great news for parents. Although we may not always be able to provide the right answer on math or geography homework, every parent can provide extraordinarily powerful support for the emotional resilience and psychological endurance of their children. The power of emotions in test preparation is an essential element of parent support. This is why "Let me help you with your homework" is far less powerful than "You're a smart kid and I believe in you; I *know* that you can do this!" As parents, we want to help our children. It is only natural. It hurts to see them struggle. It would be instructive, however, to recall the first steps of our toddler. The parent cannot walk for the child, but can only hold out loving arms and offer earnest encouragement." Come on, *you can do it!*" And they do. Our praise is genuine, enthusiastic, and encouraging. That praise, confidence, and encouragement set a standard in the minds of our children that is a difficult bar to reach in later years. "You can do it!" gives way to "Turn off the darn television and finish your homework!" "I believe in you" is replaced by "I just don't understand how you messed this up so badly." The emotional connection of parent and child has been replaced with one more layer of anxiety and stress.

Building Confident, Capable, and Empowered Children

Although few children enjoy tests, most children love games. They particularly enjoy games they can win. Think about it: Children's games, from Crazy Eights to Monopoly to a host of board and card games are typically a combination of knowledge, skill, strategy, and luck. Clever game designers know that part of maintaining the interest of children is the reasonable prospect of success. Parents help to build confident, capable, and empowered children every time they participate in an activity in which it is possible for children to succeed. This does not mean that parents deliberately lose and children win every time. Such games, children quickly learn, are boring and unrewarding. They know that the rewards that come too easily have little value. Part of building emotional resilience and persistence in the face of difficulty is the habit of trying again after a failure, full of confidence that success is a function of endurance, skill, and a little luck.

My youngest child, James, is on a basketball team. A 10-foot basketball hoop appears to be an insurmountable goal for a group of six- and seven-year-olds. During practice, the balls fly everywhere, it seems, but into the net. But once in a while—perhaps once every five to ten minutes—there is a "swish" of the ball through the net that keeps the enthusiasm of everyone in the room at a high level. There is a lesson here: We do not build capable, confident, and empowered children through the contrivance of easy tasks and low expectations. Whether the challenge is the ten-foot basket or two-digit subtraction, the prospect of success is what keeps the players engaged. They do not need the certainty of success every time, but they need to know precisely what the rules of the game are so that, when success comes, the delicious moment of victory can be savored for a moment before the players return to the game.

The game scenario has practical applications for how parents interact with children about homework and tests. Many parents tend to one of two extremes, in which one parent demands, "Go to your room and don't come out until all the homework is done!" and another parent hovers over the nervous student, correcting every error and focusing exclusively on every misstep. Can you imagine the same parents exploding with disappointment at every missed basket? Can you imagine these parents saying, after the ball goes into the basket, "Well, he made the shot, but he's no Michael Jordan!" On the contrary, these parents wait and wait, offering encouragement and perhaps a few sympathetic groans, and then they roar with approval and applause when a child—any child—makes a basket. When was the last time we roared with approval and applause for a homework assignment well done, a test question answered correctly, or a project completed on time? In some arenas, parental feedback is immediate, positive, and relevant to success. In other cases, parental feedback is infrequent, negative, and related to vague expectations of perfection that seem unreachable by the student.

The Confusion of Self-Esteem and Self-Confidence

Much has been written and said about self-esteem, with most of these words substituting rhetoric for evidence. The facts are clear: Self-esteem is important. When students, or for that matter, adults, feel a sense of self-worth, they tend to perform at higher levels. The issue is not whether self-esteem is important, but how this elusive quality is best achieved. Some parents believe that we build self-esteem through challenge and rigor, in the way that the movie stereotype of the Marine drill sergeants "build men" in boot camp through a mix of ridicule, shouting, and demands. Other parents, and an astonishing number of teachers, believe that we build self-esteem through constant affirmation of children, including reassurances that children are always great, wonderful, and terrific even when the children know that they are not always great, wonderful, and terrific. Both extremes are wrong. Parents must balance affirmation with honesty. We cannot tell a child that she made the basket when her own observation is to the contrary. It is equally unwise to tell a child that his performance is inadequate when the child just scored a point for his team.

Let us move the context from the playground to schoolwork. We should not tell the child that her paper is wonderful when she knows and we know that it is careless and inaccurate. We should not tell the child of her shortcomings because her paragraph of second grade work falls short of Hemingway. Honesty, rather than excessively high or low expectations, best serves children. We build self-esteem with clear, honest feedback, not with impossible challenges or improbable reassurances. "This was great and I'm really proud of you!" is as appropriate as "You are really getting good at this!" With a little more work you're going to be even better. I know you can do it!"

While the distinction may appear subtle, the difference between self-esteem and self-efficacy is an important one. Esteem alone is not sufficient. Humans must not only feel a sense of worth, but they must also have the bone-deep conviction that their efforts make a difference. In other words, their self-esteem is the result of their genuine worth and effort, not merely awarded by someone out of sympathy for an incompetent child. Anyone who has listened attentively to the conversations of children about the important adults in their lives knows that children have a profound and insightful understanding of the difference between sympathy and confidence. The patronizing compliments of adults can be withdrawn, but the capacity that children have to make a difference in their own lives is enduring. Thus, it is not merely esteem that our children must develop and maintain, but efficacy. In the words of Dr. Jeff Howard, president of the Efficacy Institute, "Smart is something you get, not just something you are." When students believe that they have the capacity for improvement, they are far more resilient and persistent than when they depend on another person for compliments, assurances, and affirmation.

The Limits of Tests

As important as tests are, it is essential that parents and children understand what tests tell us and what they don't. The best any test can do is to report the performance of a student on a particular set of questions on a particular day. Just as a blood pressure test does not represent a complete physical and just as blood pressure is subject to change from one reading to the next, so also test results do not represent a complete analysis of student ability and those results can change radically depending on testing conditions and student preparation.

The most meaningful tests report not only a score, but also how to get better. This is one of the most significant advantages of student self-evaluation. Rather than submitting work to an all-knowing teacher who then awards a grade, the student who engages in self-evaluation must understand the difference between acceptable and unacceptable work. Rather than communicating only a letter or numerical grade, the most effective tests challenge the complacent student and encourage the discouraged child. On letter-graded tests, the complacent student might receive an A or a B and receive the message, "I'm doing pretty well, so there isn't much else to learn." The discouraged student might receive a low grade and receive the message, "That's as well as I can do, so I guess I'm just not a very good student." The best tests not only evaluate, but educate students. These tests communicate to parents about the performance of their children, and also provide specific information about what students know and where they need to improve. Supplied with these insights, parents can help their children improve. Of course, these ideal tests are rare in most schools. Parents receive a score, and that's it. Rather than attempt to draw conclusions from a score alone, parents need to be advocates for tests that educate. In addition, parents must be careful to avoid "over-interpreting" a test score or grade.

Consider the case of the child who brings home a "C" on a test. One parent's frame of reference might be that a C is acceptable, if not great work, so perhaps it's best not to make a big deal out of it, and another parent might exclaim, "You obviously didn't do your best work on this test—what went wrong?" Both conclusions are unhelpful and probably inaccurate. The focus of the parent-child conversation should not be on the evaluation, but rather on the learning that did and did not take place. Rather than begin the conversation with evaluative statements, we should reframe every discussion as a learning conversation. It is always wise to begin with something positive, such as, "You did a great job on number 17—I didn't know you knew all of that! Tell me more about it." Then we must do what is one of the most essential, and rare, activities of parents: We must listen. Parents and teachers routinely engage in the fantasy that because they are talking, children are learning. While there is value to talk from parents and teachers, conversations are far more constructive when they are informed by the child's point of view. Thus, we begin with what the child does know and the places on the test where the performance was satisfactory. After giving the child an opportunity to elaborate on the good parts of his performance, we can then ask, "What do you wish you had done differently on this test?" This opens the door to a discussion of the questions that were blank or answered incorrectly. You might learn that the child ran out of time. You might learn that the child had failed to study. You might learn that the child does not understand fundamental concepts necessary to performance on this test. But my experience suggests that it is far more likely that you will learn that the child knew the material, but failed to understand the instructions. You might learn, for example, that the child was so confident that the haste to display her knowledge got in the way of taking time to read the instructions. You might also learn that the instructions were unclear and that many reasonable test takers, including you, might have had the same misunderstanding as your child. And it is possible that you will learn that the response was correct after all and that the scoring of the test was wrong. None of these learning conversations will occur, however, if we respond to the grade on the test rather than the content of the test.

focus on learning

Report Cards and Learning Conversations

Just as learning conversations should prevail in our discussions of tests and homework, so should the communication between parent and child about report cards focus on learning rather than evaluation. This is difficult. As I write these words, I reflect on the times I have reacted in haste to report cards, with joy at the "A" and with disappointment at lower grades, and in neither case conducting a learning conversation with my children. Taking a deliberate break from our natural reactions toward evaluation rather than education requires intellectual and emotional discipline, and those qualities can be in short supply when any parent, including a professional educator, first sees a report card. But the skill can be learned. Consider the physician who looks at your test results and exclaims, "Oh boy, are *you* in trouble!" And with those words, orders you to "work harder in the future" and then quickly leaves the room. The bewilderment, fear, and rage that might be our natural reactions to such a confrontation with a preoccupied physician are not unlike the reactions of children to typical discussions of report cards with their parents. We expect the physician to stop, think, reflect, and then not only to offer the results of medical tests, but to engage in a conversation about how we can improve. If there is ambiguity or if the results indicate a problem, the wise physician might order additional tests or conduct additional examinations before coming to a hasty and potentially inaccurate conclusion. Even a physician who reports that a patient is in perfect health might be expected to offer analysis, insight, and discussion of how such excellent health can be maintained. We owe our children no less than the wise physicians owe their patients.

Inappropriate Uses of Test Scores

Just as we expect the wise physician to have a sound basis for drawing a conclusion, so must the wise parent and teacher have a reasonable body of evidence for the determinations they make about children. Incredibly, single tests are used inappropriately to make instant decisions on a routine basis. When this occurs, parents must become advocates not only for their children, but for the cause of accuracy in tests and the analysis of test results. By far the most common error made in the use of test scores is the overgeneralization about children, teachers, and schools. Based on a single test, a child can be denied promotion, a teacher's effectiveness can be questioned, or a school can be labeled as a failing institution. Worse yet are the life-changing decisions made based on a single test. Such decisions are typically associated with "high stakes" tests such as high school graduation examinations, but in fact many tests with significant consequences for children occur on a regular basis and do not have the label or the publicity associated with high stakes tests. Such important tests in which a few hours can make an enormous difference in the education and life of a child include the assessments used to label children as gifted or learning disabled, tests that grant or deny admission to special learning opportunities, and tests that claim to predict the ability, aptitude, or interests of children.

Parents should be deeply suspicious of tests that claim to draw conclusions about children, particularly when those conclusions are linked to words such as "intelligence" or "ability" or "aptitude." There is a sorry history of such tests stemming back to the early years of the 20th century when the test results were appropriated by the eugenics movement to support their racist conclusions. With the jargon, statistics, and confidence of testing experts, the nation was assured of the scientific "proof" of the genetic inferiority of people of Irish, Italian, and Jewish descent, particularly if they came from southern or eastern Europe. These absurd conclusions were based on the low scores of recent immigrants taking the "Army Alpha" tests during the early days of World War I. Interestingly, the same populations displayed much higher scores a generation later as their language skills and familiarity with cultural references in the tests improved. Such changes prove that those tests did not measure anything like "intelligence" or "aptitude" because such qualities theoretically are not subject to change. If, however, the tests provide only a snapshot of the present knowledge of the test taker, then the results can change with the active decision of the test taker to improve. While the reader may find the racism of the test advocates of 1917 to be shocking and unacceptable, there is no logical distinction between the inappropriate conclusions based on a single test then and the overgeneralizations based on a single test for children in the early years of the 21st century.

Defenders of the use of tests for important decisions frequently refer to the objectivity, reliability, and validity that experts have claimed for these tests. Although this is not the forum for a professional discourse on the attributes of testing, there is one concept with which all parents should be familiar: validity. In lay terms, a test is valid when we test what we think we are testing. While this may seem simple on the face of it, the element of validity in testing is quite inconsistent. Consider the driving test we require in every state. Success on a multiple-choice test would not be a valid representation of driving ability. That is why every prospective driver must also get behind the wheel and demonstrate to the examiner some degree of proficiency in driving. Similarly, pilots do more than pass a multiple-choice exam; they must complete their flight examinations with an equal number of take-offs and landings. If the driving and pilot examinations result in the granting of licenses to unqualified applicants, the public safety is at risk. Conversely, if these examinations result in the denial of licenses to qualified applicants, it is not only inconvenient, but probably will result in litigation by the person to whom a license is denied. Such a reaction is possible because the test taker knows the impact of each test and is aware of the link between the test and an adverse decision.

While the requirement for validity is the same in every test, whether the subject is driving or kindergarten placement, the quality of testing is very different. We routinely make decisions about the educational opportunities for children based on test results, and in many cases the link between the test and the adverse decision is unclear or even secret. Counselors, teachers, and administrators give or deny students a variety of opportunities such as special reading groups or enrichment programs based on their performance on a single test. Worse yet, sometimes the decisions are based on tests that were taken during the prior school year.

The defenders of such decisions sometimes maintain that the students in special programs do better than the "average" and thus such tests must have been valid. In this context, validity becomes a self-fulfilling prophecy. A student does well on a test and then receives extra instruction from teachers who have high expectations. They come home to parents who have been told that their child is superior. If there is a challenge in school for such children, they assume that they can work harder, ask for help, and ultimately succeed. That is, after all, what smart kids, gifted kids, successful kids such as themselves would be expected to do. Of course, this combination of strategy, encouragement, expectations, persistence, and self-confidence would serve any student well. The converse is true. When a test indicates that a student has a poor math aptitude or is unlikely to become a good writer, then the subsequent expectations of teachers, parents, and the students themselves will assure that the negative prediction is accurate.

Does this mean that we should abandon all tests? Of course not. It is the use of the tests and the inappropriate interpretation of their results that should be reformed. The distinction that must be drawn is between tests as information and tests as prediction. Tarot cards provide information because the names of the cards are clear to any observer; few people outside of the Psychic Friends Network, however, would argue that the interpretation of the tarot cards can become transformed into accurate predictions. Consider other measurements in life. The bathroom scale may be mathematically accurate, but the next step—interpretation and prediction—can take one of two markedly different paths. A reading of 180 pounds can result in the inference, "I'd feel better if I lost 10 pounds and I know just how to do it," or "I'm fat and stupid and ugly and can never change." The test was the same and the numbers were the same. The difference in the two responses involves interpretation and prediction.

Although parents may not always be able to influence the content or results of tests, we can make a profound impact on the interpretation of those tests and can fight the predictions that might be inaccurately made based upon those tests. The first challenge is in our own conversations about tests, focusing on learning and information rather than on evaluation, interpretation, and prediction. If parents fail to model learning conversations with children, they cannot influence the self-talk by children that inevitably occurs when parents are absent. Self-talk is powerful and, in the absence of strong logical challenges, can seem persuasive to anyone, particularly a child. Cognitive therapists challenge the illogical conclusions of their patients by helping them to identify the logical errors and destructive consequences of their self-talk. We do not need a therapist, however, to help our children think through why they believe as they do about their own successes and failures in school. If we listen, we might find thought patterns revealed in such self-talk as "I'm no good at math!" The source of such self-talk is rarely a scientific examination in which the algebra gene was found to be missing. Rather, there was some test, some conversation, some announcement of student proficiency in mathematics, and on that tenuous basis, an inappropriate conclusion was drawn. Sometimes the parent's first response is to offer assurances to the doubtful child such as, "Sure, you're good at math," or worse yet, "You think you were bad? I had trouble in math as well." It would be more constructive if we ask, "Why do you think that?" And then complete the conversation in a way that children can challenge their own conclusions. This might require some gentle inquiry and lots of listening by the parent. While the encouragement, love, and high expectations of parents are undeniably important, we must also develop the self-confidence of our children by giving them the skills to challenge their own negative images that stem from inappropriate interpretation and predictions of their past performance on tests.

fair tests

Standards: The Path Toward More Fair and Meaningful Tests

Because the words "standards" and "testing" are frequently used in the same sentence, some people have associated bad tests and inappropriate usage of test information with the standards movement. In fact, the proper application of academic standards leads to tests that are more fair and educational than traditional tests that are shrouded in mystery. Standards-based tests are fundamentally different from traditional tests in that student performance is compared to a standard rather than to the performance of other students. An academic standard is a simple statement of what students are expected to know and be able to do. Because the standards are public documents, students need not guess about the expectations of teachers. Thus, with standards, tests are not a game of *Jeopardy* in which the student with the most encyclopedic memory of many disconnected facts is the winner. Rather, any student who meets the standard can be a winner. Student success in a standards-based environment is a matter of what you know, not who you beat.

Because standards-based tests reject the notion of comparing one student to another, the traditional bell-shaped curve is rejected as a method of analyzing student performance. When schools use the bell curve, they assume that there are a few students who perform significantly above the average, a few students who are significantly below the average, and the vast majority of students who are in the middle. The last group forms the "bell"—the large hump in the middle of the curve. Although the bell curve is widely used in statistics and has been a staple of educational evaluation for more than a century, there is just one thing wrong with it: It is an inaccurate way to describe student achievement. When educational evaluation is based on a comparison to the average—the middle of the bell curve—then we have another self-fulfilling prophecy. If the instrument used to evaluate children only allows for a few students who are very much above average, then the use of that instrument—not the nature of children being tested—establishes the proof of the bell curve.

Test designers have a clever way of avoiding any evidence that does not fit their theory. If, for example, all children get a particular question right, then some observers might be delighted at the obvious result of diligent work by teachers and students. But in a test dedicated to the bell curve, such a question is simply discarded. The "good" questions are those that clearly differentiate one student from another. Ironically, the technical term for such differentiation is "discrimination," a term whose connotation of unfairness might be more accurate than the statistical meaning of identifying differences among students.

There are some instances in which a bell curve approach to testing might make some sense. If there are scarce resources to be allocated—such as admission to a selective college or selection for a high-paying job—then some people argue that only a bell curve test can rank students from best to worst. This sounds great in theory. After all, isn't the 98th percentile always better than the 96th percentile? The answer is, not necessarily. In fact, on many tests, the difference between those two rankings might be the response on a very small number of questions and student mastery of the those questions may or may not be related to success in the college or job under consideration. In fact, the difference between those two might be random or, at the very least, not relevant to the decision at hand. Consider other examinations, such as those for firefighter or jet pilot. In both cases, it is not sufficient for one candidate to beat another candidate. Any successful candidate applying for these positions must meet demanding physical and mental requirements. If no one meets those standards, the examiners do not say, "You can't carry someone out of a flaming building, but you're above the average of the other candidates, so we will accept you." Moreover, if there are several qualified candidates, the examiners do not say, "You are both highly qualified candidates, but Mary knew a little more about particle physics than Joe did, and therefore we will select Mary for the job." The candidates meet the standards or they don't, and if more people meet a standard than are needed to fill a vacancy, then the appropriate decision is not to resort to irrelevant information. In the context of education, the ultimate objectives should be accuracy and fairness. When schools use standards, teachers are liberated from the ancient and inaccurate practice of grading "on the curve" and instead can speak the truth: The student is proficient or not proficient compared to a standard, and a comparison to the work of other students is not relevant to my decision.

Standards are hardly a revolutionary approach to education. In fields as diverse as music and athletics, educators have long used standards. When a student wishes to play in the orchestra or participate on the basketball team, the requirement is not merely to beat other students, but rather to play scales, shoot baskets, or otherwise meet a standard that the conductor or coach has prescribed. The rules of the game are clear, and students need not guess about the height of the basket or the number of strings on a violin. Chapter 2 provides more detailed information about academic standards and what they mean for your child.

What about Talent and Intelligence?

Some readers are thinking, "Wait a minute! In the real world, everybody can't be a winner. Besides, there are some things that just can't be taught, and those things include talent and intelligence. You can't teach a golfer to be a Tiger Woods or a violinist to be Yehudi Menhuin." This controversy about the relative impact of "born" traits versus taught skills has been at the center of educational debates since Plato. The Greek philosopher believed that there were "men of gold" who ruled over the "men of bronze." Not much has changed in the more than two thousand intervening years, as many people assume that "some kids have it and some don't."

Consider the example of musical talent, a quality many people assume is "born, not made." The Suzuki method of musical instruction has influenced literally millions of students and parents on every continent on the globe. As a result of the influence of Suzuki training, students without obvious genetic heritage of musicianship have found places in symphony orchestras throughout the world. Although the debate over talent and intelligence continues, those who discount the primacy of teaching and learning over inborn traits are deliberately indifferent to the evidence. There are surely cases of the most exceptional musicians, mathematicians, and athletes who may have some genetic predisposition toward their chosen careers. Nevertheless, the experience of the legions of students who have benefited from the Suzuki method make clear that the existence of exceptional talent and intelligence in a very few cases does not negate the general principle that talent and intelligence of the many can be nurtured, encouraged, and expanded. As Dr. Howard said, "Smart is something you get, not just something you are."

constructive conversations

Talking with Your Child about Standards and Tests

Children attribute an unusually high degree of credibility to what they hear at school, and thus the potentially negative conversations surrounding tests and standards that your child may encounter must be the subject of serious home discussion. Parents, not the local rumor mill, must determine the appropriate way for each child to react to standards and testing. This is not an issue on which the final parental word is, "Because I said so!" In our discussions with children, we must seek to equip them to stand on their own in the conflicts of the classroom and hallway. Thus, the following "point/counterpoint" dialogues are designed to suggest ways for you to talk constructively with your child about standards and tests.

"Those tests tell you how smart you are. If you don't do well, it means you're a dummy."

"Tests don't tell how smart you are, but tests do tell you a couple of things. They tell you what you have learned and they also tell you how good you are at figuring things out even when the right answer isn't very clear. That's why it's a good idea to pay attention and

study, and it's also a good idea to sit down with me and look at some of your old tests. If
there is ever a test where you don't do well, we'll just work on it a little more. You're
smart—and if you don't do well on a test, it just means we need to think through what
happened and figure out how to do better. I know you can do it."

"If I don't do well on this test I'll be ruined! I won't get to go to the next grade with my friends. I just know I'm going to blow it!"

"It sounds as if you're pretty nervous about this test. Tell me how you're feeling about it
right now? (Pause.) It's pretty scary, isn't it? Now, tell me how you felt when you did a
great job in school. Remember that time when you got a perfect score on the spelling test
and when you were so happy about your geography test? Tell me how you felt then?
(Pause.) When you feel smart and good and happy, what did you do to make yourself feel
that way? Let's make a list. Maybe we can discover the things that you have done when
you felt smart and good and happy and we'll figure out how to do those things again now.
If you do those same things, I know that you'll do a great job. And you know what? Even if
your pencil breaks, the wind blows your test paper away, and the teacher turns into a
green-eyed dragon and breathes fire on everybody's test, I'm going to love you anyway.
Do we have a deal? Let's start making that list. . ."

"I can't possibly memorize all these things. My teacher said that the standards were impossible anyway and that no kids our age could do them. Mrs. Johnson said the same thing in the car on the way to school today. There's just nothing I can do. I give up!"

"I don't know. I've heard a lot of people say that kids can't do things, like play soccer or
go on the Internet or create plays and make up songs, and then the kids do a great job
anyway. When you said that the standards were impossible, which standards were you
talking about? (Pause.) Well, I haven't read them either, so do you want to look them up
and see if they are really impossible or if you can do most of them after all? What's your
best subject? Let's start there . . ."

"I don't want to meet the standards—I want to be me! All my teachers have said I was a great writer ever since first grade. Now they tell me that I can only write the same way, every time, with a beginning, middle, and end. I used to write funny stories with crazy characters and goofy conversations, but now they say I have to be more serious. I hate standards, and so does everybody else. I have a dumb assignment because the dumb standard says that I have to compare two different dumb things. It's just stupid, and I don't want to do it. I want to write my stories!"

"I love your creative stories, too. In fact, would you like to write one right now? You can have all the crazy characters and goofy conversations that you want. I've saved some of the ones that you've written in the past. While you're working on your new story, I'm going to read some of my favorites. (Let the child write, and make clear that the love of creativity and the act of writing will always be of value to you. In half an hour or so, when the new story is done, continue the conversation.) Wow—that's great! You always amaze me with your stories and I can see why you love to write them so much. It sounds as if you think that the essays in school with a beginning, middle, and end are a lot more boring than your stories, is that right? I wonder if we could figure out a way to do both your wonderful stories and the essays the way your teacher likes them. Let's start by thinking about the way that the story you just wrote is similar to the story you wrote a few months ago. Then let's think about how it's different. Then you decide which one you liked better and why. By the time we're done, I think you might have that homework assignment done, and I know that I'll have another one of your great stories that I can keep to read again and again."

Your Right to Know about Tests in Your Child's School

Testing need not be mysterious or filled with terror. In fact, federal law establishes a parent's right to know what tests their children are taking and what the tests are about. This right includes everything from the weekly spelling tests to psychological tests to diagnostic tests to high-stakes graduation tests. If tests are mysterious, it is because parents do not ask the right questions. A sample letter from a parent to school officials requesting access to test information appears on page 92.

Parents' Checklist:

☐ Ask questions about your child's day based on his feelings and emotions, rather than events.

☐ Find out what tests are given in your child's school and how they are used to make any decisions about your child. Enter each of these test dates on your family calendar so that you can help to provide encouragement and reduce anxiety for your child.

☐ Celebrate your child's school accomplishments with the same enthusiasm you found in her first steps or her latest victory in a game.

celebrate
accomplishments

Chapter 4

Parents' Questions about Standards and Tests

This chapter is the result of hundreds of encounters with parents in focus groups, interviews, casual conversations, and letters. My research included parents from a wide variety of economic, educational, and cultural backgrounds. Although the parents with whom I spoke frequently expressed the conviction that their concerns were unique, the themes of these conversations were remarkably consistent. Parents have heard many rumors about academic standards, and much of what they have heard is the cause of significant fear and apprehension. The most consistent and significant desire expressed by parents is for specific communication from teachers about what children need to know and be able to do. Parents want more than a report card and annual parent-teacher conference. Parents want to play a role beyond working at a table at the school carnival or operating the copy machine in the school office. Parents, in brief, want information that is accurate and relevant to their children.

Despite the differences among the parents interviewed for this chapter, all of them have one thing in common: They care deeply about the educational opportunities for their children. Whether the parent was a Harvard-educated attorney or a high school dropout, the message was the same: Parents want their children to have more opportunities than they had and they are willing to support schools that provide such opportunities. They also insist on fairness for their children and clear communication from schools. Parents detest jargon, slogans, patronizing speeches, memos, and notes that appeared to diminish the importance of the family. At the same time, parents were leery of the implication that they were primarily responsible for the education of their children. Whether the subject of discussion was math homework, test preparation, or summer reading, many parents bristled at the notion that they were responsible for doing a job that the school was supposed to do. Finally, the parents with whom I spoke were deeply concerned about the impact of a single test on their child, and most parents saw more threats than opportunities in the high-stakes testing movement.

The questions and responses that follow are hardly exhaustive, but they represent a synthesis of the attitudes, feelings, beliefs, and concerns of parents throughout the nation. You might recognize some of your own questions in the dialogue that follows.

reduce anxiety

What Should I Say to My Child about Standards and Tests?

This is a great opportunity to move your children away from test terror toward becoming confident and capable students. Start with a clear definition: *Standards are the things that you should know and be able to do.* Then identify some of the standards that your children are already meeting. Review just a few of the standards in this book and tell your child, "You are already doing this. You see, standards aren't always something new and extra that you must learn; you already know many of these things right now!"

It is difficult to have a discussion with your child about academic standards without also discussing the tests based on your state's standards. This conversation is about emotions, not just about facts. Some parents are tempted to say something like, "You'd better study hard or you'll flunk the test!" In fact, the primary emotion of fear is already overwhelming, and the role of the parent is not to add to that anxiety, but to reduce it. How can you reduce your child's anxiety? Avoid false reassurances such as, "It's no big deal!" or "I'm sure you'll do just fine, so don't worry about it." When, in the life of parents, has the statement "Don't worry about it" served as a useful reassurance? What children most need to know is that their parent has heard and understood their fears. It is better to say, "Yes, tests can be pretty scary. When you fear something, it's always better to talk about it than to pretend that it's no big deal. What is there on this list of standards, or what have you heard about the test that is the most scary for you?" The parent finally has the information that can take the conversation from a dialogue filled with fear to the realm of the confident and empowered child. You will know that you have succeeded in these conversations—don't expect the matter to be resolved with a single discussion—when your child starts saying things such as:

"I know what I'm supposed to do in school."

"If I don't know how to do something, I know that I can figure it out or I know where I can get some help."

"I may not get a perfect score on the test, but I know most of the things on there. And if I miss a few questions, it doesn't mean I'm stupid. I'll just continue to learn all I can and do my best."

These are the words of a confident and empowered child. Parents need not give their children illusions, as if the Test Fairy will come to their aid in time of need. Rather, parents must give their children facts: what the standards are, what the tests mean, and how children's own efforts will improve their ability to achieve standards and do well on tests.

Is This Just Another Fad?

fairness

Y ou have probably heard of educational terms that sounded like fads, from "new math" to "whole language" to "learning styles" to "brain research" and a host of other labels that seem to dominate the discussion of educational matters from one year to the next. How do you know that the term "standards" is not just another passing fad? First, let's remember what standards are all about. The label is not important, but the essence of standards is vital. Standards are just about fairness. Because standards express what students should know and be able to do, and because standards-based schools expect teachers to give children the opportunity to meet those standards, there is nothing new or fancy at work here other than a simple commitment to fairness. Standards will not go "out of style" unless the desire of parents and teachers for fairness becomes a passing fad.

Who Sets the Standards?

I n every state except Iowa, academic content standards are established by the state. In Iowa, every school district sets its own standards. Thus, some form of academic standards exists in every public school in the nation. Indeed, whether or not the term "standard" is used, most private and parochial schools also have a clear set of academic expectations for students.

One frequent misunderstanding is that "national standards" govern the content of the academic disciplines. In fact, a few groups such as the National Council for Teachers of Mathematics, National Council for Teachers of English, and other academic and professional organizations, have offered suggested standards that frequently are used as resources by state departments of education and local school districts. There is not, however, a "Federal Department of Standards" in Washington, D.C. where busy bureaucrats wake up every morning plotting new ways to remove the local authority of school boards. There are no federally established academic standards imposed on schools. Although the federal government has broad authority with respect to protecting individual civil rights in school—particularly with regard to discrimination on the basis of ethnicity, gender, or disability—the federal role in curriculum is strictly advisory.

The evidence of state and local control over the curriculum is best revealed in the wide variation in the academic content standards of the states. Some states, such as New York and California, have very specific academic expectations, and those academic requirements are linked to curriculum documents and test objectives. Other states, by contrast, have academic requirements that are much more vague, leaving the discretion to select specific curriculum and test objectives to local school districts.

Despite the differences among state standards, there are some important commonalities. The most important distinguishing characteristic of standards-based schools is the comparison of students to a standard rather than to the average of other students. Many states blur this distinction in their testing policies. Rather than refer to the percentage of students who meet a standard, some state documents continue to make reference to "percentile" or other methods of ranking students. It will take some time before every state policy maker and administrator applies standards carefully and accurately.

Do Standards Place Too Much Emphasis on Academics?

Many parents expressed the concern that standards emphasize academic subjects to the exclusion of extracurricular activities, the arts, and simple fun in school. Some of these parents have heard alarming news stories (and more than a few unsubstantiated rumors) about schools that have been transformed into academic boot camps. In these dreary places, students do nothing except prepare for tests all day long. Work sheets and mock tests have replaced recess and painting. A number of popular writers have fanned the flames of this hysteria, fueled more by anecdote than by evidence.

It is true that when standards have been established with care, some traditional activities have been replaced by lessons with a greater academic orientation. This does not, however, imply the elimination of holiday celebrations and the systematic removal of fun from the school day. Students in standards-based schools will, for example, probably continue to bring Valentines to class in February. It does not hurt the cause of student enjoyment, however, if in addition to exchanging Valentine cards and having a party, students also read about the holiday, write their own cards rather than purchase them from a store, and otherwise incorporate academic relevance into fun activities. Indeed, the activities in this book make it clear that fun, engagement, and academic standards are not mutually exclusive.

Why Can't School Just Be Fun?

One of the frequent concerns expressed by parents I interviewed was the lament that school is no longer fun. Parents have heard tales of multi-hour homework assignments and children who complained that "Monday is the worst day of the week" because school was so terrifying. Some of these parents assumed that the appropriate reaction to the state of affairs must be a reduction of the academic expectations for their children. Parents should consider that it is entirely possible that the difficulties the students are facing arise because previous teachers did not have sufficiently high expectations of them. When everyone is focused on making school fun, the teacher who insists that students learn something is accused of being demanding and mean. This reinforces the notion that learning is burdensome and that school is dreadfully dull. The problem compounds itself in middle school, high school, and even in college, when the expectation of rigor is abandoned and students are viewed as "customers" who must be satisfied by credits that are easy, fun, and worthless.

What about the Basics—Reading, Writing, and Arithmetic?

Some parents are concerned that an emphasis on the higher order thinking skills included in many academic standards will reduce an emphasis on the "basics"—that is, skills in reading, writing, and arithmetic. In fact, there is not a contradiction between the requirement for higher order thinking and basic skills. Students cannot learn to master the challenge of mathematical problem solving if they do not have arithmetic skills. Moreover, students cannot respond to the challenge of critical thinking in social studies and science if they are unable to read their social studies and science textbooks or write a lab report.

The controversy over basic education has been particularly acute in mathematics. Partisans of pure "problem-solving" believe that an emphasis on mathematical concepts is essential, and that the dreary "drill and kill" of traditional worksheets must be discarded in favor of an emphasis on thinking. Of course, most mathematics teachers and parents recognize the intuitively obvious proposition that problem-solving and math skills are inseparable. Even in an age of calculators and computers, students must have "number sense." This means that students not only must be able to compute that $9 \times 9 = 81$ but they must also be able to understand that the number 81 is comprised of nine groups of nine and comprehend the notion that there are many other ways to achieve a product of 81. For example, consider these three levels of mathematical understanding, using the same example that begins with the question, "What is 9×9?"

The lowest level of understanding is expressed by the student who grabs the calculator and punches the buttons: $9 \times 9 =$ receives the answer 81. The next level of understanding is the student who recalled from memory that the product was 81 and did not need the calculator for assistance. But neither of these levels of understanding approaches the sophistication of the student who not only understands that $9 \times 9 = 81$, but also understands that since $3 \times 3 = 9$, then 81 is also the product of $3 \times 3 \times 3 \times 3$. For this student, the study of exponents in a future grade will be intuitive and easy. He will immediately grasp that $3^4 = 81$ rather than perceive exponents as a new and foreign mathematical concept that must be memorized without understanding. In other words, students need both the basics and thinking skills. The two are complementary, not competitive concepts.

Similarly, we expect students to have a deep understanding of causes and effects in history and science. But these deep understandings will elude students who do not have the ability to read and understand the paragraph before them. Moreover, the thinking skills involved in understanding the interplay of politics, geography, economics and conflict will elude students who did not study the factual details of those subjects. Thus, anyone who contends that an emphasis on standards excludes a commitment to basic skills has not carefully read the standards. I have met with angry parent groups whose concerns about standards were allayed when presented with the actual words of the standards. The academic standards make clear that students must not only master thinking, reasoning, and analysis, but also must understand how to read, write, and compute, as well as know the content associated with the foundational academic subjects.

a high level of understanding

Will Standards Mean the Elimination of Music, Art, and Physical Education?

There is a legitimate concern expressed by many parents that the overwhelming emphasis in state tests and standards on mathematics and language arts will exclude music, art, and physical education in some schools. In most successful schools I have studied, mathematics, social studies, science, music, art, and physical education are an integral part of the academic life of the school. For example, students in music class routinely use melody, rhythm, and song lyrics as a bridge to better understand history, learn new vocabulary, and master fractions. Students in art class use the visual images of art to expand their vocabulary and enhance their ability to compare and contrast different images. Moreover, students in effective art classes are able to master the art of scale and ratio, measurement, and the relationship between different geometric figures. There are wonderful physical education classes in which students acquire a better understanding of measurement. When the coach has given students the choice to run a millimeter or a kilometer, and the students make the wrong choice, the lesson on metric measurement tends to remain with them for a long time. Moreover, I have seen effective physical education teachers conduct vocabulary relays and math relays in which students must not only run fast but also must understand vocabulary and mathematical information in order to continue the race. This is the ideal intersection of the academic, the aesthetic, and the athletic.

Similarly, science and social studies need not be neglected because the state tests emphasize language arts and mathematics. Wise teachers know that science requires reading and writing, as well as the collection, measurement, and display of data. Perceptive social studies teachers know that students who frequently write essays about the relationships between geography, history, and economics will better understand both the content and the concepts of those subjects. The students in these science and social studies classes are not neglecting the importance of literacy and math, but are applying those essential skills in a different context.

the ideal intersection

Does My Child Really Have to Meet All of the Standards?

One of the weaknesses of standards as they have been articulated in most states is the failure of prioritization. In fact, not every standard is of equal value. Some standards recognize the need of basic skills, including reading, writing, and arithmetic. Moreover, the standards recognize the need of students to analyze and understand a relatively narrow set of facts. But neither every fact nor every skill has equal value for the student. Thus, it is not accurate to say that children have to meet every single standard elaborated by the state. One method of distinguishing the more important standards from those that are interesting but less valuable is the concept of "power standards." Chapter 5 provides more detailed elaboration on this concept.

What Happens If My Child Doesn't Meet the Standards?

When children do not meet academic content standards, the most immediate response should be the opportunity for additional learning. In other words, the immediate consequence for the failure to achieve a standard should be neither a low grade nor the repetition of an entire year of school. Rather, the initial consequence should be the opportunity for additional learning. This recognizes what all parents know to be true: Students learn at different rates. Many states have implemented high-stakes tests that are associated with academic content standards and some of these tests have dramatic consequences. For example, in some states, students must pass a reading proficiency test in order to enter the fourth grade. In other states, students must pass middle school proficiency tests in order to enter high school. A growing number of states—26 at this writing—have established high school graduation examinations, which must be successfully completed by students in order to receive a high school diploma.

In the best school districts, the student performance on these examinations is rarely a surprise. In fact, students have multiple opportunities to prepare for important tests. Parents also have many opportunities to know well in advance of the test whether their children need additional help. Unfortunately, many school districts have a reactive response to high-stakes tests. Remediation and opportunities for additional learning only take place after a student has failed a test. Worst of all is the fallacy of remediation in high school for problems that have their roots in elementary and middle school.

If you are concerned about the performance of your child on a high-stakes test, then the use the letter format on page 92 to inquire of your school administration what specific testing policies will affect your child. Once you have this information, identify the particular knowledge and skills that your child will be required to have. Then you will be able to identify the gap between what your child knows at this time, and what your child will need to know and be able to do when the test is administered.

Parents frequently make the same mistake as schools, becoming involved in a child's academic challenges only after a student is experiencing difficulty in school. The most successful parental involvement occurs long before a child has experienced academic difficulty. Therefore, if you are concerned about the performance of your child in an upcoming test, the time to become involved is now, not after you receive your child's score.

My Child Just Doesn't Get It. What Do I Do?

Lots of frustrated parents share your concern. Most of us attempt to teach our children in the same way that we learned. In other words, if we learned by having someone read to us or speak to us, we assume that our children learn the same way. If we learned by having instructions written out for us, then we assume that our children will benefit from our own written instructions. Fortunately, children have a way of emulating some but not all of our characteristics. One of the things that they may not inherit is your learning style. As result, please do not assume that your child "just doesn't get it" simply because the child is not learning the same way that you did.

You can discover your child's learning style by identifying the circumstances in which your child performs at a very high level. For example, perhaps your child plays a game exceptionally well. Perhaps your child enjoys a particular story so much that she is able to repeat it word for word. Perhaps your child enjoys writing to a relative or receiving mail. These will give you clues about the ways in which your child acquires information, processes that information, and applies information to the task at hand. Of course, just because a person prefers one learning style does not mean that the rest of the world will always accommodate that need. Therefore, children need to be able to process information from written text, oral instructions, and the context of the world around them. By finding your child's preferred method of learning, you can capitalize on that strength and also be more attentive to building skills in those learning methods that do not come so easily to your child.

When you become frustrated with your child's performance, one of the most important things that you can do is to stop the common practice of giving your child a single set of instructions involving the performance of multiple tasks. The most common example is, "Clean up your room!" For some children, this instruction is clear. For others, we must be more clear by breaking down the tasks: "Take the clothes off the floor and put them in the hamper." Then, after the successful completion of that task, "Empty the trash." Then, "Let your brother out of the toy chest," and so on, until the task of cleaning the room is completed. The breaking down of complex instructions into individual tasks is essential in the academic context as well. The only way you can isolate the difficulty your child is having is by providing clear instructions in a step-by-step manner. You may find that the problem is neither an inability to comprehend your instructions, nor an unwillingness to act on them. The difficulty, rather, may be that your child, like all of us, prefers some types of instructions to others. It is also quite likely that there is a difference in understanding when your child hears instructions compared to when the same instructions are printed on a page and your child must independently read and respond to them. The difference between oral and visual strengths is not the only learning style you should consider. Some children who do not respond well to oral or written instructions can perform the same tasks well if they see a physical model of the expected result, watch a demonstration, or engage in trial and error. The point is not that one of these learning styles is "right," but rather that every person learns in different ways, yet all of us occasionally are compelled to acquire information in a manner that does not correspond to our strengths. By understanding the need to listen, read, or observe demonstrations, a parent can support a child's strengths and offer encouragement and practice to deal with learning styles that are less familiar and, in the past, less successful.

Another common reason for children having difficulties in school is the disconnection between previous learning and current expectations. For example, students are bound to have difficulty in fourth grade location division if they failed to master addition and subtraction in earlier grades. Students are not going to be able to create a satisfactory paragraph in fifth grade if they were unable to write coherent sentences in earlier grades. One of the principal benefits of the standards movement has been the requirement that teachers communicate with one another so that, in the best standards-based schools, there is a seamless transition from one grade to the next. A fourth-grade teacher has confidence about what students learned in the third grade because the third grade curriculum was not based on the personal preferences of the teacher, but rather on a coherent curriculum that led directly to the instructional needs of the fourth grade classroom. It is fair to say, however, that this ideal, seamless transition from one grade to the next is the exception rather than the rule in most American schools. Moreover, many schools have high rates of student and teacher mobility so that it is impossible to assume that every child in every class had a common foundation of learning.

The final consideration with respect to children who are having difficulty in school should be evaluation for learning disabilities. When you have tried to analyze a child's learning style with few results, and when you have attempted to help your child fill in the gaps from previous grade levels, it may be that your child continues to have immense difficulties in school. In these cases, it is appropriate to request an evaluation of your child for a variety of learning disabilities. Some parents fear that if they request an evaluation of their child, a label with negative connotations such as "special education" may be applied to their child. It is essential to note that both federal laws and public perceptions have changed markedly in the past several years on this issue. If your child is among the 11 percent of students nationwide with an identified learning disability, it does not mean that your child is "stupid" or otherwise incapable of great performance. The fields of law, medicine, music, and governmental leadership include many men and women who have learning disabilities. Indeed, identification of and compensation for a learning disability are the keys to their success. It is also very likely that children who are evaluated will not have a learning disability, and that work by those children, along with parents and teachers, on academic and behavioral issues will help them reach their full potential.

What If My Child Has a Learning Disability?

More than 11 percent of students across the United States have some sort of learning disability. We have made great strides in this country in diagnosing, understanding, and even valuing the diversity of learning styles that different students bring to class, and this includes learning disabilities. The notion of "valuing" a learning disability is not merely a politically correct posture designed to make students and parents feel good about a bad situation. Marcus Buckingham and Donald Clifton of the Gallup Organization, one of the leading polling and management consulting firms in the world, provide examples of how even the profoundly challenging reading disability, dyslexia, can result in positive effects for students and adults who recognize the disability and carefully plot strategies for dealing with it. Students with learning disabilities have clear legal rights expressed in the Individuals with Disabilities Education Act (IDEA). Moreover, the students frequently have rights that are protected by local district policy and state law.

Foremost among the rights of learning disabled students is the right to have the "least restrictive environment" for learning. This typically means that learning disabled students are sitting next to students in regular education classes with regular teachers. The students, therefore, must have accommodations and adaptations made for them, particularly when it is time for a test. The most frequent accommodations and adaptations include time, environment, reading, and writing. The adaptation of time is provided to students who process information slowly, but accurately, and thus taking more time on a test allows them to accurately express what they know. The adaptation of environment provides for a quiet and secluded test-taking environment for students whose learning disability limits their concentration. The adaptation of reading allows students who understand words, but cannot process words in printed form, to have tests read aloud to them. Finally, the adaptation of writing allows a student who can speak words, but cannot write them, to dictate test responses to an adult for the writing portion of the test. Of course, these are only some of the many adaptations that are available to students with disabilities.

It is absolutely vital that parents and teachers distinguish between appropriate accommodation and the reduction of rigor for a test. Many professions include members who are extraordinarily gifted and intelligent, and yet suffer from some learning disability. The gifts of these professionals would never have been recognized had their teachers and parents reduced rigor rather than seek the most appropriate adaptation for the needs of the students. There are instances in which parents and teachers harbor grave misconceptions about the distinction between appropriate accommodation and an inappropriate reduction in rigor. Such misunderstandings are usually revealed in the form of a statement such as, "She's in special education so I had to give her a B," or, "He has a learning disability, so even though he didn't take the test or complete the project, I had to give him a C." Such statements are at odds with both federal law and the best interests of the child. The focus of IDEA is appropriate consideration of individual needs. There is not a single sentence in the law or accompanying regulations that requires teachers to lie to parents about the nature of student performance. Indeed, the requirements for individual considerations in curriculum and assessments are not a prescription for "dumbing down" requirements, but rather a requirement for appropriate accommodations and adaptations. When those adaptations are offered to students, it is typical that the report card will indicate that the student "achieved standards with appropriate adaptations and accommodations." Moreover, when a student does not meet an academic standard, the appropriate and accurate report should reflect that "the student met these objectives in the educational plan and did not meet the other objectives in the educational plan." The path to improved performance by all students, including students with learning disabilities, is accuracy and honesty in assessment.

For more information on students with learning disabilities, please consult Chapter 9.

accuracy and honesty

What If I Disagree with the State and Local Standards?

Standards are political documents. They represent the efforts of a group of people who have endeavored to identify what students should know and be able to do. Nevertheless, as with any product of any committee, the documents are typically flawed. One can accept the obvious notion that some standards are too broad, some are too narrow, and most remain "works in progress," and nevertheless grasp that standards are superior to the poorly described curriculum or pedagogical anarchy that preceded them. It is entirely reasonable, and even likely, that thoughtful parents may disagree with some of the standards. Perhaps you disagree with the quantity of standards, with their specificity, with their vagueness, or even with their content. For example, I have heard a parent exclaim, "I don't care if my children can write, as long as they can read!" This was in direct response to the requirement of the state academic standards that children must be able to write coherent paragraphs. While this parent has a legitimate right to express such a point of view and, ultimately, to remove the children from the state school system, the parent should not have the right to require teachers to have a different set of standards for those children than for other children.

In many districts, parents have an extraordinary degree of influence on what the expectations are for their children. Unfortunately, these expectations are often used to reduce expectations and rigor and, as a result, dumb down the curriculum. In the example cited above, I confess to a prejudice. The research is clear and unambiguous: Writing is an effective way for students to think, reason, and learn. The fact that some parents may wish that their children did not have to write is not a sufficient justification for the absence of the requirement. I have worked in other schools where parents have asked the rhetorical question, "Why do these kids need algebra anyway? They will never use it." These parents, too, deserve a thoughtful hearing, but do not deserve to have their advice govern the curriculum standards for the school, district, or state that must serve all children.

There are other circumstances, however, in which the standards genuinely have deep flaws that contradict the philosophical, moral, or religious beliefs of parents. In these cases, parents have an opportunity to make their concerns known. Parents can exclude their students from tests and from subjects of study that they find objectionable on religious or moral grounds. Most schools ask parents specifically for permission to discuss issues involving human sexuality, birth control, religion, and other sensitive subjects. Schools routinely offer an alternative area of study and alternative literature to respond to parent wishes.

How Can I Deal with Stress and Anxiety about Tests?

Stress and anxiety are undeniably important parts of test performance. Most readers of this book can recall an instance in which they were well-prepared for an examination, or other challenge, and nevertheless performed below their ability. The reason for their poor performance was the stress and anxiety associated with a circumstance under which they had to perform. Although parents cannot completely eliminate childhood stress and anxiety, they can mitigate the negative impact by giving students healthy coping skills. These skills include the "second look" view of any situation in which children feel unprepared or uncomfortable. If the first look at a test question or other challenge reveals the student does not immediately know the answer, some students will simply assume that the challenge is impossible, emotionally shut down, succumb to the pressure at hand, and give up not only on the question before them but on the entire test. Other students, by contrast, have the ability to take a second look at a question or challenging circumstance. The second look of the student is comparable to the runner's second wind. This boost of energy occurs when students are able to use strategy, rather than mere recall, to address the question or challenge at hand.

Although parents need not conduct a test preparation academy from their home, they can give their students the ability to maintain and expand their repertoire of second look skills. Examples of second look skills include the following:

Two-pass technique—This technique suggests that students focus first on the questions to which they know the answer. Because every question typically has the same point value, students can generate the greatest yield on their investment of time when they focus first on those questions to which they immediately know the answer. After they have made the first pass going through all questions on a test, students can return to the beginning of the examination and devote additional energy to those questions that are ambiguous or more difficult. In most cases, students are well served to eliminate one or two obviously wrong answers, then guess the answer to these questions and quickly move along to the next challenge.

Outlining—Whenever students are faced with an essay question, there is a direct relationship between the amount of time spent outlining an answer and the time saved in creating the final answer. When students immediately launch into writing the final answer, they frequently produce an aimless and disorganized essay. When, on the other hand, students take the time to outline an answer first, they have the ability to produce a crisp and well-organized essay. Moreover, the very presence of the outline makes it clear to the teacher that the student understands the question and has taken the time to provide a detailed and well-organized response.

Process of elimination—In some cases, the right answer is not clear. Sometimes this is due to the difficulty of the test item. In many cases, however, this is due to the deliberate ambiguity of the test items. This is particularly true in the case of national standardized tests in which the test writers have determined that there must be a wide variation in the "difficulty value" of the test items. That is, some items are constructed in a manner so that many students will get them correct, and other items are constructed so that very few students will get the correct response. In the latter category, the cause for such a few number of students finding the correct answer is as likely the ambiguity as it is the difficulty of the question. In such cases, the students with the ability to persevere and take a second look at the question will find that, despite the difficulty or ambiguity of the question, they can at least eliminate one wrong answer and therefore have a higher probability of guessing the correct response. There is a great deal of mythology with respect to guessing on tests. In most cases, however, guessing strategy need not be mysterious at all. On many examinations, there is no "guessing correction factor" and therefore students should always guess if they do not know the right answer. On other tests, students are penalized for every wrong answer. In those cases, it only makes sense to guess if the student can eliminate one or two wrong answers. Consider these examples:

> Mary is taking a test without any guessing correction factor. It is a multiple-choice test with four possible answers: A, B, C, and D. After reviewing her work, there are still eight questions that she just can't understand. Should Mary guess? Absolutely yes. If she just marks "A" for each of those eight questions, she has a one-in-four chance that "A" is correct, and thus she is likely to get two out of the eight questions correct. That is an extra two correct answers that she otherwise would have missed if she just left them blank.

In our second example, however, the rules are a little different. Bob is taking a similar test, with four possible answers. But for each question Bob misses, he will be penalized $\frac{1}{3}$ point. Bob also has the same chance of guessing correctly that Mary had, and indeed, he answered two out of eight questions correctly. But what about the other six questions? Because Bob lost $\frac{1}{3}$ point for each of those six, he was penalized two points ($\frac{1}{3} \times 6$), and thus he gained no advantage guessing.

What if Bob was able to eliminate two possible wrong answers? In other words, he is not guessing among choices A, B, C, and D, but only among choices A and B, because he determined that C and D were not possible right answers. Now Bob has a 50/50 chance—it's either A or B—of guessing correctly. With eight questions, he probably will get four correct. He will be penalized $\frac{1}{3}$ point on the other four, for a total of $1\frac{1}{3}$ points ($4 \times \frac{1}{3}$). Because Bob could eliminate two possible wrong answers, it was a good strategy for him to guess.

perseverance

The suggestions offered here are essential elements of educational and psychological strategy. One of the most powerful forces operating in the life of the empowered child is emotional resilience. Children with the ability and willingness to persevere in the face of seemingly great odds have the gift of emotional resilience. This lifelong ability has importance that extends far beyond test taking and academic pursuits. We routinely see parents encourage the skill of perseverance and emotional resilience in athletic competition. "You can do it!" the proud parents exclaim. The same level of perseverance can be encouraged through parent support for the resubmission of student work after the first draft did not meet the standard, encouraging more than one attempt at an essay, and encouraging one additional try for success at the mathematics homework. This encouragement is the source of emotional resilience that will be as valuable in algebra class as it is on the soccer field. In the future, this sense of empowerment, perseverance, and resilience will serve your child well in college, in relationships, and in any professional endeavor.

What If My Child Is Not Ready for a Test?

It is relatively uncommon for children to say with confidence, "I'm ready for this test and I'm going to ace it!" More often than not, we have created a sense of fear and loathing for tests, including those tests for which students are reasonably well-prepared. Parents have an important role to play here. First, parents have an obligation to help students be prepared for tests. The first step is simple: Mark test dates on the family calendar. When it is clear that Thursday is a test day, then Wednesday is not the ideal evening for a movie or an appeal for a later than usual bedtime. Most teachers—particularly at the secondary level—confirm that the difference between the superior students and the vast majority of their students is more a matter of time management and organizational skills than intellect. While parents cannot take tests for their children, nor should they, parents can give students the gift of organization and that includes a calendar, appropriate focus on test preparation, and a consistent theme that performance on tests is improved with preparation and hard work. Parents must obliterate the notion that prevails among many children that, "either you've got it or you don't —studying doesn't make much difference." In fact, the harder they work, the better they will perform in school and most other areas of life.

Consider the typical exchange between parent and child: "Do you have any homework tonight?" When the response is in the negative, parents need to ask a few more questions. The absence of homework might be genuine. On the other hand, the absence of homework, particularly in middle school and in upper elementary school, might be due to the fact that there is a test the next day. Students of every age should maintain a calendar with important dates on it. This is one of the key lifelong time management skills that everyone must master. The skill and discipline of maintaining an accurate and up-to-date calendar and task list not only separates successful students from unsuccessful students, but also distinguishes people in the professional and business world from one another. When there is a test the next day, the result need not be endless anxiety, trepidation, and fear. Rather, there must be a systematic approach to test preparation.

The systematic approach to test preparation includes the following steps. First, students must outline exactly what the test entails. Sometimes it is clear, such as all the traditional spelling tests in elementary school. At other times, a chapter test in a book will provide a clear and accurate preview of the test that students must face in the classroom. At other times, however, the content of the test may not be so clear, and some questions must be asked. If this inquiry takes place at half past nine o'clock the evening before the test, there are few alternatives other than an investigation into the mysteries of the backpack and notebook. If, by contrast, this inquiry takes place several days before the test, there is an opportunity to give the student responsibility for asking the teacher for help and for seeking additional guidance from other sources.

Second, students should prepare a sample test. One of the most effective learning exercises is for students to create a test. For younger students, acting as a teacher is a fun and engaging way to learn. For older students, such an activity may lack pure enjoyment, but the intellectual advantage is nevertheless very significant. In addition, when students practice creating and taking a test, they have not only provided themselves with a cognitive edge over their peers, but they also have provided themselves with an emotional safety net. By facing the unknown in friendly circumstances—the family room or bedroom—the student has the opportunity to endure natural test jitters in an environment that is far less consequential than in the classroom the following day. Moreover, it is my experience that students generally ask themselves far more difficult questions than those posed by the teacher.

In a Technological Age, Why Should Kids Take Paper and Pencil Tests?

It is a common parlor game for people to fantasize about the future. For years we have contemplated a world in which pencils and paper would become obsolete. The "paperless office" has been a concept considered by business people for years. Alas, the reality of our daily lives flies in the face of our fantasies. In fact, both students and people in the world of work must be able to create visual images, words, sentences, and paragraphs using pencil and paper, white boards, chalkboards, and a host of other media. In addition, the use of pencil and paper to slowly and carefully express ideas offers students the ability to think through problems without necessarily resorting to the guesswork involved in a multiple-choice question.

It is true that 21st century students must achieve a degree of technological literacy. Nevertheless, we also expect students to achieve a high degree of thinking, reasoning, and analysis. Those skills are best reinforced when students must take pen or pencil in hand, express an idea, communicate their thinking, and subject their reasoning to the critical review of others. Although computers clearly will play a role in the classroom and the future of today's students, technology does not replace the need for students to communicate clearly, accurately, analytically, and yes, legibly, in written form.

appropriate help

How Can I Help My Child with Homework and Projects Without Doing the Work Myself?

The subtext of this question is quite revealing. Every parent has observed instances in which the work presented to the teacher is clearly the product of a parent rather than the student. Such projects reveal far more about parental ambition than they do about student ability. The problem is that parents do not like to see their children become frustrated, angry, and ultimately disengaged from school. So how much "help" is appropriate and when do we cross the line from appropriate coaching and assistance to the inappropriate substitution of our own efforts for those of our children?

Parents are best served when teachers provide clear expectations for student performance. Some teachers are also clear about the nature of acceptable help and the instructions will clearly say, "Ask a parent or friend for help on this part," or, "Do this part all alone—don't get help from anyone else." Unfortunately, this level of clarity and specificity is the exception rather than the rule. One method that is particularly helpful when students are doing projects is the use of a scoring guide (sometimes called a "rubric" in educational jargon). When there is a clear set of teacher expectations, parents are able to help students not by doing work for them, but by asking students this critical question: If you were the teacher and you were grading this assignment using the scoring guide or rubric that the teacher provided, what grade would you give?

The cognitive scientist Benjamin Bloom made a tremendous contribution to the field of education when he recognized that the abilities to synthesize and evaluate information were essential for the intellectual development of children. When parents ask students to evaluate their own work, they are challenging students to engage in the advanced skill of evaluation, something too frequently left only to the teacher. If the teacher has provided a clear scoring guide or rubric—particularly a scoring guide that is expressed in student accessible language—then students can place themselves in the role of the teacher-evaluator and ask themselves how they would evaluate their own performance.

Too frequently, however, students merely do their best work, or do the work in the minimum amount of time given the exigencies of an upcoming television program, and assume that the teacher will evaluate the work in his or her own mysterious wisdom. This common practice of reserving evaluation responsibilities exclusively for the teacher denies students the opportunity to evaluate and learn. Make no mistake: This is not an exercise in making children feel good about themselves or engaging in unwarranted self-congratulatory smiling faces affixed to non-proficient work. Rather, the practice of evaluation and reflection requires thoughtful criticism, evaluation, and in many cases, rewriting, correction of errors, and the improvement of the quality of work. When parents insist that students engage in evaluation, they are doing far more than helping students on an individual homework assignment. These parents are giving their children the lifelong skills of reflection and evaluation.

a sense of accomplishment

How Much Homework Is Reasonable?
How Much Is Too Much?

In the early elementary grades, students revel in sharing school work, stories, and projects with parents. It hardly seems like "homework," but rather is a chance to share a daily sense of accomplishment. Some practice and reinforcement on basic skills, as well as a review and revision of school work, might require 15 to 20 minutes each school night. As students enter the fourth and fifth grades, teachers are mindful of the need to prepare students for the homework demands of middle school. Most upper elementary teachers require about 30 minutes of homework each evening. In the middle grades (usually sixth through eighth grade), students should expect about 90 minutes of homework each evening. It is important to note that these are averages. Before you conclude that your child has too much homework because of a project that requires four hours to complete, it might be useful to note whether the project was assigned three weeks ago. If that is the case, don't be surprised if, the night before the project is due, you hear the claim that "my teacher gave me five hours of homework!"

If the averages noted above are consistently exceeded, then it might be reasonable to have a conversation with the teacher about how the student can better use classroom time to finish work and how the homework burden can be made more reasonable.

In addition to the quantity of homework, parents should attend to the quality of homework assigned by teachers. Are students building skills, conducting independent research, reading for understanding, and building confidence? These are the characteristics of effective homework assignments. If, on the other hand, students are bewildered, unfocused, bored, or completing worksheets on skills they have already mastered, then the value of the homework assignment is subject to question. The best way to approach the teacher is not with a complaint about "too much homework" but rather with the request that homework be challenging and meaningful. "I understand your desire to instill discipline and daily work," you might say, "and I want to be supportive of those habits as well. Perhaps we could work together to find assignments that will be best suited to my child's needs."

The most important contribution that parents can make on the homework front is to make it a priority, with a consistent place and time for the completion of daily work. When no homework has been assigned, the place and time remain available for learning activities in this book as well as those that you and your child create. In this way, you have a regular commitment to learning at home that will sustain your child whether or not homework has been assigned by the teacher.

What If I Can't Help My Child with a Subject in School?

I have a confession to make. I studied and taught mathematics, and yet sometimes I find my own children's homework in that subject baffling. Even more embarrassing, I have given my children the wrong answers when I violated my own rules and helped them too much with their homework. If these mistakes can be committed by a former teacher and professor, how much more likely is every parent to make them? If you have ever felt intimidated by your children's homework, you certainly are not alone.

Even if you can provide the answer, this is rarely the most appropriate way for you to help children. When your children ask for your help, here are some steps that will produce better results than insisting they do everything themselves, or doing their homework for them.

First, ask the child to make an attempt. In some cases, this means breaking the problem down into steps. For example, if there is a multi-step story problem in mathematics, and the child does not know how to frame the answer to the problem, an appropriate step toward solving the problem might be creating a picture that accurately describes the problem. This is particularly effective coaching because many children understand visual images of a problem better than they do the words of the story problem. This also makes the point that the key to answering a problem successfully is the accurate understanding of the problem, not merely asking the parent for help.

Second, ask the child to solve a single part of the problem. If, for example, the problem involves a complex series of geography questions, and the child does not have all the answers, encourage the child to answer only one or two of the possible problems. Every time we break a large and complex problem down into its component parts, the problem becomes more approachable. This gives your child not only excellent task and time management skills, but also reduces the anxiety associated with the majority of complex and difficult problems.

Third, it is entirely legitimate for the child to write down these words: "I don't know the complete answer—I tried, but this is as far as I got." The child then makes a good faith attempt to respond to the challenge at hand. This demonstrates to the teacher that the child considered the problem, thought about the problem, and genuinely did not know the answer. This is far more important information for a teacher than when a child merely leaves a piece of paper blank or turns in nothing at all. In such cases, the teacher is unable to distinguish between work that has been ignored and work that was attempted, but completed unsuccessfully. Moreover, this builds a skill too rarely discussed in the context of homework and academic achievement: the skill and habit of intellectual honesty. Leaders in professions, businesses, and academic institutions can all attest to the rare circumstances under which the words "I don't know" have been uttered. Nevertheless, the courageous people who say those words are often well regarded by their peers. When leaders express this trait, it becomes clear that honesty, rather than bluffs, is the acceptable code of conduct.

What about Extracurricular Activities?

The research involving extracurricular activities is unambiguous. When students are participating in extracurricular activities such as sports, music, leadership, service, drama, debate, and a host of other wonderful activities, their academic achievement improves. Although these activities do take some time, and occasionally they even take time away from homework and academics, the overall research is not even a close call. Attendance and grades improve when students are busily involved in extracurricular activities, and the most effective schools seek to encourage every student, not just the most talented athletes and the most gifted musicians, to participate in activities beyond the classroom. Parents are well advised to encourage their children to participate in extracurricular activities. Moreover, schools must challenge themselves to give recognition to the most inclusive extracurricular activities in addition to the most exclusive extracurricular activities.

As valuable as extracurricular activities are, involvement can be carried to an unhealthy extreme. I know of children whose days begin with 7:30 chess club, followed by a full day of school, followed immediately by science club from 3:30 to 4:30. Religious school follows from 4:45 to 6:00. Eating a sandwich in the car, the child barely makes the 6:15 piano lesson. Basketball practice starts at 7:00 p.m. sharp and the child arrives home, exhausted, about 8:30 p.m. The cycle will repeat itself tomorrow, with soccer practice in place of basketball practice, a violin lesson replacing the piano lesson, and student council replacing science club. A reasonable rule might be, "one sport at a time" or "no more than one private lesson per week."

What If My Child Is Assigned to a Bad School?

The first question that must be considered is what makes a "bad" school. More often than not, parents evaluate schools the same way that real estate agents do, with a review of test scores. It is more than ironic that the same parents who seek out schools with high test scores express shock when those schools demonstrate that they take tests seriously. Moreover, it strikes administrators and teachers as deeply distressing when parents choose a school based on its academic excellence, and the same parents immediately try to change the policies of the school, expressing discontent that it is "too serious" and requires too much work for their children.

It is essential to identify what choice parents have in your school district. There is a national trend toward giving parents greater choice with respect to the assignment of students to different schools, but this is by no means a universal characteristic. Frequently, students are assigned to a school and parents have no choice within the public school system. Chapter 6 provides step-by-step procedures for exploring your school choice options.

Conclusion

When you are confronted with uncertainty, there is no substitute for information. While opinions and rumor abound, solid evidence and reliable information are frequently scarce. Because you want to have information that is directly relevant to *your* needs and the education of *your* children, there is no substitute for direct personal inquiry. You may be more comfortable with letters than with personal meetings or telephone conversations. However difficult the initiation of communication may be with the teachers and administrators at your children's schools, or the leaders at the district office, this challenge is worth the effort if you are able to begin the process of open dialogue, respectful communication, and accurate information.

seek reliable information

Chapter 5

What Your Child Is Expected to Know and Do in School

The academic standards at the back of this book can seem intimidating to parents, students, and teachers. You may experience many common apprehensions as you ask these questions: How can one child possibly do all that? How can a teacher possibly cover all of that material? What were these people thinking when they wrote all of these expectations for my children? This chapter puts the list of standards into focus by identifying some of the most important expectations for your children.

Before we begin, consider the most important question: What would parents be doing to help their children if we had no standards at all? We would probably do our best to build skills in reading, writing, and mathematics. We would help our children to understand that school is important, that diligence is a worthy character trait, and that perseverance in the face of difficulty is the way that one learns to master difficult tasks. In other words, if you simply followed your instincts as a good parent, you would impart to your child many of the most important elements of academic standards. With standards to augment common sense and good parenting, you need not guess at the details. You will understand what every student is expected to know and be able to do to become a successful student.

The inevitable question arises: Does my child have to master every standard in order to be successful? The straight answer is no. The details of academic standards—particularly with respect to social studies and science—represent more content than many teachers and parents understand. That even successful students have not mastered 100 percent of this material should be no surprise. In addition, each of you will find important information—perhaps things you learned in school—that appears to be missing from this chapter and from the state academic standards. This presents every teacher and school leader with a paradox: There are simultaneously too many and too few standards. The standards that exist require more time than is available in the school year; the standards that exist omit some subject matter that many parents and teachers find interesting or even vital. This paradox simply establishes what most parents are forced to admit rather early in the lives of their children: Perfection is not an option. The use of standards in school is no exception to this maxim. Therefore, use the standards as a guide, not a straitjacket. If you follow your instincts and help your child build academic skills in reading, writing, and mathematics, and if you consistently model and reinforce the development of sound character traits, your child will be successful in school.

Reading

Chances are that you began reading to your children while they were still babies By your early efforts, you were building a love of books, an understanding of the power of stories, and the belief that words on a page have meaning. In addition to reading, you probably provided plastic books on which your baby chewed, drooled, and even appeared to "read" as the vivid images captured the attention of the infant. As babies become toddlers and new words seemed to spring from their lips every day, reading together becomes a magical experience. Even before they know letters, very young children associate words with images and thus can fill in words in the picture books that parents are reading. When I ask parents about their favorite times of learning together with their children, these early days of eager discovery, quick mastery, joint experience, incredible wonder, and lots of laughter are the times recalled most fondly.

By the ages of four and five, the association between print and words is clear to most children, and they appear to "read" because they have memorized certain symbolic patterns. These so-called "sight words" help give children confidence, and therein lies one of the early misunderstandings about what it means to become a successful reader. While we naturally celebrate the ability of children to memorize symbols and their meaning, we also must understand that reading is more than the memorization of symbolic patterns. In order to become successful lifelong readers, we must build on the initial skill of memorization and add the following critical elements: decoding, comprehension, summarization, conclusions, and predictions.

Decoding—The End of the "Phonics Wars"

One of the most hotly debated issues in education over the past 30 years has been the battle between advocates of phonics (the use of letters and letter groups to "sound out" words) and the partisans of "whole language" (the use of literature as the principal basis of reading instruction, with students encouraged to use context clues rather than stopping to sound out each letter and word). Although there are still zealots on both sides of the issue who claim that allegiance to their true faith requires rejection of the other side, the clear consensus of researchers and the American Reading Association is that both approaches are essential, and the exclusion of either one damages learning.

We cannot rely on a whole language approach to the exclusion of phonics. Children must learn their ABC's and the sounds associated with them. They cannot successfully decode text without this fundamental skill any more than they can develop an understanding of mathematics without knowing that the symbol "8" represents two more units than the symbol "6" does. In some schools, a generation of children was systematically denied access to the skill of decoding with disastrous results. If students are dependent only on context clues to understand new words, then they are limited to relatively simple reading passages. As the reading passages become more difficult in a larger number of subjects, both the words and the contexts are unfamiliar. Neither memorization of sight words nor a reliance on context is helpful. The students quickly decide that "either I know it or I don't, and I guess I just don't know it." The

What Your Child Is Expected to Know and Do in School

good news is this: It is never too late to teach phonics and decoding skills. This is the starting point, though surely not the ending point, of good literacy instruction.

Instruction in reading that is solely dependent on phonics is also fundamentally flawed, and thus the exclusive reliance on simple reading texts to the exclusion of a rich variety of literature will result in the loss of complexity, challenge, and rigor in the reading experiences of children. Professor Sandra Stotsky of Harvard University conducted an exhaustive analysis of the literature commonly used in classrooms over the past century. She found that the richness of the vocabulary and the complexity of the plots steadily declined over the past several decades. As the use of complex—and, I might add, fun, interesting, enjoyable, and creative—literature declined, so did the children's interest and proficiency in reading.

We can synthesize the best practice as follows. First, phonics are essential. Teach your children not only the alphabet, but also the sounds associated with each letter and, eventually, with combinations of letters. Second, phonics are necessary but not sufficient for complete reading instruction. Do not leave the wonderful children's classics that your parents and grandparents read to you on the shelf because the words are "too hard" for your children. They will thrill to the settings, characters, and plots in the stories and poems of Edgar Allan Poe, Laura Ingalls Wilder, E.B. White, A.A. Milne, and many other authors of the past. If the vocabulary of these books is too challenging at first, take turns reading. Let your child read a sentence, then a paragraph. Then you can read a page or two. The pure joy of allowing the story to unfold before their very eyes is one of the many wonderful gifts you can give to your children.

Independent Reading and Reading "On Demand"

You also can encourage independent reading by encouraging friends and relatives to give books for birthdays and special events. Although the notation on the birthday party invitation that "Julia loves books!" may seem a breech of etiquette, it is a risk worth taking to avoid one more mindless electronic game or other stultifying toy that the purveyors of Saturday morning television trash have convinced children are necessities of life.

In addition to independent reading, it is also appropriate to encourage your child to read material that someone else has selected. Once children have developed fluent reading skills—certainly by the second or third grade—they can read stories to the blind, to someone who is in the hospital or homebound, or into a tape recorder to send to relatives. The requirement for children to read passages selected by a parent is an excellent opportunity to balance fiction—the overwhelmingly popular genre for most classrooms—with some nonfiction text. This is also an opportunity to break the association that many children build between nonfiction text and the conviction that factual material is boring. The sports page of the newspaper, a column from a magazine about an interesting topic, a news item from a nature magazine all provide opportunities for parents to balance the literary diet of their children with both fiction and nonfiction texts.

Beyond Decoding: Comprehension, Summarization, Conclusions, and Predictions

A graduate student completed an interesting study that asked this question: What do children think "good reading" really is? The answer, not surprisingly, is that most children (and quite a few of their parents) equate proper oral pronunciation of words with good reading. For children lucky enough to have parents read with them, the greatest encouragement occurs when children successfully read a passage, say the words correctly, and add some expression to their voice while they read. The researcher found that these skills are certainly important, but far from qualifying as "good reading." In order to take reading skills from the level of decoding to competence, parents must form the habit of stopping periodically in a story and asking these questions:

What happened? Listen for the accurate statement of the sequence of events and description of the characters and setting. It is not uncommon for a child to focus so hard on the words that the meaning is lost. That has certainly happened to me. When I catch myself simply going through the words without understanding the meaning of the page, then I have no choice but to stop, go back to the top, and start over. When we ask our children, "What happened on that page?" we are not subjecting them to cross-examination. Rather, we are building the skills of reflection, challenge, and perseverance. If you don't understand a page, that's okay. It happens to all of us. But you don't give up; you persevere, start again, and learn what really happened on that page of text.

Tell me the story in your own words. This is a wonderful opportunity for children to mimic voices, use rich descriptions, and portray the story to the most important audience: their parents. Interestingly, this technique is appropriate not only for fictional stories, but for nonfiction as well. In a stunningly comprehensive analysis conducted by Dr. Robert Marzano of the most effective teaching strategies, one of the most effective techniques he discovered was the use of dramatization. By allowing students to tell the story in their own words, we not only encourage factual recall, but also help to develop a sense of context and the use of creative vocabulary to convey ideas.

Why do you think the story ended this way? If there is another book about the same characters, what do you think might happen and why? When we ask children to connect a pattern of events and associate them with a conclusion, we are building the skill of drawing inferences. Effective reading comprehension is more than mere factual recall. Students must not merely remember the facts and characters, but also must draw conclusions based upon those facts.

Books: Just *SO* 20th Century

This book, as with most of those published in the 21st century thus far, is written on a computer. Much of the research that I conduct comes from Internet searches and electronically published journals. If computers and electronic communication are to be the future of the written word, why should parents invest money and time in old-fashioned books? You might as easily ask why you should attend a live symphony orchestra concert when there are so many fine compact discs available. Why should you write a thank-you note with pen in hand rather than send an e-mail? The answer to these questions is that there are intangibles to the heft of a book and the resonance of the symphony hall, and to holding a letter that someone else took the time to write that are absent when technology, no matter how elegant or sophisticated, replaces physical contact.

There is, of course, an important role that technology will play in the future of our children. There are some wonderful computer programs that are successfully used to help children develop skills. As I write these words, my seven-year-old is explaining the nature of pulleys and levers to his five-year-old friend using illustrations from a clever science program. As with many education matters, this is not an "either/or" proposition. We can nurture a love and respect for books while encouraging an understanding of appropriate uses of technology. Our priorities, however, must be clear. My observation is that there are many more students who can troll the Internet than who can write a sentence with appropriate grammar, spelling, and punctuation.

the most effective strategy

Writing

Although most educators and parents properly place an exceptional emphasis on reading, we dare not neglect the importance of writing. It is also essential to recall that language development does not proceed in a neat linear fashion in which we first perfect speaking skills, then polish reading skills, and only then proceed to writing. In fact, as students improve their writing, they also improve their ability to read, particularly with regard to the advanced skills of comprehension, summarization, and prediction. Student proficiency in writing also is associated with improved student achievement in mathematics, social studies, and science. In fact, of all the strategies that teachers and parents can use to boost student achievement, improved formal writing is the single most effective strategy that provides benefits in every other area of the curriculum.

Some parents may question whether writing is really that important when state academic tests and college admissions tests are typically multiple-choice exams. The answer is not that there is some magic in a number two pencil, but rather that writing—particularly formal nonfiction writing—requires students to think, reason, analyze, and communicate. Those skills will help students deal with multiple-choice tests and every other challenge that they face in school. Indeed, the best teachers I have observed do not see writing as a trade-off with multiple-choice tests, but rather combine these two testing methods. They routinely require students not only to choose the correct response, but also require written explanations of why one response was chosen and another possible answer was rejected. Such an approach transforms multiple-choice tests from a guessing game into a challenging and engaging intellectual task.

Some parents and teachers regard writing with pen or pencil as an ancient craft, soon to be displaced by computers. I respectfully dissent. If we think of writing not merely as a means of communication, but also as a means to enhance thinking, reasoning, analysis, and communication, then writing will not "go out of style" until thinking goes out of style. Moreover, children and adults who are able to convey in handwritten form their deep emotions and sentiments such as sympathy, appreciation, and encouragement, will find that they have a far more profound impact on those with whom they communicate than if they are brought up to rely solely on a word processor. Technology will replace neither emotions nor the need to communicate them. Thus writing, including the ability to write legibly and without the aid of a computerized spell-checker, remains an essential characteristic of the educated child.

developing skills

Rewriting: The Key to Improved Writing

Think of the things your child does well. Perhaps she plays soccer. Maybe he plays the violin or piano. She might be a great swimmer. Every child has something in which enjoyment and skill coincide. Now consider how that skill was developed. It never—not once—occurred with a single effort. Many soccer balls were kicked far from the net before that first glorious goal. A fair amount of screeching preceded the successful completion of "Minuet in G" on the violin. The first attempt at the G-major scale probably omitted the F-sharp. Skills are never developed in one-shot endeavors. Children know intuitively that practice makes perfect, and that the remedy for failure is additional practice. Why then, is so much written schoolwork submitted on a one-shot basis? The habit of writing a rough draft, submission to a parent or teacher for correction, and rewriting, is not merely a habit for writing; it is a habit of mind that displays perseverance and character.

The Basics: Spelling, Grammar, Punctuation, and Legibility

Some of the best support for the proposition that the basics of English communication are important in every academic and vocational setting has come from several unexpected sources. The president of an urban electricians' union, for example, addressed an audience of technical school students and parents and provided a passionate defense for the literacy requirements. "Successful members of this union must be able to read and write instructions. Mistakes in writing can mean putting yourself and others at safety risk. We require people to be good writers." Many high schools have conducted focus groups of former students who were invited to share their responses to the question, "What do you wish you would have had in school?" With remarkable consistency, students in universities noted that they were required to write not only in English class, but in history, music, economics, and every other discipline. They needed more formal writing, they admitted. Individuals in technical schools and the world of work similarly expressed their concern that they were required to write on a regular basis and that they needed additional training to do so. Whether the former student was a dispatcher in a truck stop or an undergraduate in the Ivy League, the consistent theme was a request for more writing. Of course, none of these chastened high school graduates requested more writing during the course of elementary, middle, or high school classes. The role of teachers and parents in this and many other areas is not to give children what they want, but what they need. Writing is, in brief, a skill that they need, but rarely request.

It is important that parents and teachers are specific about what "writing" really means, for too often students have been left with the impression that aimless reflections in journals fulfill the requirement for written expression. Whatever merit journal writing may have, the self-absorbed and frequently scatological reflections of teenagers do not develop the formal writing skills that students need. They need to write paragraphs with topic sentences and essays with a clear beginning, middle, and end. They need models of good writing and clear criteria for what constitutes acceptable and exemplary composition. In any other area of skill development, specificity is essential. Children would laugh at the notion that they should be creative with regard to where the soccer ball should go. Thankfully, they do not find the need to be creative with regard to the tones to which the violin is tuned. Yet, there are remarkably creative and gifted soccer players and musicians. The strict application of structure, in other words, does not remove creativity, but rather creates a clear framework within which creative expression can occur.

The overwhelming majority of writing by students in elementary and middle schools is in the form of a creative narrative. While this genre of writing is important, it is not sufficient. Specifically, students must be able to write for several purposes. First, students must write to inform. That is, they must describe an object, sequence of events, person, or situation with clarity and accuracy. Second, students must write to analyze. Typically, analytical writing involves the comparison of two different events, people, or activities. When students write analytically, they carefully explain similarities and differences between the objects of their analysis. Third, students must write to persuade. Effective persuasive writing is not an expression of personal preference, but rather an argument supported by evidence, examples, and illustrations. Although the labels of these types of writing may vary from one class to another, students must understand differences between creative writing and description, analysis, and persuasion. Second and third graders can be asked to compare different books or describe characters. Fourth graders can be expected to state a point of view and support their opinion with evidence. My interviews with secondary school and college faculty members reveal that the single greatest deficiency among their students is writing, and in particular, nonfiction writing in the form of description, analysis, and persuasion. College students who persist in the illusion that a successful argument begins with the words "I feel" have, at some early point in their academic career, been denied the opportunity to learn the craft of writing.

Mathematics

The controversies involving mathematics education have mirrored the phonics vs. whole language debate. Typically, the terminology of the math wars includes "problem-solving" and "number operations," with advocates of the "new, new math" preferring the former over the latter and traditionalists taking the reverse point of view. While few thoughtful people doubt that problem-solving is a useful skill in mathematics, it is baffling to me that anyone would think that skill in solving mathematical problems can be developed without an understanding of calculation. Conversely, no mastery of the times tables replaces the necessity to read a story problem and write a clear explanation for a solution. The debate between these extremes implies a dichotomy that is illogical. Students must have both the ability to read and write about mathematics, as well as a sound grounding in the fundamentals of arithmetic.

One common source of friction is the use of calculators. Indeed, calculators are commonly used in math classes, based on the "obvious" proposition that students would be foolish not to make use of the best technology at hand. Evidence reported in the *Wall Street Journal* (December 15, 2000, p. A1) indicates that students who make frequent use of calculators in class perform at much lower levels on state tests than students who use calculators only two or three times a month. This is no surprise to the parent or math teacher who has witnessed a child instinctively reach for a calculator when asked to multiply three times three. Worse yet, if the student hits a wrong key and the screen says that the answer is 25, she may have been conditioned to place more confidence in the calculator than in her own understanding that three groups of three cannot conceivably yield a product of 25. This is not merely an issue of discipline and the "basics." Some of the most sophisticated mathematics at the secondary school and collegiate levels requires students to be able to estimate. Their ability in "mental math," and their confidence in making a judgment about what a likely answer might be, is an important input into some statistical and financial equations. In sum, calculators do not replace the need for the disciplined thinking in mathematics any more than word processors replace the need for thoughtful analysis in an English class.

If You Are Intimidated by Math

It is possible, even likely, that your own experiences in mathematics were not favorable in school. Moreover, the format, content, and sheer size of mathematics textbooks can be intimidating. Nevertheless, there are many things you can do to help your children develop sound mathematical skills. In addition to the many activities suggested at the back of this book, there are four common household themes that will build the math skills of your children. These include games, money, time, and measurement. Children love games, and keeping score is normally part of this family activity. Parents may be tempted to take on the scorekeeping duties in the name of accuracy or speed. This is a missed opportunity. My experience is that if one child is keeping score, every other child at the table will be doing the same thing, keeping an eagle eye out for errors. When the parent keeps score, children may passively accept the calculations. Money offers an exceptional opportunity to build mental math skills. If children are paid an allowance or compensated for chores, parents should make a point of providing money in different denominations and combinations. Playing store, running a summer lemonade stand, selling Girl Scout cookies, and a host of other activities surrounding money will provide children with well developed skills, not only in arithmetic, but in percent, decimals, fractions, and ratios. Time is a theme that governs many households, yet the predominance of digital clocks prevents many children from learning to tell time or to solve problems regarding the intervals between different time periods. Daily reinforcement of these skills can occur with questions such as, "What time is it now, and how many minutes before school starts?" Finally, the theme of measurement offers abundant opportunities for the building of math skills in the kitchen, the yard, home construction jobs, or marking off athletic fields. Because measurement refers to space and volume, these lessons cannot be learned by reading a chapter in a math book about measurement. Students learn about measurement by measuring, by observing the impact of measurement mistakes, by making corrections, and by learning the carpenter's rule to "measure twice, cut once."

a spirit of inquiry

Science

As intimidating as mathematics may be, the science curriculum can be even more baffling to many parents. The traditional curriculum of weather, dinosaurs, and volcanoes has been replaced by an early emphasis on the physical, chemical, and biological sciences. Both state standards and school texts can present remarkably sophisticated challenges for students. Despite these challenges, there are several things that parents can do that will improve the scientific thinking of their children.

Parents can encourage a spirit of inquiry, helping children to understand that science is not just about providing answers, but also about asking questions. Real scientists are not just smart people who have all the answers. Even very famous scientists, such as Galileo, have been spectacularly wrong about many of their theories. Science advances through the process of generating a theory, developing alternative hypotheses, and then systematically testing those hypotheses. For science to advance, we must disprove hypotheses. This means that for every gain in scientific knowledge, some very smart scientist was proven wrong. This does not diminish the credibility or importance of scientific work. Indeed, the researcher's aphorism is, "We learn more from error than from uncertainty." This is a good rule in the lives of students as well. When they don't know the answer, testing an idea—even if such a test proves their previous conceptions to be untrue—is better than proceeding in ignorance.

Scientific observation can occur in the home every day when children pose the hypothetical question, "What will happen if I do this?" If we announce the answer, we deny our children the opportunity to generate a hypothesis and then test it through systematic observation. Children are full of "why" questions that are directly susceptible to the generation of hypotheses and systematic testing.

- **Why do ice cubes melt in water?**

- **Why does the metal pan stay hot longer than the wooden spoon in the pan?**

- **Why does the bathtub water get cold?**

The list is endless. The key is not for parents to attempt to become walking encyclopedias, but to build a spirit of inquiry and testing in which children are not afraid to generate thoughtful guesses and then test those guesses. Real scientists, and thoughtful students, are not afraid to routinely write the words, "My hypothesis was not supported by the evidence." This approach to learning values evidence over alchemy and thus is not only a sound intellectual trait, but an opportunity to build sound character as well.

Social Studies

The amount of content in social studies curricula can be overwhelming. Spanning the subjects of history, geography, civics, and economics, social studies texts can add many pounds to your child's backpack and nevertheless omit many important subjects. Despite the bewildering array of complex ideas in the subjects involved in social studies, parents can reinforce some fundamental understandings that every child should have.

The first and most important principle to understand is that advancement in social studies is directly related to student proficiency in reading and writing. Make no mistake: If your child needs help in reading and writing, then you and the teachers must devote time to these areas as a priority. Of course, it is possible to use reading texts that include history and government. There is, however, no substitute for absolute proficiency in literacy as an antecedent to the study of social studies. I have never heard a secondary school teacher say, "I wish that more students knew the capital of South Dakota," but I have heard hundreds of them say, "I wish that more students could read my textbook."

Government and Civics

At the end of the Cold War, President Gorbachev of the former Soviet Union famously said to General (now Secretary of State) Colin Powell, "General, you will have to find yourself another enemy." While Americans who grew up in the 1940s and 1950s rejoiced at the diminution of world tensions, and the reduction in the likelihood that our own children would face the prospect of nuclear war, the demise of the Soviet Union also changed conversations in schools and homes. For the last decade, we rarely talked about the difference between democracy and authoritarian forms of government with the same urgency that we did when our own form of government seemed to be threatened. These are distinctions that remain important and are among the fundamental concepts that students must know. If you can take your children to see any democratically elected body in action, it is worth the trip. If you live near the state capital, watch the legislature in session. Better yet, arrange to have your children serve as a page in one of the legislative chambers for a day. If distance from the capital prevents such an excursion, then take your children to a meeting of the school board, county commission, or city council. The concept of representative democracy is fundamental and every child should understand that one of the distinguishing parts of our heritage of freedom is the ability to vote, selecting men and women who do the public's bidding. Of course, parents who wish to encourage good civic behavior by their children must vote, and you may wish to consider taking your children with you to observe this most fundamental civic right and obligation. There can be little doubt in the aftermath of the presidential election of 2000 that every vote has an important influence on the future of the nation.

History

History has been the subject of the most hotly debated state standards. Part of this controversy stems from the idiosyncratic manner in which history has been taught in schools, with the principal source of differentiation being the personal preference of the teacher. Some teachers devote weeks to the building of scale models of the Coliseum as a substitute for the study of ancient Rome, while others devote the month of November to an historically inaccurate drama inevitably focusing on Pocahontas and

John Smith. Other classrooms devote weeks to Custer's Last Battle, while others linger for months on the Civil War. Few, however, stop to ask what the study of history is all about and many leave students with the conviction that it is simply "a bunch of facts" that are regurgitated on demand. If the teacher deliberately avoided the fact-based approach to history, then students have the impression that history is a series of disjointed dramas and personal stories. The presence of social studies standards offers the beginning of some coherence to the study of this discipline.

Let us first put to rest the "facts vs. themes" controversy. Students need to learn historical facts. It is preposterous to assume that students can apply higher order thinking skills to history, geography, and economics without understanding that the Civil War preceded Vietnam, that the Balkans are not the Baltics, and that there is rarely a singular cause for an historical or economic effect. While not every date is of equal importance, a sense of sequence in the broad sweep of history is essential if students are to have an appropriate context for their understanding of historical events, political decisions, and cultural artifacts of the time. The words of the song, "Battle Hymn of the Republic" have a profoundly different meaning for students who have studied the words as part of their understanding of 19th century history.

Parents can reinforce this understanding of historical context by talking about family history. Family trees and time lines can lend context that many children do not understand. If your children have parents, grandparents, or great-grandparents who fought in a war, then encourage serious family discussion about those events. For today's students, Vietnam is simply one more piece of history, as removed from their reality as the World Wars of the last century, or the many conflicts of centuries long past. If you can add profound family context to these events, the lessons learned by your children will have value far beyond a few paragraphs in a textbook. Every community has historical landmarks and most have museums. Although the events commemorated in those monuments may not be the focus of your school's textbooks, there is nothing to match the visual impression of personal observation. If your family has the resources to take a vacation, then plan to spend a week or more in the nation's capital. Let your children see the Constitution, the Declaration of Independence, and the words of Lincoln beneath his majestic statue.

adding context

Foreign Language, Music, and Art

Although this book focuses on the core academic areas of language arts, mathematics, social studies, and science, parents are wise to reinforce their children's pursuit of studies in foreign language, music, and art. At the very least, study of a foreign language will help to build English vocabulary, and at best will improve your child's understanding of other cultures. Much of the world's classic literature first appeared in languages other than English, and by opening the door to the study of other languages, you will provide a lifelong gift with which your children can explore other cultures and lands. Even a slight familiarity with another language allows your children to recognize the value of courtesy when they are guests in other nations.

The study of music is one of the most important disciplines for children. It is not necessary for your child to become a concert pianist or to play first chair in the saxophone section of the school band. The study of music, however, will improve your child's understanding of mathematics with the study of rhythm and notation. The study of songs will build your child's vocabulary and reading skills. The occasional performance will build confidence and presence.

The study of art allows your child a creative outlet that can be successfully combined with many other disciplines. Because vivid images are one of the best ways for children to acquire understanding and knowledge, the study of art should include not only the creation of original pieces of art, but trips to the museum and the observation of the art work of the world's great artists. The connection between art and written expression is particularly important. A wonderful way to build your child's skills in analytical writing is the comparison of two pieces of art. Moreover, students can illustrate their creative and nonfiction work with vivid illustrations that reflect their words.

Behavior

No discussion of learning at home is complete without addressing the issue of behavior. Veteran teachers frequently complain of the extent to which behavioral education has been transferred from parents to schools, and teachers readily acknowledge that schools are ill-equipped to begin teaching respect, teamwork, and integrity in a classroom for six hours a day if those values were not taught before a child's schooling began and reinforced before and after the school day.

Although every family has its own code of behavior, these differences need not obscure some fundamental obligations that people, including school children, have in a civil society. Parents may differ about the need to call adults "sir" and "ma'am," but every parent has an obligation to instill in children a respect for the authority of teachers and school leaders. No amount of parental guilt due to absence and no amount of parental recollections of unsatisfactory relationships with their own parents justifies the wholesale abandonment of behavioral training. Even more shocking than the abandonment of parental attempts to instill codes of civil behavior in children is the frequent support of student behavior that is disruptive, rude, and dangerous, as if the school had an obligation to conform to the behavioral code of the children, rather than the reverse.

In addition to encouraging a fundamental respect for adult authority, parents can build sound behavior in their children by insisting upon good organization in everything from the toy box to the dresser, closet, and backpacks. The adage, "A place for everything and everything in its place" may not conform to the adults who routinely display messy desks and ridicule their more organized colleagues. Nevertheless, secondary school educators routinely speak of students who fail not because of poor intellectual skills, but due to lack of the most fundamental organizational skills. The teachers assumed that children would learn these skills at home, while parents assumed the children would pick up these traits at school. Meanwhile, school lockers resemble toxic waste dumps, completed homework assignments are lost in a backpack full of trash, and bright students flounder because they lack simple organizational skills and habits.

The most important consideration with regard to building strong organizational skills is to establish the fact that good student organization is a skill, not an inherited genetic trait. Writing assignments in a notebook, making daily lists of things that must be done, and putting away books and toys are not matters encoded in DNA; they are skills and habits that are taught, learned, practiced, and developed over time.

What to Do When You Can't Do it All: Power Standards

Having reached the end of this chapter and not yet confronted the list of standards at the end of this book, the skeptical reader might be tempted to exclaim, "Twenty minutes a day? He's got to be kidding! I could devote hours every day to the reading, writing, mathematics, science, music, and art, and never even get to the behavior and organizational stuff. Attempting to make a difference in 20 minutes is sheer fantasy."

Your skepticism is understandable. Moreover, this perception of standards and school curricula as overwhelming burdens is shared by many teachers and school leaders who know that even the most diligent teacher may not produce students who know and understand every single standard. Nevertheless, the plain fact remains that your time does matter, and that 20 minutes a day makes a world of difference. Without question, the homes in which independent reading routinely takes place probably have other characteristics, including access to books, caring adults, quiet space, and time. Nevertheless, the evidence is clear. Student achievement can dramatically improve without transforming school and home into a joyless test prep center. Rather, the ideas in this book, implemented incrementally and balanced between academic and behavioral objectives, serve to have a clear and dramatic impact on student success.

Given the overwhelming number of standards and the many activities in this book, a fair question to ask is, "Where do we start?" The concept of "power standards" provides one mechanism for parents, teachers, and students to choose wisely among many available alternatives. The notion of power standards suggests that the choice is not necessarily based on popularity, but on impact. Power standards must pass three thresholds. First, they must have endurance. In other words, some information memorized for a particular test is liberated from our neurons within nanoseconds after the completion of a test. While the knowledge that Pb is the chemical symbol for lead may be of use when the *Jeopardy* category is Chemical Symbols, it is not a piece of knowledge that has endurance. While the scientific method endures, memorization of chemical symbols and, for that matter, the dimensions of the stegosaurus do not.

The second criterion for power standards is leverage. This chapter has already highlighted a skill that provides students with leverage, that is, it has impact on many different subjects. When students write more frequently, particularly when that writing includes formal submissions with rewriting based on teacher feedback, student achievement improves not only in writing, but in mathematics, social studies, and science. Another example of leverage is the skill involved in creating tables, charts, and graphs, and the understanding necessary to draw inferences from the graphic representation of data. This requirement not only appears in the mathematics standards, but also in academic standards for science, social studies, and language arts. Time invested in the development of a skill with leverage will pay dividends in many different academic areas.

The third threshold that power standards must cross is that they be necessary for success at the next level of instruction. Whenever I have challenged teachers to narrow the focus of their curriculum and omit a chapter, activity, or unit, they frequently respond that "everything I do is important" and besides, "The children will need this information for the next grade." When I ask the same teachers to provide advice for a new teacher who has the responsibility for students in the next lower grade, the story changes. While the 5th grade teacher may insist that "everything I do is important," the sixth grade teacher is quite willing to provide a very brief list of requirements for fifth grades. The fifth grade teacher is similarly willing to provide clarity and focus for a suggested fourth grade curriculum. In contrast to the lists of standards and test objectives that include scores of items and extend to several pages, the lists of requirements for the next lower grade that I routinely receive from teachers rarely exceeds a dozen items and seldom exceeds a single page. Part of this phenomenon may be the very human characteristic that it is easier to give advice than to take it. The inescapable conclusion, however, is that teachers and parents know that hasty and superficial coverage of massive amounts of curriculum is not as effective as thorough student knowledge of the most important elements of the curriculum.

While reasonable people may differ with regard to the ideal curriculum, no parent wishes students to be in a classroom where reading is not valued. Few parents would find competent the teacher who provides writing requirements only on rare occasions. In other words, while reasonable people may disagree about the universe of standards, most parents and teachers can apply the three criteria—endurance, leverage, and readiness for the next grade—and quickly arrive at a consensus on the most important pieces of information that are the non-negotiable. These are the areas of knowledge and skill that students must absolutely, positively have in order to be successful. This might mean that the scale model of the Coliseum gives way to improved reading instruction, that the 18th annual dramatization of Pocahontas yields to the need to master fractions, and the recollections of summer vacations are supplanted with a better understanding of the Constitution. In brief, power standards help teachers and parents make choices in the real world of limited time.

be a proactive advocate

What's Worth Fighting For

Although it may appear that the burdens of standards are staggering, there are only a few areas on which parents must absolutely insist both with regard to student work at home and the curriculum in school. Those areas worth the assertion of parental authority include thinking, reasoning, and communication. If you find that students are only being asked to complete drill sheets rather than engage in deep and thoughtful analysis, it is essential that such practices are challenged with the evidence that the path toward greater student achievement lies not in mindless test preparation, but in extensive analysis, reasoning, and writing. If you find that students are taking exclusively multiple-choice tests and rarely if ever are required to write, then it is essential that such practices are challenged with the evidence that more frequent student writing not only builds thinking and reasoning skills, but also improves student performance on multiple-choice tests.

Although parents may not win every issue of contention over curriculum and testing, these discussions with teachers and school officials will make clear that the obligation of the parent is not merely to support homework and reinforce the skills required by the school. Sometimes the most important obligation of the parent is to provide complementary skills in those areas that the school is short-changing. If writing is underemphasized, then it is important that parents pay particular attention to writing requirements as part of your 20-Minute Learning Connection. If math calculation is underemphasized in the name of improved problem-solving techniques, then parents must make up the shortfall with an emphasis on the development of sound basic skills in addition, subtraction, multiplication, and division. If the teacher emphasizes literature to the exclusion of phonics, or phonics to the exclusion of literature, then the parents must help to make up the gap at home. When parents are proactive as advocates for their children, then they not only help future generations of children, but also immediately and decisively intervene in the educational lives of their own children.

Chapter 6

Before School Begins: Planning for School Success

The 20-Minute Learning Connection begins long before children enter school. Part of the success of parent planning is a commitment to being proactive rather than reactive when dealing with school issues. This chapter addresses the strategies parents can use to maximize their influence on their children's educational opportunities.

Much of the recent discussion about parent choice in schools has been focused on the politically volatile issue of school vouchers. Although only a very few school systems in the nation offer publicly funded vouchers that parents may choose to use for a private school education for their children, there is frequently a great deal of choice that parents can and should exercise with regard to the educational opportunities for their children.

Choosing Schools

In some school districts, a parent's request for school "choice" is welcomed as an indication of positive involvement. Even some large urban school systems pride themselves on the claim that more than 90 percent of parents and children receive their first choice of school. In other school systems, however, choice of school is something exercised only by the administration, with boundary lines, program assignment, and bus schedules, all matters that are announced to parents, rather than decisions that invite participation and comparison among alternatives.

If you wish to get the straight story about parent rights and choice in your district, it is important that you ask the right questions. Figure 6.1 provides an easy guide to the specific questions you should ask school administrators in your district about your rights as a parent. Don't settle for a form letter or impromptu policy statement by a harried administrator. Ask the questions and write down the answers.

FIGURE 6.1
What Are My Choices?

School Administration Telephone Number:_____

Name of Administrator:_____

Introduction:

"Hello. My name is _____ and my child is a student in this district. I would like to ask some questions about the choices of schools available to my child. Are you the right person to talk with about this matter?"

If "no": "Thanks very much. Who should I speak with about this?"

 Name:_____

 Phone Number: _____

If "Yes": "That's great. Do you have a moment so that I can learn more about this?"

"Does the district have a voucher program that provides funding for private schools?"

❏ No

❏ Yes

❏ Details:_____

"Does the district have any charter schools?"

❑ No

❑ Yes

❑ Details:_____

"Is my child required to attend the school nearest to me, or may I select any of the public schools available?"

❑ Your child must attend local school. That is:_____

❑ Your child may choose any school.

❑ Your child may go to another school, but must deal with certain restrictions.

❑ Your child may go to another school, but families living close to each school have first priority, and people outside of the boundaries of that school are only permitted to enroll if there is space available.

❑ Additional details:_____

If no choice at all: "I understand that you are saying I have no choice of schools at all. Is that correct? So that I understand this clearly, are you saying that there are no situations in the school district at all in which students are attending a school other than their official assigned school? Could you please tell me about these exceptions to your normal policy?

If choice is available: "That's great. Is there a written policy that governs the choices that I have as a parent? Would you please send me a printed copy of that policy?"

"Just one more question. Where can I find information about the different schools? Is there an accountability report or other document that will provide detailed information about the enrollment, teaching staff, and academic programs of each school in the district?"

"Thank you very much."

Although most public school systems are far from a genuine market system in which consumers can make informed choices from among a variety of alternatives, there is frequently much more choice available than parents recognize. Although only a tiny minority of school systems offers publicly funded vouchers and only a few school systems offer charter schools that may appeal to some parents, virtually every school system with more than one school will provide some level of parent choice if the matter is pressed. The purpose for the inquiry is not necessarily to engage in political advocacy for vouchers, charters, or other forms of school choice. Rather, the purpose for your question is simply to ensure that you have the best possible information with which you can make a reasoned judgment.

choose wisely

Making the Best Choice

Once you have determined that you have some level of school choice, it is important that you choose wisely. The label of the school tells you very little about the quality of the curriculum and teachers. For example, some charter schools are among the very best in the nation; some charter schools have been abject failures. The label "charter" does little to assure a parent of educational quality. Rather, you must make specific inquiries about the curriculum, teaching, and leadership of the school. Sometimes these inquiries may be uncomfortable, as many schools have a history of operating free from parental scrutiny. Many other schools welcome parent questions and provide easy-to-understand accountability information for parents or any other member of the community. Regardless of the ease with which you acquire this data, the following questions will serve as a useful guide for your conversations about schools, curricula, teachers, and leadership.

Your inquiries must be specific. First, you'll want to know what the academic expectations of the school are. The assurance that "we are standards-based" or "we follow the state standards" is not sufficient. You deserve a direct answer to this question: "What is my child expected to know and be able to do at the beginning of the school year and at the end of the school year?" You should receive a specific list of the knowledge and skills with which your child should enter and leave each grade level. Anything less than a straightforward response to this inquiry is evidence that the school is "standards-based" in name only, and that curriculum anarchy prevails. The extent to which individual teachers can choose to make extraordinary departures from the curriculum is stunning to many parents. Some teachers offer little or no science, while others emphasize science to the exclusion of essential literacy programs. Some teachers invest extraordinary amounts of time in student performances, often with the enthusiastic encouragement and support of parents, omitting large amounts of academic requirements. A great number of teachers emphasize arts and crafts more than academic requirements. Kati Haycock, president of the Education Trust, recently observed that in classroom after classroom she witnessed more coloring assignments than reading, writing, and mathematics assignments. You must ask, "What is my child expected to know and be able to do?" The principal and individual teachers must be able to answer this question clearly and without hesitation. If the response is unclear to you, academic expectations will be the subject of mystery and ambiguity for your child.

Another important part of your consideration of curriculum is testing and assessment. Curriculum without testing is wishful thinking. All the elegant lesson plans, detailed curriculum documents, and heavy textbooks in the world have little impact if there is not a systematic method of determining the extent to which students are learning what is expected. Do not settle for unspecific assurances such as, "We do regular testing." Ask to see the results for the past two years of the state and district tests that are related to the academic standards and curriculum requirements of the school. Determine for yourself whether students in this school are learning what school leaders believe that students are learning.

Second, you want to know about the teaching qualifications of the staff. Teachers typically receive certifications for specific subjects, particular groups of grade levels, or both. While certification is no guarantee of quality, the evidence is overwhelming that students taught by noncertified teachers perform at significantly lower levels than students under the tutelage of certified teachers. Many school systems have emphasized reductions in class size. Unfortunately, they have filled some classrooms with well-intentioned, but untrained, people. You must insist that your child be taught by a certified teacher. In addition, the educational background and experience of the staff should be examined. Advanced degrees and extensive experience is no guarantee of quality, but you may wish to consider carefully whether your child should be in the classroom of a teacher with little or no experience.

Third, you want to learn about the leadership of the school. In some schools, the principal operates autonomously, with little or no oversight. In other schools, a collaborative decision-making body includes teachers, parents, and administrators. Sometimes these committees operate differently in practice than the theory with which they were originated. The best way for you to address this is to ask when the next meeting of the decision-making committee will be and plan to attend the meeting. Does the group make substantive contributions to the decision-making process? Do some groups dominate the discussion? Do parents have a real voice on matters such as curriculum, instruction, and policy? Finally, ask this specific question: "Can you give me an example of how parents have influenced the curriculum and instruction policies of the school?"

There is no doubt about this fact: You have a right to make these inquiries. Information about curriculum and teacher qualifications is not secret. If you receive anything less than completely forthcoming information, then you should make a written inquiry to your district superintendent. Figure 6.2 provides an example of how you can make these inquiries in a courteous and businesslike manner.

FIGURE 6.2
Inquiry Letter to School Superintendent

(name), Superintendent of Schools
(district name)
(address, city, state, zip)
Re: Information concerning _____ school
Dear (Dr./Ms./Mr.) _____:

On (date) I met with the principal of _____ school. The purpose of my meeting was to learn more about the curriculum, teaching, and leadership of the school my children may attend next year. I still have some questions about these matters and I would appreciate your assistance in responding to them.

With respect to the curriculum, I am particularly interested in the specific academic expectations of my children and how those expectations are assessed. If there are specific curriculum standards that every child is expected to meet, I would like to see them. In addition, I would like to know if there are district or state tests that address the extent to which the school has met those academic expectations in the past. I would also appreciate seeing the results from those assessments for the past two years. Please let me know if there are differences among the curriculum based on choices made by each teacher or if the curriculum is the same for each teacher. If there are differences, please elaborate on those differences.

With respect to the faculty, I would like to know about the subject matter and grade-level certification of the staff, their educational backgrounds, and teaching experience. If some faculty members have particular interests or areas of expertise, please share that information as well.

Finally, I am very interested to learn about the leadership of the school and particularly about the manner in which parents are able to participate in school decision-making. If there is a governing or advisory body in which parents participate, I would like to learn more about the operations of this group and when its next meeting will be held.

Thank you very much for your assistance.

Sincerely,

(your name)

**be courteous
but persistent**

Choosing Teachers

Parent choice of teachers is a delicate subject. Reasonable people may disagree on the matter. Those advocating parent choice see it as a way of encouraging parent involvement and ensuring that parents have a vested interest in supporting the teacher and encouraging their child to succeed. Certainly most parents believe that they know their children better than anyone and are therefore best equipped to determine which teachers and educational programs are best suited for their children. Those opposing parent choice of teachers see this practice as an inequitable device in which activist parents get better teachers for their children than parents who do not have the time, ability, or interest to attempt to influence school administrators. Moreover, some administrators fear that parent choice is more of a popularity contest fueled by rumor than a choice based on professional abilities. In addition, some administrators worry that teachers might make unwise educational decisions in an attempt to be popular with parents. Finally, there is the concern that since teaching ability and popularity never will be equally distributed among various teachers in a grade level, some classes might be overburdened with too many students in a quest to meet the demands of parents.

Whatever the policy of your local school, it is important that parents take the time to understand the extent of their ability to influence the assignment of students to the classroom. Even if there is an official policy against parent choice, parents are entitled to ask questions about the differences among teachers with regard to certification, education, experience, and educational practices. While some of this information may be obtained through public documents, other matters, such as the educational practices of individual teachers, will only be revealed through interviews and observation.

When you make your initial inquiries about teachers, you will likely be told, "All of our teaching staff is excellent. Besides, we all have state standards, so you'll find that pretty much every class is the same. That's why we handle teacher assignment." You should be courteous but persistent in pursuing your inquiries. After you have learned the basics—certification, education, experience—you will need to dig deeper. Talk with your child's prospective teacher, preferably in the classroom. Plan to spend more time listening than talking. This is not the time for you to articulate your educational philosophy, but rather the time for you to determine what the philosophy and practices of the teacher will be. This is a difficult but important consideration: Your time is better spent finding a school and teacher that conform to your philosophy than attempting to convince a school and teacher that they should change their philosophies to agree with you.

Here are some things to notice as you enter the classroom:

❑ **Student work:** Is student work prominently posted around the room? If so, is there clear and specific feedback on what work is acceptable and what work needs improvement? Does every paper, including poor work, have a "smiley face," or does the teacher provide encouraging but clear guidance on how to improve? Are there samples of exemplary work that represent the educational target for students?

❑ **Class rules:** Are there high standards of behavior that are clear and unambiguous? Does the appearance of the classroom indicate that students take good care of their personal property and school property?

❑ **Teacher's desk:** Does the teacher set an example of organization and neatness?

❑ **Availability:** Were you welcomed into the classroom at any time or was your entry into the classroom restricted to specific pre-announced times? Were other parents actively volunteering, participating, and improving the learning environment?

Following is a list of things you should discuss with the teacher. It is absolutely important to take the time to listen to the responses without interruption. You want to solicit clear and unambiguous answers. You might need to draw the teacher out with some encouraging phrases such as, "Please tell me a little more about that."

❏ **What should a child know and be able to do at the beginning of the school year? In other words, what preparation should a successful student have before coming to your class?**

❏ **What should a student know and be able to do at the end of this school year? Please be as specific as possible.**

❏ **How do you assess student progress? May I please see an example of one of the tests you routinely use to assess student progress? What is the consequence when a student does poorly on a test? Can you please provide an example of a time when you changed the curriculum based on your analysis of the assessment results of the class? If my child does badly on a test, how soon will I be informed? Are there reports of student progress other than the report card?**

❏ **Please tell me about your favorite things to teach. Are there certain areas for which you provide extra emphasis based on your personal interest and knowledge?**

❏ **Are there some areas that you are not as comfortable teaching? Are there certain areas that you tend to emphasize less as a result?**

❏ **As a parent, how can I be most supportive of my child's education? Are there particular things that the parents of students in your class should do?**

❏ **Please explain your homework policy. How much homework should students normally have? What is the consequence when a student fails to turn in homework?**

❏ **What is your policy with regard to parent volunteers in the classroom?**

❏ **What is the practice of the school and your class with regard to extracurricular activities? If these activities occur during the regular school day, do students make up for lost instructional time? If so, please explain.**

❏ **May I please see a copy of the report card form? Please explain how grades or other marks on the report card are determined. Is there a written grading policy? May I please have a copy of it?**

❏ **What happens when students learn and complete their work at different levels of speed and proficiency? What assistance is provided to students who are slower or less proficient? What enrichment is provided to students who are quicker or more proficient? If enrichment work is provided, could you please show me an example of such a task?**

While these questions are certainly not exhaustive, they provide the basis for a continuing conversation and mutual understanding between parent and teacher. Even if there is absolutely no parent choice with regard to teacher and class assignment, this conversation will allow you and your child to begin the year with greater clarity and less ambiguity. Such a conversation also makes clear to the teacher that you are genuinely interested in the education of your children and that you are willing to be helpful and supportive of the teacher.

When You Need to Change Teachers

Many teachers are wonderful. They are dedicated professionals who work extra hours, take a personal interest in every child, and who are remembered by generations of students who were lucky enough to be in their classroom. Students in these classes may not come home every day having had fun, but they always come home having been challenged to do their best. Many teachers are solid practitioners, perhaps a little cynical because of their treatment at the hands of administrators and school boards. These teachers have had a few run-ins with parents, and those experiences left the teacher wondering whether the parents really wanted to support education or just wanted a babysitting service for their child. These teachers can provide a solid education for your children, but they are not the exceptional educators who will inspire a child to excellence. A few teachers are truly incompetent. Their classrooms are out of control, perhaps dangerous. Sometimes they scream; sometimes they are silent in the face of belligerent behavior that appears to be tacitly approved by their silence. They play favorites and the incomprehensibility of their evaluation system makes it impossible to tell how grades are awarded. Some of these terrible teachers embrace every new fad, sometimes to the exclusion of educational basics; others have learned nothing since they left college, perhaps decades ago. They rarely ask students to write, and the teacher's own writing is full of errors in grammar and spelling. Their personal understanding of the subjects that they teach rarely extends beyond the textbook, so that if there were errors in the science or social studies text, they would be unlikely to notice.

In the course of 13 years of education from kindergarten through the completion of high school, your child will probably have more than 50 different teachers, assuming one or more teacher for each elementary grade and at least 7 different teachers each year for secondary school. Of these 50 teachers, some will be wonderful, some will be solid practitioners, and perhaps a very few will be incompetent. If that is the case, you have an obligation to intervene. In some cases, such as with an unclear grading policy, the situation may improve with a simple request. In most cases of a true incompetent, however, no amount of cajoling or complaining will change the fact that the person in the classroom is not equipped to do the job. Whatever the inconvenience, you will be less aggravated and your child will be better educated if you insist on a change. You may be able to change to a different teacher within your school or it may be necessary to change schools. In extreme cases, where the district and school administration are extremely uncooperative, it may be necessary to change to a different public school system or to find a charter or private school that will meet your child's needs. The impact of this disruption is negligible when compared to the impact of a lost year of learning.

If you request a change of teacher, you must have your facts straight. Present to the principal a written request, identifying the specific objections you have. If there were particular behaviors by the teacher to which you object, identify with as much specificity as possible the circumstances, the exact behavior (not the attitudes or motivation, just the behavior) that you observed, and precisely when it occurred. You should expect to have the principal listen to you politely, and then refuse your request for a change. In general, school administrators deplore change and are supportive of teachers in most instances of teacher-parent disagreement. Remain calm, make your case with clarity and specificity, and ask for a written notice of the principal's decision. If the decision is against your wishes, ask also for the written notice to include information on the next level of decision authority. There is no such thing as a decision that cannot be appealed, and you must pursue the matter with the district administration if necessary.

One final issue should be considered before you proceed to change teachers, schools, or systems. You must ensure that the alternative is genuinely better. That means that you have taken the time to have the same conversation with the prospective teachers in the other classrooms or alternative schools that you had with your child's current teacher. You cannot assume that simply because a school has a good reputation, is a charter school, is a private school, is exclusive, or is expensive that the individual classroom to which your child is assigned will be one of quality and challenge. There is no substitute for asking the questions listed above, starting with the simple, "What is my child expected to know and be able to do at the end of this year?"

Parents' Checklist for the Week Before School Begins

☐ **Gradually begin to move your child's bedtime back (getting up at 6 a.m. can be quite a shock after "summer hours").**

☐ **Do any last minute shopping for school supplies. Try not to leave it all until the week before school starts, as the shelves may be stripped. Instead, try to start shopping for school supplies two or three weeks before school starts.**

   ☐ **Plan ahead. Know what you need to buy before you're in the store.**

   ☐ **Try office supply stores and warehouse stores. You'll find better prices.**

   ☐ **Try to involve your child in the shopping and decision-making. After all, these are the notebooks and pencils she'll be using.**

☐ **Let your child choose something special to wear or bring on the first day of school. A new backpack or his favorite shirt may help make things less overwhelming.**

- [ ] Take your child to the school and look around. Locate:
    - [ ] Rest rooms
    - [ ] Counseling office
    - [ ] Main office
    - [ ] Nurse's office
    - [ ] Gym
    - [ ] Cafeteria
    - [ ] Where to buy lunch tickets
    - [ ] Playground—maybe even play for awhile before all the other kids get there
    - [ ] Where to catch the bus
- [ ] Get a copy of the bell/class schedule and look it over along with a map of the school.
- [ ] If your child will be bringing a sack lunch to school, consult her on the menu.
- [ ] If your child will be walking to school or to the bus stop, make sure he is familiar with the route and with "safe places" along the way (friends' houses, stores you frequent, etc.).
- [ ] Be open, alert, and sympathetic to any and all questions about school, as well as to moods and behaviors that may indicate fear and anxiety on the child's part.

Parents' Checklist for the First Week of School

- [ ] Once again, be alert. Ask a lot of questions and make eye contact and affirming comments when your child answers. Make sure he knows you want to be involved and that you are listening to him.
- [ ] Some direct questions to ask:

- ❏ Where is your locker? Is it conveniently located? How often can you go to it? Do you have to carry all your books all day long?

- ❏ is lunch? Do you have someone to sit with? Do you know how to get through the lunch lines? Do you know where to buy lunch tickets?

- ❏ Are you having trouble with any kids?

- ❏ Are you thinking of trying out for any sports or plays, or joining any clubs? How can I help?

❏ If you happen to have one of those kids who doesn't answer direct questions, here are some indirect ones to try:

- ❏ What was your favorite part of the day?

- ❏ Was there a high part? What was it?

- ❏ Was there a low part? What was it?

❏ Pay close attention to any handouts your child brings home. The important guidelines and forms tend to be sent home in the first few weeks. If your child is not forthcoming with handouts, a "backpack search" may be in order.

❏ With your child, go over any homework, artwork, tests, or other papers she brings home. Talk openly about what was difficult and what was easy, her likes and dislikes about the assignment or project.

❏ Never be afraid to call the teacher! If something doesn't seem right or is simply unclear, a phone call at the beginning of the school year can often ward off bigger problems later.

❏ Realize that your child may be tired, overwhelmed, and even cranky the first week of school. Try to help him relax.

❏ Leaving notes of encouragement in a backpack or lunch box is a pleasant surprise that even older kids enjoy. Help them remember that you support them even if you can't be there.

The Emergency Supply Cabinet

We all remember running home from school one day saying, "Mom! I have a project due tomorrow! I have to make a replica of the Coliseum... do we have three pounds of clay and a yard of brown felt?" If it hasn't happened to you yet as a parent, it will. You can't get through even one child's school career without a school supply emergency of some sort. Here are a few things to keep on hand so that you'll be better prepared for such an occasion:

❑ Glue and/or glue stick

❑ Construction paper

❑ Extra computer paper

❑ Extra toner or ink cartridge for the printer

❑ Blue and black ink pens

❑ Lined paper

❑ Poster board

❑ Colored pencils

❑ Markers

❑ Tape

❑ Scissors

❑ Ruler and/or yardstick

❑ Stapler and staples

❑ Paper clips

❑ Stickers

❑ Glitter

- ❑ **Dictionary**
- ❑ **Thesaurus**
- ❑ **Atlas**
- ❑ **Globe**
- ❑ **Encyclopedia**

Chapter 7

But **What** Do I Do *Tomorrow?*

The 20-Minute Learning Connection is not a quick fix. Rather, it is a commitment that will become a habit for you and for your child, leading to success in school as well as learning, discipline, intellectual development, discovery, and most importantly, the connections between parents and children that are far more important than any test or homework assignment. The path to this commitment, as with all great achievements, begins by recognizing what could go wrong and anticipating these developments. One of the first things that might go wrong is that your child might not share your enthusiasm for spending these 20 minutes together every day. This chapter suggests some practical ways for dealing with the typical differences between what children want (freedom, television, and Nintendo) and what they need: guidance, discipline, and the development of skills and knowledge that will last them a lifetime. We will consider some typical responses of children who will resist your attempts to engage them in new and challenging enterprises.

"I Can't Do This!"

Perhaps the most frequent complaints of school children and, for that matter, adults, is the allegation that because they cannot do something, it must be impossible. I am reasonably certain that the young Michael Jordan did not sink his first basket, nor did Tiger Woods ace his first golf shot. Van Cliburn probably muffed a scale or two long before achieving stardom as a concert pianist. In the abstract, we know that hard work and many mistakes, along with an occasional dose of frustration, are part of learning. When the abstract becomes our reality, however, it is much easier to succumb to the logic that the past is prologue, and that what I was unable to do yesterday I cannot do today, nor will I ever be able to do it.

Children do not invent such a negative image of their ability to learn. They are taught this pernicious lesson through the example of many adults, including teachers and parents. Every parent knows that there is a wide gulf between pride in the accomplishment of a difficult task and the anxiety that preceded the first step toward such an achievement. Whether the challenge is the first step of the baby, the first word of the toddler, the first chapter of a book, the first soccer kick, or the first sonata, there is an inevitable sequence that includes challenge, doubt, failure, perseverance, and ultimate success. The chasm from challenge to success is a wide one, but it is not filled merely with obstacles and heartache. This path also includes encouragement, small victories, glimpses of future success, and growing confidence that the goal is worth the effort. When we hear the fear-filled complaint from children, "I can't do this!" our response must be more than superficial encouragement. Rather, we must provide an immediate shift in focus away from the insurmountable goal and toward an immediately achievable objective. In other words, our focus must continually be on what children can do now and our encouragement must be focused on the immediate next step. This establishes a clear incremental process: challenge, self-doubt, encouragement, small steps, and then, the next challenge.

"I Don't Have Any Homework! Why Should I Have to Do This?" learning

The 20-Minute Learning Connection offers parents an excellent opportunity to make learning part of life rather than mere drudgery confined to the school day. This habit can be developed as a routine, no more onerous than making one's bed or washing the dishes, and no less pleasurable than a short walk around the neighborhood or enjoying a hot cup of tea. Even though there are many other things to be done, parents and children still manage to engage in the ordinary duties and pleasures of everyday life. Learning ought to be one of those simultaneous duties and pleasures.

In order to develop the habit of learning, parents must counter the prevailing notion that the only context in which structured learning should take place is when homework is assigned by the teacher. Indeed, some parents may be skeptical about asking their children to engage in any additional activities because of what they have heard about excessive homework that today's children must endure. The myth of the kindergartner with five hours of homework every night should be challenged for what it is: either the result of the most grievous educational malpractice or, far more likely, the result of the fevered imagination of those who are persuaded by rumor rather than evidence. In fact, the far more common problem in many schools is the complete absence of homework, even at the secondary level. Teachers increasingly find that it takes too much time to grade, that students refuse to complete it, and that parents and even administrators fail to support the requirements that teachers place on students. When I hear complaints about excessive homework, including in my own home, I am generally inclined to examine the facts. The "five hours of homework" was, in fact, 30 minutes of homework, plus $4\frac{1}{2}$ hours of phone calls, computer games, television, and other diversions. Even when there is an extensive homework assignment that might have required many hours of work, further investigation reveals that the teacher provided the requirement weeks in advance of the due date, and it was poor planning on the part of the student that caused all of the work to be required in a single sitting. The plain fact is that for the vast majority of elementary and secondary students, the problem is not too much homework, but the habitual absence of homework that has convinced students that they ought to be liberated from anything resembling learning beyond the confines of the school day.

The skills and knowledge contained in this guide will, in fact, build confidence, speed, and efficiency in the completion of homework. Moreover, these activities offer the opportunity for parents and children to enjoy learning together, whereas the typical homework assignment is something that the teacher expects students to complete independently.

figure it out together

"It Doesn't Make Any Difference What I Do! I Just Don't Get It!"

I wish that I could offer a response to the frustration of a child that would mix the wisdom and certainty that Dr. Spock (the pediatrician and best-selling author, not the alien on *Star Trek*) offered to parents of the 1950s. Readers would recognize and challenge the superficiality of easy answers to challenging problems. In fact, children can become plagued by self-doubt, and their absolute knowledge that "I just don't get it" quickly becomes the ingrained belief that "I just *can't* get it." Here are some ideas to consider when dealing with a child who expresses feelings of inadequacy, self-doubt, and hopelessness.

First, recognize the value of these feelings. When children accurately say, "I don't get it," they are expressing the first step toward understanding. After all, it is far more difficult to convince someone to accept instruction when they think that they have the right answer and are unwilling to admit that they don't know everything. Thus, the parent's response to uncertainty and self-doubt should be clear and unequivocal affirmation. "You're right," the parent can acknowledge. "You don't know it. And you know what? You have to be *really* smart to know that you don't know something! Let's see if we can figure it out together…"

Second, determine what the child knows. For example, if the child is bewildered by multiplication or exponents, start with addition. "So you're saying that six times five is pretty hard, is that right? Well, let's start with five plus five— what's that? Ten! You're right—I knew that you could do it! Now let's do five plus five plus five? Fifteen! Right again…" The pattern is clear. Start with what the child knows, and then honor it, build on it, and work together to create the next level of understanding. To complete this example, we will eventually arrive at the point in which the patient and loving parent can exclaim, "You did it! You just said that when I add five six times, that's thirty! You just told me that six times five is thirty! I *knew* that you could do it!"

Third, break the task into incremental steps. Too many textbooks, academic standards, and test requirements involve many different tasks masquerading as a single step. If the student does not recognize that there are many separate tasks, then frustration is inevitable. For example, consider this typical item from an upper elementary school math test:

"Herb is a gardener who loves tomatoes. In fact, that is all he plants in his backyard garden. In his side yard he has a 12-square-foot garden with zucchinis and azaleas. In the front yard, he has a pond in the middle of his 32-square-foot flower garden. However, the backyard garden is all tomatoes. His backyard garden is 7 feet wide and 24 inches long. There are 4 tomato plants in each square foot. If each tomato plant has an average of 3 ripe tomatoes, how many tomatoes will Herb harvest?"

Some students might tackle this problem with gusto. In fact, they might do it so quickly that they will include information about the side yard and front yard gardens or forget to convert 24 inches into two feet. Other students will find the sheer quantity of information so overwhelming that they will become bogged down in some of the irrelevant details. An effective method of helping students tackle a multistep problem is the clear identification of each step. A good rule of thumb is this: If you are not sure whether you need to add an extra step, then add it. It is much less risky to have a step that you do not need than to skip a step that you did need.

Here is one approach to breaking this problem down into incremental steps.

First, circle the question—what am I supposed to know? In this case, the question is, "How many tomatoes will Herb harvest?" Whatever I do, I know that the final answer is not about feet or inches, it is about the number of tomatoes that Herb will harvest.

Second, make all the units the same. The garden is "7 feet wide and 24 inches long." To make this the same units, I need to know that there are 12 inches in one foot, and that 24 inches is the same as 2 feet. Third, draw a picture. Why? Because pictures are easier to understand than words. On some tests, students are required to draw a diagram for math problems. However, even when such a drawing is not required, it is a great idea to convert words into pictures because it makes the problem easier to understand. My picture might look like this:

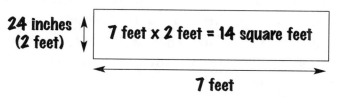

But What Do I Do *Tomorrow*?

Fourth, write the problem in words. It might look something like this: "The number of tomatoes that Herb will harvest is equal to the number of tomatoes on one plant (3) times the number of tomato plants in one square foot of his garden (4) times the number of square feet in his garden (14)." Some tests require that students explain their answer in writing. However, even if it is a multiple-choice test and no one but the student will see the diagram and sentences, it is an excellent idea to write out the sentences that explain the answer. Fifth, put numbers with the words of the sentence. "The number of tomatoes that Herb will harvest is equal to 3 tomatoes per plant times 4 tomato plants per square foot times 14 square feet, or 168 tomatoes." Sixth, go back to the question in step one. Ask yourself, "Have I answered the question?"

This may seem to be a laborious process for a relatively simple math question. On the contrary, the easiest way to tackle this or any other math problem is to break it down into simple steps. Some of these steps will be the same on every single math problem, from fifth grade math through graduate school statistics. For example, the first step is always, "Circle the question—what am I supposed to know?" The last step is always, "Go back to the question in step one—have I answered the question?" This process is essential for a student to move beyond calculation into real mathematical problem solving. There are many students who know the times tables and math facts, but who cannot solve the problem of Herb's tomatoes. They do not read the problem carefully, they include irrelevant data, or they provide elaborate answers in square feet when the question is asking about the number of tomatoes that Herb will harvest.

This problem illustrates an important component of the 20-Minute Learning Connection. In this illustration, the parent was not imperiously demanding, "Don't you get it? It's 168 tomatoes!" Rather, the parent was breaking down a complex problem into steps and the child proceeded systematically through the problem.

"Everything Is Okay. Just Leave Me Alone!"

Self-reliance is a wonderful thing. A few school children still read Emerson's essay on the subject and are enjoined to revel in the independence of spirit enjoyed by that rare individual who is dependent on no other person. As a student and as a parent, I have experienced both sides of the tension that results when a parent wishes to be helpful and the child prefers to assert independence. It is at this point that the normal stress of homework can explode into a tearful confrontation. Thus, the parental response to "Just leave me alone" must be careful and measured.

Start with a positive statement. "You must be very confident to want to do this yourself without any help. I am proud of you. Please show it to me when you are done." This is not a request; it is a requirement. If the Emersonian spirit is alive and well, your self-reliant student will submit flawless work that will elicit unrestrained praise. When that daydream is interrupted, however, it is far more likely that "Just leave me alone" was a way of saying, "I don't know how to do this, but I really don't want you to think that I'm stupid. If you would just stay away, then I won't know it, but at least you won't know that I don't know it."

This is a delicate point in a conversation with any child. Whether your child is in second grade (my youngest) or twelfth grade (my oldest), the need for independence is strong. There is a world of difference between the parent who in exasperation demands, "Let me show you how to do it right," and the parent who says gently but firmly, "I'm really proud of your independence. Please show it to me when you are done." Your time is limited. Invest it wisely. If the child's confidence is appropriate, then parental support for that confidence should follow. If the child needs help but will not admit it, then no humiliation is required. The certain knowledge that a loving and supportive parent will look at the final work product will lead to a request for help. For the strong-willed, independent child, the response to a request for help is far better than imposed assistance.

a positive beginning

Daily Checklist for School Success

Whether you have one child or six, checklists are helpful ways to transform the chaos of the morning into a positive beginning to the school day. While every family has its own rituals and requirements for the start of the day, here are some items you may want to include in a visible checklist for daily review by children and parents:

❑ **Assignment notebook complete.**

If not, call a friend, call the "homework hotline" if your school has one, or call the teacher at home. If it is not written down in the assignment notebook, it will not happen.

❑ **Backpack empty and repacked.**

Archaeologists of the future will find some student backpacks and be unable, in at least a few cases, to differentiate them from time capsules. The accumulation of literature, culture, and food represent the accumulation of epochs of civilization. Let your child find a better way to be famous than in the diorama of a natural history museum of future centuries. Empty the backpack completely every night and repack it, with a place for everything and everything in its place.

update the calendar

❑ **Projects, tests, and other important dates on the family calendar.**

There are few more discouraging moments than finding "important" notes squashed in the residue of the bottom of a backpack that involve dates that have already passed. There should be a single large family calendar that has everything from the volunteer activities and business trips of parents to the school activities, project due dates, and tests of children. Without such a combined calendar, conflicts are inevitable.

❑ **Homework checked.**

This does not mean homework done by the parent, nor does it imply homework completed at all. It means that the parent knows what has and has not been done. The child knows that accountability begins at home and that the requirements of the parents are at least as stringent as those imposed at school.

❑ **Long-term projects reviewed.**

The myth of "five hours of homework" is frequently revealed as the month-long project that has been concealed and postponed until the night before it is due. The requirement of 15 minutes a night for 20 nights thus became five hours in a single night, with the teacher portrayed as the architect of student misery. While it is important that parents ask about projects due "tomorrow," it is equally important that future projects and tests become the subject of daily conversation.

The "Refrigerator Curriculum"

Ray Simon and Janine Riggs are leaders in one of the most remarkable stories of educational progress in the nation. Their "Smart Start" initiative in Arkansas focused on literacy and math and created nationally recognized progress among students of every economic and ethnic group in the state. Their methods were hardly revolutionary. They set high standards and clear expectations for every child. They also had the wisdom to know that parents were essential contributors to student success. One of their most successful innovations was the "Refrigerator Curriculum," so named because it was designed to be affixed next to student work proudly displayed on the refrigerator door. This document expressed on a single page the essential knowledge and skills that students needed for each grade level. Unless you have a large refrigerator, you will not have enough space to display every state standard. Nevertheless, you can identify the most important skills that your child must acquire, and reminders of those essentials should roughly correspond to the frequency with which you open the refrigerator door.

If your child's school does not offer a refrigerator curriculum, then consider creating one. The plain fact is that every standard and academic requirement is not of equal value. Determine those that are most important and reinforce them frequently. Ask your child's teachers and school administrators this simple question: "If I can't do everything that you'd like me to do at the end of the day, what are the most important things for my child to know and be able to do in order to be successful in the next grade?" When the question is phrased in this way, the response should be brief. It will not include a laundry list full of scores of standards. Rather, the list will include some academic requirements, a focus on literacy, and an emphasis on appropriate behavior, time management, and organizational skills. These are worthy of a place on your refrigerator door.

Conclusion

Advice about how to raise the perfectly behaved and flawlessly educated child can be overwhelming, unreasonable, and silly. There is simply too much to do and not enough time to do it all. One of the central themes of this book is that even on the typical day when perfection is elusive and you cannot "do it all," there are nevertheless important and constructive things you can do in order to make a positive difference for your child. As this chapter suggests, not every conversation is easy, nor is every offer of parental support welcomed by a child. Nevertheless, in 20 minutes you can update the calendar, check the backpack, help break a complicated problem down into small steps, provide some encouragement, and maybe even share a laugh. In other words, even on the busiest day, you can make a difference.

make a positive
difference

Chapter 8

Standards and Tests in New York

Putting It All Together: Standards, Tests, and Accountability

"Standards, Tests, and Accountability"—the very words have the rhythm of "Lions, Tigers, and Bears" from Dorothy's scary walk along the Yellow Brick Road. That which is unknown and mysterious is, to both children and adults, the source of fear and anxiety. This chapter will demystify elementary school tests in New York. While the tests are not easy, the more students know what to expect, the less fearful they will be. It is important to note that this chapter is not a definitive guide to the content and format of the New York State elementary school tests. You should expect to see periodic changes in testing policy on everything from the standards addressed to the grades tested. What this chapter does offer is sound advice for helping your child succeed on any state test. Even if the format and content change, your child will learn sound test-taking principles and, most importantly, will discover the importance of reading comprehension and written analysis as the keys to test success in every subject. For the latest information about the content and format of the New York State elementary school tests, visit the New York Department of Education's website at www.nysed.gov.

Is Test Preparation Unethical?

There is an important difference between mindless test drills and the teaching of a curriculum that is thoughtfully linked to the assessments that students must take. Although the phrase "teaching to the test" is often used critically by those who oppose any sort of testing, consider the alternative. If teachers did not link their curriculum to state assessments, then children would be set up for failure, with every test a mystery and every question a surprise. Inevitably, anger, frustration, fear, and anxiety would stem from the failure of schools to link their instruction to the requirements placed on students during tests.

Parents are rightfully concerned when they hear rumors that a thoughtful and rigorous academic environment has been transformed into a boot camp for test preparation. I personally have investigated many such claims, including the complaint that "all students do all day is prepare for the state tests." Each time I hear such a statement, I make a point of asking for more detail. "Tell me," I inquire, "about the schedule of the most test-obsessed teacher in the entire school. How much time every day is spent on test preparation? For how many weeks does such a regimen last?" The most recent inquiry resulted in the admission that the "test-obsessed" teacher devoted one hour a day for three weeks to test preparation. That is 15 hours out of 1,080 instructional hours (180 school days times 6 hours a day), or about 1.4 percent of the time in school. That is not, by anyone's standards, an inappropriate obsession with test preparation. My typical recommendation to educators is that they devote about 20 minutes a week to the "life skill" of test taking. We teach children many life skills, including pedestrian and bicycle safety, avoidance of alcohol, tobacco, and drugs, and a variety of skills that extend beyond the academic curriculum of school. Test taking is also a skill that students use throughout their lives. Twenty minutes a week—about 12 hours a year—is hardly transforming American schools from an academic paradise into a test preparation boot camp.

Finally, let us consider the ethical issue itself. Even at 20 minutes a week, does test preparation cross an ethical boundary? Certainly it would be unethical if a teacher were to procure questions from the state test, copy them, and encourage students to memorize the answers. Such behavior can result in felony convictions and jail time for teachers and administrators in some states. No thoughtful person recommends such behavior. It is, however, entirely fair and reasonable for teachers and school administrators to say, "This test will require reading and, more specifically, require students to write a summary of the stories and nonfiction passages that they read. This is not only a test requirement, but the requirement for any well-educated child. We would do this even if there were no state test. Therefore, every day when students read a passage in their textbook or read a story, we will require students to write a brief summary of what they have read."

This is good educational practice, not unethical "teaching to the test." The same is true of requirements for students to write, know their geography, or understand mathematics. It is good education, not any sort of ethical breach. In fact, the real ethical challenge is presented by teachers who refuse to give students the information they need to be successful on tests and in the next grade. Some teachers refuse to acknowledge the value of aligning their curriculum with the skills and knowledge students need to succeed on tests. These teachers are committing an ethical violation as serious as the driver education teacher who sends students to take a driving test without an understanding of stop signs or the operation of the brake pedal.

reading, writing, and math
What Children Need to Know for the Tests

The most important clarification with regard to standards and testing is this: Children do not have to be proficient on every single standard in order to be successful on the New York tests. Although the New York State Learning Standards provide excellent guidelines for teachers and parents, it is impossible for any test to address every standard for each grade level. Therefore, the New York tests, administered to fourth grade students each spring, cover only a small part of the school curriculum, with a particular emphasis on reading, writing, mathematics, and science. So if someone were to ask, "What does a child need to know and be able to do in order to be successful on the New York tests?" the answer would be, "The child must read, write, and understand elementary mathematics. Some understanding of elementary science content is helpful, but the most important areas for students are reading and writing."

There are three tests of concern to elementary students in New York: English Language Arts, Mathematics, and Science. All are administered in the spring to fourth grade students. The English Language Arts test takes place over three days. On the first day, students devote 45 minutes to 5 reading passages and 28 multiple-choice questions. On the second day, students listen to an adult read a passage of several paragraphs. The students then write responses to three questions; two of the answers are brief and one is long. This requires about 30 minutes. Also on the second day, the students write an essay, a process that takes another 30 minutes. On the third day, students read two related passages and respond to four questions. Three of the responses are short and one is long. This requires a total of about 60 minutes.

The Mathematics test also takes place over three days. On the first day, students spend 40 minutes responding to 30 multiple-choice questions. On the second day, students have seven short, open-ended questions and two longer open-ended questions, requiring a total of about 50 minutes. On the third day, students again respond to seven short, open-ended questions and two longer open-ended questions, also within about 50 minutes.

The Science test has two parts. The first part is an hour-long multiple-choice test that includes 45 questions. The second part is called a "performance test" and involves hands-on tasks at five stations. Over the course of about an hour, students work individually at four stations and with another student at the fifth station. The five tasks are described below:

1) *Liquids*—Students use measuring equipment and their observation skills to determine the physical properties of objects, make inferences, and formulate new questions.

2) *Grouping Objects*—Students sort a set of eight objects into appropriate groups and create their own classification system by forming subgroups for the objects.

3) *Ball and Ramp Game*—two students work together, gathering data about problems associated with the development of the ball and ramp game, measuring distance and making inferences based on the data. Each student completes an answer sheet and makes predictions about how to modify the game.

4) *Magnetic and Electrical Testing*—Students use a magnet and electrical tester to collect data about a set of eight objects. They record their findings and use the data to make inferences about the magnetic/electrical properties of the objects.

5) *Unknown Object*—Students are given an unknown object and must describe it in a letter that a scientist might read. Observation skills and nonstandard measurement must be used to describe the object, communicate the information in writing, and ask additional questions of the scientist.

The English language arts skills questions on the New York test require students to understand the meaning of common vocabulary words, spell correctly, identify misspellings, identify mistakes in sentences, and understand the meaning of reading passages that vary in length from single sentences to several paragraphs.

The mathematics skills questions on the New York test require students to read questions (this is very important: the "math" test is, in fact, very much a test of reading ability as well), understand what the question is asking, solve simple number operations (addition, subtraction, multiplication, and division), and find the "next step" in solving mathematical problems. Make no mistake: math facts are important. Just as was the case when you were in school, children must know addition and subtraction facts from second grade on, and multiplication and division from third grade on. If your child is in a later grade and was told that, in the age of calculators and computers, math facts are not really important, then it is not too late to break out the flash cards and correct this omission in his or her education. If your child has a teacher who believes that learning the "times tables" and other drudgery is unimportant, then you need to seriously consider changing teachers. There are many areas in education about which reasonable people may differ, but this is not one of them. While the logical and analytical skills involved in mathematical problem-solving are important, they are not a replacement for understanding and knowing—and yes, that means memorizing—the facts of addition, subtraction, multiplication, and division.

Writing: The Best Way to Build Thinking Skills

One of the best ways that parents can help children gain the essential knowledge, not only for the English language arts portion of the tests, but for success throughout the school years ahead of them, is to require students to read for at least 20 minutes, write a summary of what they have read, and then edit and correct their summary. While reading is important, the creation of a written summary, along with the editing and revision of that summary, provides one of the best ways to build the skills of thinking, comprehension, analysis, synthesis, understanding, and communication. Students may not think that they have time to create a brief outline of what they are going to write. In fact, students will find that the creation of a brief outline will save time and improve organization.

Student writing is required on every element of the New York examinations. Whether the subject is reading, mathematics, or science, students must write clearly and coherently. Of all the skills acquired in elementary school, the one with the greatest weight on the state tests is, by pleasant coincidence, the skill with the greatest impact on student success in secondary school and college: nonfiction writing. If parents and teachers feel overwhelmed with too much academic content and wonder where they should focus their energies, the development of writing, editing, and rewriting skills would be at the top of my list.

It is important that parents understand that the term "writing" can be applied to many different activities, and some are more helpful to students than others. While journal and story writing may be entertaining, these activities are not as useful as writing that requires students to hone summarization, analytical, descriptive, and explanatory skills.

Writing Activities to Build Thinking Skills

■ **Summarization:** Listen to a parent read a story or an article. While the story is being read, make a few notes about the events, characters, and setting. Write a brief summary of that story.

■ **Comparison and Analysis:** Listen to a parent read two related but different stories. Make a list of what is similar and what is different between the two stories;

then write three paragraphs. The first paragraph should contain a brief introduction, followed by a statement of how the two stories are similar. The second paragraph should contain statements describing how the two stories are different. The third paragraph should draw conclusions about the stories and make an evaluation about which one the student prefers.

- ■ **Description:** Look at an object, animal, or activity for five minutes. Write down what you notice, using as many senses as you can. Then write a paragraph describing the object, animal, or activity in as much detail as possible.

- ■ **Explanation:** Look at a process—perhaps a math problem or a scientific procedure. Explain in writing how to solve the math problem or how the scientific procedure works.

Some readers may wonder about such an emphasis on writing. Aren't the majority of questions on the test in a multiple-choice format? It is true that, for example, the Math test includes 30 multiple-choice questions and 18 questions that must be answered in writing. Student skill in writing, however, not only improves performance on the 18 open-ended questions (14 requiring short responses, 4 requiring extended responses), but it also helps on the multiple-choice questions. The research is unambiguous that a greater emphasis on nonfiction writing builds the thinking, analysis, and reading skills of students. These skills, in turn, are associated with improvements on multiple-choice test scores. Finally, writing is a complex skill that improves only with consistent effort and reinforcement. Because writing takes on even greater importance in secondary school and college, elementary school educators and parents are well-advised to place an exceptional emphasis on writing.

Test Format and Test Preparation

The majority of test questions are multiple-choice in format. This means that students can choose an answer from among the four or five possible responses provided by the test. The multiple-choice format has an important implication for students, teachers, and parents:

It is not only important to know the right answers to test questions, but also to find the wrong answers and eliminate them.

Although this may seem obvious to parents who have experience in taking multiple-choice tests, the implications for students are profound. This means that test taking need not be a game of mere memorization in which students conclude, "Either I know it or I don't, and if I don't, then I might as well give up." Rather, this focus on knowing both the right and the wrong answer gives students multiple opportunities to be successful on the test. It also gives students an incentive to persevere on a problem even if the right answer is not obvious to them. Most importantly, this insight gives teachers and parents the ability to move far beyond traditional practice tests and enhance the thinking and reasoning skills of students.

Consider this sample question:

George sold these items at a garage sale.

Cap: $2.15   Lock: $0.85   Toy Mower: $12.23

About how much did he make?

A) $10   B) $12   C) $15   D) $20

The intent of the question is for the student to estimate (the clue "about" suggests this) and then add $2 + $1 + $12 to get the sum of $15. Even an excellent fourth-grade mathematician may, however, add the decimal figures and then be bewildered by the fact that the sum—double and triple-checked—is actually $15.23, a figure that does not appear among the possible answers. In this and many cases like it, we can coach our children to use their powers of reasoning to *eliminate the wrong answers.* First of all, since a single toy costs more than $12, we know that answers A and B must be wrong. If we only get that far, we now have a 50 percent chance—either C or D—of selecting the correct response. That is far better than leaving the answer blank or randomly guessing. It is also important to know that, from an educational point of view, this sort of practice is not the "mindless test prep" that critics of standards and testing so frequently assail. In fact, this approach to the practice problem improves students' reasoning, reading, estimation, and problem solving—all skills that are essential even if state tests were eliminated tomorrow. Moreover, the habit of moving from the search for the right answer to the elimination of wrong answers builds a student's power of logic and reasoning, helping to improve success on tests for many years to come.

When parents and teachers analyze multiple-choice problems in this way, they are moving far beyond the low-level test preparation that critics of standards and testing have so frequently criticized, toward the thinking skills that students need. It is fair to ask this question: If all tests were eliminated tomorrow, would my child still need to think, read, write, and compute? If you answered in the affirmative, then these exercises are not merely a matter of preparation for tests, but preparation for life.

editing and revising

Student Writing

The New York exams include questions requiring short and long written responses. The long responses require students to develop skill in organization and planning to gain the maximum score. Students typically will have plenty of time to create an outline, write a rough draft, and then produce a final copy. Students who immediately start writing in response to the question frequently submit work that is poorly organized. One of the most important skills that you can instill in your child is the habit of rewriting. Children never should presume that their first written product is their last. Most editors would argue that this is a good rule for authors of any age. By focusing on the habit of rewriting, parents provide both an intellectual and an emotional advantage for their children. Successful writers must not only write, but also rewrite and after thought, reflection, and feedback, rewrite yet again. This intellectual attribute is directly related to the emotional trait of persistence. Students will not have the ability to rewrite unless they have the emotional strength to persist in the face of difficulty and challenge. One of the most important gifts any parent can give to a child is the habit of persistence, resilience, and rising once again to a challenge. In simple terms, rewriting is an emotional and intellectual gift to children, and it is as important as the initial gifts of reading and writing that were bestowed by parents in the earliest days of literary exploration.

Does *Every* Student Have to Take the Test?

New York laws and administrative regulations place a heavy emphasis on the inclusion of all students in testing. Although extensive accommodations have been made for the provision of the Math test in alternative languages (Spanish, Chinese, Haitian, Creole and Russian, at this writing), that option is only available to students scoring above the 30th percentile on the English Reading test. If students are to be exempted from the test, special permission is required from the local account-ability committee. Thus, the vast majority of students must take the tests prescribed by the state. The clear intent of both the law and the commissioner's statements is to have maximum participation. Students with disabilities must take the assessment with appropriate accommodations and adaptations, unless their Individualized Education Plan (IEP) specifies in writing that the student must be excluded from testing. Even in those cases, the IEP must provide for other means of assessing student progress.

What If Parents Object to the Tests?

Because of the clear emphasis on 100 percent participation in the state test-ing program, some parents may be legitimately concerned that their chil-dren are being subjected to inappropriate testing. Because of the complexity of feder-al laws guaranteeing the rights of individual students to appropriate testing and the New York statutes that intend to have 100 percent participation, parents must serve as advocates for their children in those cases where testing may not be appropriate. In gen-eral, every student, including the profoundly disabled and those unable to speak English, will be assessed. The vast majority of those students will be assessed using the English Language test forms, although teachers are required to provide reasonable accommodations to students with specifically diagnosed learning disabilities. Only in the most rare cases can students be excluded from state testing, and even in those cases, it is the responsibility of the school to administer an appropriate alternative assessment.

What About the Other Tests in School?

Although the state-mandated standardized tests receive the lion's share of the publicity about testing in school, there are other tests that children routinely take that can have very significant consequences for a child's future educational opportunities. Some of these tests include so-called I.Q. (Intelligence Quotient) Tests and Aptitude Tests. These tests frequently are used to determine the eligibility of a student for "gifted and talented" programs or for participation in special education programs. Educational assessment experts have strong differences of opinion on what these tests mean. One leading national testing company explains "aptitude" as follows:

> A combination of characteristics, whether native or acquired, that is indicative of an individual's ability to learn or to develop proficiency in some particular area if appropriate education or training is provided. Aptitude tests include those of general academic (scholastic) ability; those of special abilities such as verbal, numerical, mechanical, or musical; tests assessing 'readiness' for learning; and tests that measure both ability and previous learning, and are used to predict future performance—usually in a specific field, such as foreign language, shorthand, or nursing. (Harcourt Educational Measurement website, www.hemweb.com/library/glossary)

Some scholars question the very existence of aptitude as a consistent quality in young children, arguing that interest, environment, and early education are all variables that change rapidly in the life of a young child. Moreover, the announcement of such a quality as aptitude can become a self-fulfilling prophecy. There are large numbers of children who have been told that they lack an aptitude in math and science based on a test at an early age. This test result discouraged these students and their parents from the pursuit of the more advanced—and potentially more interesting—science and math courses. Not surprisingly, the "predictions" appeared to be accurate, as these students did not perform well in high school and college on science and math tests. Consider the case of a child who is told, "You're going to be fat, so there is no reason for you to even consider diet, exercise, or a healthy lifestyle." When that child becomes an obese and unhealthy adolescent and adult, do we blame the child or would we question the wisdom of the prediction that, not surprisingly, came to fruition?

There is a cautionary tale from comic genius Matt Groening, the creator of the television series, *The Simpsons*. In one episode of the show, Bart, the ne'er do well son of Homer and Marge, is accidentally identified as "gifted" when his test paper is switched with that of another student. As Bart exhibits the same behavior that had been routinely ridiculed and berated by teachers and school administrators, he is now applauded for his wise insights and extraordinary "gifts." The test had miraculous powers of prediction, though not in the way that its creators had intended. In this cartoon, as in real life, tests do a much better job of predicting the actions of the adults to read and believe the results than they do of predicting the success and failure of the children who take the tests.

Just as the term "aptitude" has been subject to debate among researchers, so also the term "intelligence" has been the subject of considerable controversy. Although the notion of measurable intelligence was regarded as a scientific fact in the early 20th century, researchers in the last two decades have cast considerable doubt on the notion of general intelligence. These complex controversies have filled volumes. For the purposes of this book, suffice it to say that a few things are fairly clear. First, the younger a child is, the more variable the scores on intelligence tests tend to be. Therefore, it is wise for parents to avoid reading too much into the results. Tuesday's gifted child may, with a little more fatigue and distractions, become Wednesday's child in need of special intervention. The same child, in turn, becomes Thursday's child who is destined for a career in music because of the chance playing of an engaging song on the radio and the ability of that child to replicate a music and rhythm pattern on the way to the office of the school psychologist.

These observations do not indict all tests administered to all children, but only indicate the obvious: the smaller the number of measurements, the greater the opportunity for error. No adult would submit to a life-changing decision based on a single test. If a physician prescribed surgery after a single blood pressure reading, we would demand more tests. We should be no less insistent on additional measurement when someone makes life-changing decisions that affect our children.

Questions for Teachers and School Leaders

The tests in New York have consequences, both intended and otherwise, for students and parents. The most draconian consequence is the possibility of forcing a student to repeat a grade in school due to failure to pass a test. While there are many areas of educational research that yield ambiguous results, the issue of student retention is not one of them. In a tiny fraction of cases, such as those where a student started school at an inappropriately early age or where overly aggressive parents insisted on skipping the first or second grade, the requirement for a fourth grader to repeat a grade may be appropriate. In the vast majority of cases, however, the repetition of a grade is a classic example of the faulty logic demonstrated by repeating the same activity and expecting different results. It simply doesn't work. If the child has a reading deficiency, then the appropriate intervention is intensive and immediate reading instruction, not another year in which reading constitutes only 60 minutes a day of the curriculum. Because retention has such negative consequences for the children retained and, ultimately, for all children in the classroom, it is important that parents ensure that their children take the tests seriously, are well-prepared, and perform well on them. Because the consequences of inadequate preparation are so serious, it is appropriate and fair for parents to ask these questions:

- **How is the curriculum in my child's class related to the New York State tests?**

- **What opportunities will my child have to become familiar with the requirements of the state tests?**

- **If my child is not making adequate progress toward preparation for the state tests, when and how will this be communicated to parents?**

- **What intervention plan does the school have for students who are having difficulty so that children receive this intervention long before the state tests are administered?**

- **Do the teachers and administrators in the school believe that these tests are important?**

ask questions

While most parents have observed the obnoxious behavior of the Little League Dads, and their academic counterparts who are incessantly berating teachers and children about their performance, these questions are neither inappropriate nor intrusive. The unfortunate fact is that parents cannot assume that teachers know or care about tests. There is a backlash against testing in some areas of New York, and many teachers and school administrators continue to regard the classroom curriculum to be the exclusive domain of the teacher. Thanksgiving plays, Halloween parties, and scores of hours devoted to dioramas, crafts, and coloring all have hallowed traditions and have been supported by generations of teachers, students and, indeed, parents. But none of these is more important than learning to read.

While the primacy of reading, writing, and mathematics may be obvious to some readers, a backlash to the standards movement has resulted in a growing number of places where an emphasis on academic excellence is regarded as politically incorrect. Even well-meaning parents have jumped on the bandwagon, opposing standards and testing, and decrying the increased emphasis on academics in the classroom. One wonders if the same parents would protest against the physicians who delivered the bad news that kids could benefit from cutting back on the corn chips, soda, and Twinkies. If those, too, were fixtures in classrooms for generations, a reduction in them might cause frowns and protests from children. Presumably, if the matter at hand were the health of our children, we would endure the whining about a reduction in junk food. There is no doubt about this point: Success in school, including proficiency in reading, writing, and mathematics, is a health issue. Children who are forced to repeat a grade are at substantially greater risk for dropping out of school later in life, and students who drop out of school exhibit a broad range of high-risk behaviors that threaten their very lives.

achieving balance

Test Preparation Without Tests Anxiety: The Delicate Balance

The challenge for parents and teachers is the manner in which we convey this complex message to children. We want them to understand that the tests are important and we want them to be willing to work hard to learn in school. We also want them to have fun, enjoy school, love learning and most importantly, deal with the inevitable stress and anxiety that occur in school without becoming paralyzed by negative emotions. While the perfect balance may be elusive, we certainly know what does not work. Telling children that "It's no big deal" or "You're wonderful and you really don't need that stuff" may be comforting in the short term, but it lays a foundation of academic quicksand for students. False reassurances now lead to failure, stress, and anxiety later. By contrast, gentle but firm challenges now are necessary for the reduction of anxiety in the months to come. Many of these gentle but firm challenges occur in school under the guiding hand of a devoted, caring, and knowledgeable teacher. The vast majority of such challenges, however, must come from home where daily routines, including the 20-Minute Learning Connection, will give students confidence, skills, perseverance, and ultimately, success.

Chapter 9

Children with Special Needs

Your Rights As a Parent

I choose my words carefully here: The rights of people with disabilities are civil rights. The last century will be marked in history not only for technological advances, world wars, and economic booms and busts, but for the battle fought and won on behalf of the disadvantaged. If you are the parent of a child with special needs, whether the child is blind, hearing-impaired, cognitively disabled, or suffers from any other disability, then school officials are not doing you a favor when they provide accommodations for your child any more than your local officials do you a favor when they allow you to vote. Meeting the needs of persons with disabilities is a civic responsibility. Having those needs met is a right, not a privilege.

If you are already confident in the accuracy of the diagnosis of your child's needs, then you may wish to proceed directly to the end of this chapter and find more detailed information on organizations that are specifically oriented to the needs of your child. If, however, you do not know if your child has a learning disability or other special need, then this chapter may offer some ideas for you to consider as you enter this very complex and challenging area of education.

In the context of standards and testing, the discussions surrounding special needs students frequently have been polarized. At one extreme are those who stereotype every special needs student as cognitively unable to meet academic standards, and thus every effort is made to exclude these students from testing. At the other extreme are those who recognize no impairment that would interfere with testing and insist on including every child in testing. In reality, the essence of the legislation at all levels regarding children with special needs is designed to protect the *individual* needs of the child. This chapter, therefore, cannot provide guidance about all children except in the most general sense. Every sentence that follows must be interpreted through the parental lens that is best able to focus on the individual needs of your child. Whether your child is included or excluded from special education, whether your child meets academic standards with or without accommodations, and whether your child participates in regular state examinations or alternative examinations that are more appropriate, is not a matter of blind bureaucratic policy, but rather an individual decision made based on the individual needs of your child.

What Are Special Needs Anyway, and How Do I Know If My Child Has Them?

Some special needs are obvious. Children with profound physical, neurological, or developmental challenges clearly need additional assistance in order to deal with the challenges of daily life, including the challenges of a school environment. Other children may be unsuccessful in school, and yet there is no clear developmental or physical disability. How then can you tell if your child needs the additional assistance that is legally guaranteed? Parents must separate the normal challenges of daily life from the challenges faced by students with developmental impairments. As the complexity of pediatric neurology grows, the field is understandably intimidating for any parent. One thing is clear: Your child will never have any advocate that is more knowledgeable and caring about the individual needs of that child than a parent. Your lack of a professional credential must not limit you from playing an active role as the primary advocate for your child. In this respect, it is important for you to advocate accuracy. You are not an advocate either on behalf of participation in special education programs nor exclusion from them, but rather you are an advocate on behalf of accurate, complete, and meaningful diagnoses of your child's needs.

independent evaluation

The Limits of "Field Diagnosis"

The field of special education includes professionals who are gifted educators and diagnosticians. When your child is entrusted to this select group of educators, psychologists, and medical professionals, their wealth of experience and personal attention to each child, as well as their expert administration of a wide battery of tests and other diagnostic assessments, will provide a high probability that the diagnosis of your child's learning disability—or the absence of any disability at all—is accurate. Unfortunately, schools across the nation are governed by resource constraints, where one school psychologist may be assigned to serve the needs of more than a thousand students. Specialists in the diagnosis of learning disabilities are overwhelmed with the immediate needs of students whose needs are obvious and profound. In some cases, this leaves the diagnosis in the hands of amateurs who have neither the experience nor technical skills to make an accurate diagnosis. Here are the most important words in this chapter:

Before you allow your child to be categorized as "special education" or "learning disabled," it is imperative that you have an independent evaluation of your child done by an independent psychologist (doctor of psychology who specializes in learning disabilities and their diagnosis—not a practitioner, regardless of degree, who gives diagnostic tests on a part-time basis).

Why is independent diagnosis so important? The literature is full of tests and questions that appear to create a link to potential learning disabilities. Among these "diagnostic questions" I have found, a parent might be alarmed to find the following:

- ❑ **Does the child have difficulty in understanding new concepts?**

- ❑ **Is the child restless in class?**

- ❑ **Does the child fidget in his seat?**

- ❑ **Does the child seem less mature than his classmates?**

By these standards, every one of my children would have sent alarm bells ringing on any given day, even though all of them have managed to perform at very high levels in school. Indeed, by these standards, I know of few children who would not send parents scurrying to a specialist in search of a diagnosis to these obvious "problems" which, in another age, we called normal childhood behavior. This does not diminish the very real presence of learning disabilities and the need for their diagnosis and treatment. Yet, when I hear of regular schools with no greater population of disabled children than the average, and more than 30 percent of the children have been labeled as "special education," then I must wonder if the problem is really with the children or in pervasive presumptions of disabilities and the need for accompanying accommodations when, in fact, the children are quite normal.

an important clue

Context: Where Does Your Child Excel?

One important clue to your child's needs is the context in which your child has difficulty and that in which your child excels. For example, a child who does not write well in class, but who at home is able to compose wonderful stories with exciting plots and characters does not have a writing disability, but rather has a disinterest in the type of writing that is presently being required in class. The child who refuses to read aloud in class may not have the suspected reading disability, particularly if the same child is able to read with enthusiasm when alone with Grandma. Some parents have been told that the requirement for multi-step mathematical problem-solving is developmentally inappropriate for their child, and yet the same child is able to engage successfully in playground games that require multi-step conditional problem-solving and to keep the score with meticulous accuracy.

Thus, the first step in your reflection on your child's learning needs is to ask the question, "Where does my child excel?" I have heard some parents and teachers insist that there is no response for such a question and that every activity involves failures. When I persist, I will sometimes get a shrug of the shoulders and the rueful observation that, "Well, at least he can excel at Nintendo!"

Curious, I persist. "Tell me more about this success in Nintendo."

"It's awful," the parent complains. "He'll sit there for two hours, hardly blinking an eye, and proudly announce that he has made the 'next level,' whatever that means. He even compares scores with seven other kids at school who seem to devote every recess period to talking about how to get better at the dumb game, and he rattles off their scores every night as if he were announcing the league standings for the NFL."

"Please let me make sure that I understand this," I respond. "This is a child who at school appears to have memory problems and a complete inability to focus and concentrate. Homework seems futile because the child cannot remember simple facts from the previous day. Just sitting and talking about schoolwork often provokes an angry and tearful confrontation and, eventually, you both give up and the child retreats to the Nintendo game, and that way at least you both get some peace and quiet. Is this a fair summary?"

"Every blessed night," the parent sighs.

"Okay, I want to make sure I understand this," I continue. "The child has memory problems, but gives a daily recitation of seven different changing Nintendo scores. The child has attention problems, yet remains engaged in a complex game with multiple levels for hours at a time. The child does not like to discuss even for a moment his areas of failure, but will revel at length in stories of his success. Let's think about where this child can excel. The child excels first when other students are similarly enthusiastic about the activity. The child also excels when there is immediate feedback— in fact, every few moments in a Nintendo game, the child knows if there is success or failure, and every session reveals whether a 'next level' has been achieved. And, it is fair to say that this child, like most humans, enjoys talking with those he loves and respects— his parents—about his successes much more than he enjoys dwelling on his failures. And when he talks with his friends, he talks about how to get better, not about how terrible his failures make him feel."

"So what?" the parents counter. "Playing Nintendo won't get him into college. In fact, it won't get him into the third grade, and that's what we're worried about right now."

"That's true, and as someone who (I trust my children will never make it to this chapter) has hidden the family Nintendo machine for several months now, I share your frustration with what seems like a mindless game that robs time from homework and other more appropriate pursuits. But let me share what I have learned from Nintendo and my good friend, Dr. Jeff Howard. Dr. Howard is the founder of the Efficacy Institute. He's a Harvard-trained psychologist who has devoted a good deal of his life to helping students on whom many other people have given up. Jeff doesn't like Nintendo games any more than I do, but he made me pay attention to what they offer that kids need. He asked me one day, 'How long would those kids be playing Nintendo if their scores were put in a package and given to them at the end of the week?' After I thought about it, I knew that the answer would be, 'Not very long.' Then Dr. Howard persisted, 'They stay focused on Nintendo because the feedback is immediate and relevant. They know when they succeed and, even if they fail, they have an immediate chance for redemption. When was the last time a homework assignment did that? In fact, it gets shoved into the parent packet and the child sees it at the end of the week, if ever, and the feedback inevitably focuses on their failure to do something that was required many days (an eternity for a third grader) earlier. Trust me—the kid can focus, memorize, and excel, but only if there is feedback that is timely and relevant, and only if the conversations about the activity focus on success rather than failure.'"

"So," the exasperated parent demands, "You and Dr. Howard want kids to play Nintendo?"

"Not at all," I offer reassuringly. "We just want students to apply the Nintendo Effect to the classroom and to family discussions of schoolwork. What would happen if we applied these rules to learning at school? First, feedback doesn't happen at the end of the week amidst a sea of red ink in the parent packet, but it happens right away. That means that you ask the teacher for immediate feedback, so that whenever there is an error, your child has the opportunity to correct it immediately. Teachers almost always have some free time built into the day, and this could be devoted to allowing your child to leave the school day with success rather than with ambiguity or failure. At the very least, your child could take the work home and deal with it Monday night rather than over the weekend—typically Sunday night after an exhausting weekend. Second, your child might be encouraged to talk with friends and parents about strategies to get better, and even an incremental gain—each time he reaches the 'next level'—is the cause of some celebratory phone calls. That might be a new chapter, a new reading level, or a new performance level in writing. Each gain may be, like Nintendo, only a few points, but it is at least as worthy of celebration as is game success."

The point of this extended dialogue is not to suggest that Nintendo will solve the development challenges of children. Rather, the central question must always be, "Where does my child excel?" Whether or not your child has a learning disability, the context, conversation, and process of those areas where your child excels will provide clues for application to other areas where your child needs help. This is one of many areas in which the lessons of special education can be broadly applied to every other area of education for learners of any age.

Adaptations, Accommodations, and Truth

Children with special needs are entitled to the "least restrictive environment" for learning. They are also entitled to adaptations and accommodations that allow them to participate in regular classrooms to the maximum extent possible. The greatest entitlement, however, for students with special needs and their parents is the truth, including the truth about what the student has and has not yet accomplished. Too frequently, the discussions surrounding adaptations have as the underlying theme that an adaptation is equivalent to a loss of rigor. This is summed up in statements such as, "She was in special education, so I had to give her a B," or, "Sure, he passed the test, but only because he received special accommodations, so it really doesn't mean very much." There is a more appropriate way to discuss student achievement, and that is with an unwavering focus on truth.

If a child were blind, few people would presume that the Braille version of the test had less rigor than the printed version used by children with no visual impairments. In fact, some might argue that success on these tests by students who are blind requires more memory and better analytical skills than are required by other students. After all, the student reading Braille has to solve the Pythagorean theorem on a middle school math test, whether the problem about right triangles is posed in print or the problem is presented in the form of raised symbols. Now let's consider a child who has a different disability that is less obvious. The child has no guide dog, cane, or other external indicator of a disability, but nevertheless this student has an impairment that prevents the processing of printed text. The accommodation in such a case might include the presence of an adult to read the test. For another child with an attention deficit, the accommodation might include testing in a different room. For another child, there might be a scribe who writes the answers as dictated by the child. But all of these children must solve the problem with the Pythagorean theorem. In other words, the presence of an accommodation does not necessarily indicate a reduction of rigor. If these students can solve that equation, then it would be prejudicial in the extreme to conclude that they didn't "really" know that the square of the hypotenuse is equal to the sum of the square of the two sides.

Let's consider the case of a student who, perhaps due to a cognitive delay, does not correctly solve the problem. Rather than conclude that, "This child cannot do the Pythagorean theorem," or more broadly, that the child has a mathematics disability, we should focus our attention on truth and accuracy. We know what the child has not done yet, so what *can* this student do? Special educators are masterful at breaking standards and other academic requirements down into incremental tasks. In this example, the special educator might say that the real problem is text processing, not an inability to manipulate numbers. When the problem is presented as a story problem, the child "can't" do the Pythagorean theorem, but when the problem is presented with symbols and numbers, the child quickly calculates that $c^2 = a^2 + b^2$ or otherwise solves the problem without relying on text. Perhaps the student does not understand exponents, but does understand multiplication, or in this example, $c \times c = (a \times a) + (b \times b)$. Or perhaps the child does not yet grasp multiplication, but does understand the nature of addition as the total represented by groups of other numbers or objects. And so the task of incremental analysis continues. It is not done until we have more than the obvious information, such as the test item that the child missed. Our task as educators and parents remains incomplete until we have identified what the child can do, and the small incremental steps that are ahead of us, separating the present moment from the ultimate solution of the problem. A well-drafted Individualized Education Plan (IEP) will contain a series of such small increments, including a clear identification of what the student has already accomplished and the next steps to be accomplished.

The Individualized Education Plan (IEP)

The IEP is an important document that governs everything from classroom expectations to curriculum to assessment. This plan, as the name implies, must be focused on the individual needs of each student. While accommodations may be similar for several different students, the plan itself must be distinct, unique, and individual. The IEP is an evolving document, and the needs of your child may change. As a student gains skills, improves development, modifies behavior, or otherwise changes over the course of time, the IEP should also change.

The IEP is the result of the careful collaboration of a group of teachers, frequently labeled the IEP Team. This includes the classroom teacher, special education specialists, other specialists (such as speech pathologists), and school administrators. Parents should be personally involved in the IEP Team and should plan to attend meetings of the team. Your observations about the successes and challenges in the daily life of your child will provide valuable information that is more detailed and timely than may be obtained from classroom records.

Reporting Student Achievement of Standards— Beyond the Report Card

A frequent source of miscommunication between educators and parents has to do with the student report card. Many parents have contributed to this confusion by insisting that teachers must use a regular report card because parents perceive that this document is part of the "inclusion" to which their child is entitled. Although it is true that "regular" students routinely receive a traditional report card, this is among the many practices applied to regular education students that are of questionable value. For students who need very specific feedback on what they can do and have not yet done, the traditional report card provides inadequate information. Rather than focus on the report card, parents should focus on the imperatives of accuracy and fairness. What they really need to know is what standards their child has met and what specific incremental steps remain to be achieved in those areas where the student has not yet met a standard. When teachers and parents pretend that a standard has been met, or otherwise indicate achievement on a report card that is at variance with the facts, then the child does not benefit. In fact, when the adults in the system focus on factors other than objective indicators of real achievement, the child is left wondering what the meaning of success and failure really is. One of the best ways to resolve this dilemma is to make better use of the IEP and other documents that teachers and IEP members have collected. In fact, one of the best ways to individualize curriculum and instruction for a student with special needs is to start with an individualized report card that includes narrative descriptions, the IEP itself, evidence of student achievement in a portfolio, and narrative descriptions of what the child has achieved. This is far superior to the traditional set of letters and numbers that represent judgments which are typically inconsistent and poorly related to the individual needs of your child.

assistance and support

For Further Information

There are a number of national organizations devoted to helping parents of children with special needs advocate for their children. Because the needs of your child are likely to be complex and significantly different from the needs of other children, it might be helpful to find a group of parents across the nation who face similar challenges. You may feel that your circumstances are unique in your school, and thus you and your child can be made to feel very isolated. In fact, there are many parents who share the same challenges and successes, frustrations and triumphs. Here is a partial list of such organizations that you may wish to contact:

Children and Adults with Attention Deficit/Hyperactivity Disorder
(800) 233-4050
www.chadd.org

Council for Exceptional Children
(888) CEC-SPED
www.cec.sped.org

Learning Disabilities Association

(412) 341-1515

www.ldaamerica.org

National Center for Learning Disabilities

(888) 575-7373

www.ncld.org

National Information Center for Children and Youth with Disabilities

(800) 695-0285

www.nichcy.org

International Dyslexia Association (formerly, the Orton Dyslexia Society)

(800) 222-3123

www.interdys.org

Access America

www.disAbility.gov

Federation for Children with Special Needs

(617) 236-7210

www.fcsn.org

Alexander Graham Bell Association for the Deaf and Hard of Hearing

(202) 337-5220

www.agbell.org

American Foundation for the Blind

(800) 232-5463

www.afb.org

Autism Society of America

(800) 3AUTISM

www.autism-society.org

Brain Injury Association

(800) 444-6443

www.biausa.org

Tourette Syndrome Association, Inc.

(718) 224-2999

www.tsa-usa.org

Contact Numbers and Websites for the New York Department of Education and National Resources

If you are interested in staying abreast of the latest educational policy as well as finding various ways to support and supplement your child's education, the numbers and sites below should prove helpful.

New York Department of Education

http://www.nysed.gov/

National Resources

U.S. Department of Education's Main Site

www.ed.gov

(800) USA-LEARN

Individuals with Disabilities Education Act (IDEA)

www.ed.gov/offices/OSERS/IDEA

National Assessment of Educational Progress (NAEP)

nces.ed.gov/nationsreportcard/site/home.asp

(202) 502-7458

National Center for Educational Statistics (NCES)

nces.ed.gov

(202) 502-7420

No Child Left Behind (President Bush's Statement on Education)

www.ed.gov/inits/nclb/index/html

Safe and Drug-free Schools

www.ed.gov/offices/OESE/SDFS

(800) 624-0100

PART II

NEW YORK STATE

LEARNING

STANDARDS

with Home Learning Activities

New York State Learning Standards* with Home Learning Activities

• English Language Arts • Mathematics, Science, and Technology • Social Studies

Annotated with Home Learning Activities by Abby Remer

Reviewing practice questions isn't the only—or even the best—way to help your child succeed on the tests taken by New York State elementary school students. If you and your child spend 20 minutes every day on activities that are interesting, challenging, and directly related to New York's academic requirements, your child's test performance and grades will improve. Relax, have fun, enjoy your child's company, and help your child become a confident, capable learner.

The activities in this section are designed to help your child master the knowledge and skills required by the state of New York for students in elementary school. Although there are many ways to approach the standards and activities, here are some suggestions:

- Read through all the standards. This will help you understand how the "power standards" (see Chapter 5) apply to the New York State Learning Standards. Although not every standard is of equal value, reading the complete set of standards will give you a general overview of the knowledge and skills the state expects your child's school to cover.
- Choose activities that will be most appealing to your child. If your child especially enjoys writing, drawing, music, drama, or athletics, the icons will help you identify these types of activities.
- Look for activities that will build skills in an area where your child needs help in school. Ask your child's teacher to identify the standards your child needs to work on, and select corresponding activities for your 20-Minute Learning Connection.
- If you are concerned that the arts or physical education have been reduced at your child's school, this guide offers many opportunities to reinforce their importance at home. Icons for fine arts, performing arts, and physical education will help you identify activities in these categories.

Materials needed for each activity are identified by the following icons:

writing materials drawing materials Internet access newspapers

magazines TV or VCR reference books money

The following subject icons are used to indicate that more than one subject is covered by an activity:

English Language Arts Mathematics Science

Social Studies Fine Arts Performing Arts

Physical Education

NEW YORK

Learning Standards for English Language Arts at Three Levels

Elementary Level (Revised March 1996)

Standard 1: Students will read, write, listen, and speak for information and understanding.

As listeners and readers, students will collect data, facts, and ideas; discover relationships, concepts, and generalizations; and use knowledge generated from oral, written, and electronically produced texts. As speakers and writers, they will use oral and written language to acquire, interpret, apply, and transmit information.

Standard 2: Students will read, write, listen, and speak for literary response and expression.

Students will read and listen to oral, written, and electronically produced texts and performances, relate texts and performances to their own lives, and develop an understanding of the diverse social, historical, and cultural dimensions the texts and performances represent. As speakers and writers, students will use oral and written language for self-expression and artistic creation.

Standard 3: Students will read, write, listen, and speak for critical analysis and evaluation.

As listeners and readers, students will analyze experiences, ideas, information, and issues presented by others using a variety of established criteria. As speakers and writers, they will present, in oral and written language and from a variety of perspectives, their opinions and judgments on experiences, ideas, information and issues.

Standard 4: Students will read, write, listen, and speak for social interaction.

Students will use oral and written language for effective social communication with a wide variety of people. As readers and listeners, they will use the social communications of others to enrich their understanding of people and their views.

Standard 1–Language for Information and Understanding

Listening and Reading

1. Listening and reading to acquire information and ideas; discovering relationships, concepts, and generalizations; and using knowledge from oral, written, and electronic sources.

Students:

■ gather and interpret information from children's reference books, magazines, textbooks, electronic bulletin boards, audio and media presentations, oral interviews, and from such forms as charts, graphs, maps, and diagrams).

Information please

DICTIONARY, THESAURUS, ATLAS *Have your child pretend to be a librarian to whom you, as a patron, will come with questions. Pose questions where your child will need to identify and then search the correct reference book for the answers. Devise questions about weather predictions for an almanac, geographic questions for an atlas, and synonyms for the thesaurus.*

■ elect information appropriate to the purpose of their investigation and relate ideas from one text to another

Pet info

Ask your child to research information about how to keep his pet, or an imaginary one, healthy and happy. Help him conduct his research using the Internet (e.g., http://wwwanimaland.org), reference books, and speaking with veterinarians or pet store owners. Encourage him to take notes throughout the research process and discuss ways to organize the information he has collected to combine information on similar topics: diet, grooming, exercise, and so on. Based on his research, have your child write an illustrated pet-care manual from the pet's point of view, telling people what is necessary and why. Your child's manual should be legibly written in complete sentences, with proper grammar and punctuation. Encourage your child to choose words precisely to convey his ideas.

■ elect and use strategies they have been taught for note-taking, organizing, and categorizing information

Gal/Guy Friday

Dictate your weekly shopping list to your child in a random order. Next, ask your child to review the list and rewrite it in a logical order for your shopping (such as listing all the produce together, then all the paper goods, and so forth). Other notetaking/organizing opportunities include listing all the errands you have to do on a particular day, and having your child reorder the dictated list in a logical sequence in terms of their location.

■ ask specific questions to clarify and extend meaning

Find the five Ws

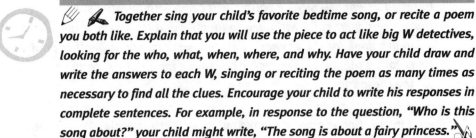

Together sing your child's favorite bedtime song, or recite a poem you both like. Explain that you will use the piece to act like big W detectives, looking for the who, what, when, where, and why. Have your child draw and write the answers to each W, singing or reciting the poem as many times as necessary to find all the clues. Encourage your child to write his responses in complete sentences. For example, in response to the question, "Who is this song about?" your child might write, "The song is about a fairy princess."

■ make appropriate and effective use of strategies to construct meaning from print, such as prior knowledge about a subject, structural and context clues, and an understanding of letter-sound relationships to decode difficult words

Funny phonic cards

Explore letter/sound relationships with your child. Write letters for a particular sound on a piece of paper, such as "st" or "ai." Help your child sound it out and then together, think of words that contain the phonic (for example, stay, stop, stand, stare, stair). Write each example on a separate note card and have your child draw a quick related illustration (such as a person with eyes wide open for "stare") on the same side as the written word as a memory aid. Have your child shuffle the cards and then say them the aloud. Eventually use a sequence to create an amusing phonic song.

■ support inferences about information and ideas with reference to text features, such as vocabulary and organizational patterns.

Seeking information

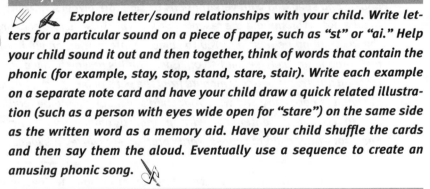

COMIC BOOKS Together, read one of your child's favorite comic books. After, create a short skit about two main characters, analyzing the story for information. When developing the characters, have your child study what he can infer or conclude about each character's personality, emotions, and physical being from the comic book. Is the character strong, brave, rich, romantic? What information supports this? Write and act out a short adventure

your characters might have, based on the type of events that occur in the comic book. Make sure that the characters in your skit speak in complete, grammatically correct sentences, and that the actors deliver their lines with appropriate intonation, rhythm, and pacing.

This is evident, for example, when students:

■ **accurately paraphrase what they have heard or read**

■ **follow directions that involve a few steps**

■ **ask for clarification of a classmate's idea in a group discussion**

■ **use concept maps, semantic webs, or outlines to organize information they have collected.**

Speaking and Writing

2. Speaking and writing to acquire and transmit information requires asking probing and clarifying questions, interpreting information in one's own words, applying information from one context to another, and presenting the information and interpretation clearly, concisely, and comprehensibly.

Students:

■ **present information clearly in a variety of oral and written forms such as summaries, paraphrases, brief reports, stories, posters, and charts**

Extinct is forever

 Have your child imagine she has been hired as a speech writer by an animal rights organization. They want your child to prepare a persuasive speech to be given at a news conference meant to gain support for their cause. Helpful background information on endangered species can be found at "Animals of the World in Danger" at

http://www.animalsindanger.com/. (Make sure your child addresses the guidelines in the Standard.) After your child has drafted and revised her speech, invite her to deliver it before family members.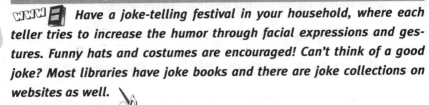

■ **select a focus, organization, and point of view for oral and written presentations**

Make 'em laugh

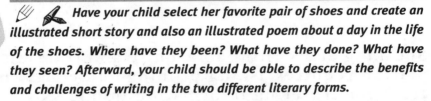 **WWW** 📖 *Have a joke-telling festival in your household, where each teller tries to increase the humor through facial expressions and gestures. Funny hats and costumes are encouraged! Can't think of a good joke? Most libraries have joke books and there are joke collections on websites as well.*

■ **use a few traditional structures for conveying information such as chronological order, cause and effect, and similarity and difference**

If my shoes could talk

✏️ 👞 *Have your child select her favorite pair of shoes and create an illustrated short story and also an illustrated poem about a day in the life of the shoes. Where have they been? What have they done? What have they seen? Afterward, your child should be able to describe the benefits and challenges of writing in the two different literary forms.*

■ **use details, examples, anecdotes, or personal experiences to explain or clarify information**

What's next?

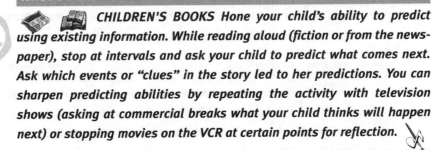 📚 *CHILDREN'S BOOKS Hone your child's ability to predict using existing information. While reading aloud (fiction or from the newspaper), stop at intervals and ask your child to predict what comes next. Ask which events or "clues" in the story led to her predictions. You can sharpen predicting abilities by repeating the activity with television shows (asking at commercial breaks what your child thinks will happen next) or stopping movies on the VCR at certain points for reflection.*

■ **include relevant information and exclude extraneous material**

✍ RADIO Listen to a radio news report together as you prepare a meal. Have your child take notes on the report, knowing that he will be a newscaster at the dinner table. As an "appetizer" at the beginning of the meal, have your child "broadcast" the story, briefly summarizing the major points with supporting evidence from the newscast.

■ use the process of pre-writing, drafting, revising, and proofreading (the "writing process") to produce well-constructed informational texts

Fine tuning

✍ ✈ Have both you and your child create separate campaign leaflets, imagining you are each running for president of your neighborhood association. What will you write to convince others that you should be elected? What personal characteristics, experiences, and ideas will you try to get across? Swap leaflets and critique one another's writing. What is clear, unclear, strong, weak, confusing, and so forth? Then each edit your own work as indicated in the Standard, and rewrite the final leaflet on plain paper, adding illustrations that will attract voters to your words.

■ observe basic writing conventions, such as correct spelling, punctuation, and capitalization, as well as sentence and paragraph structures appropriate to written forms.

Physical punctuation

Decide on three physical moves that correspond to punctuation, such as a jump for an exclamation point, a twist for a period, a shrug of the shoulders for a question mark. Say sentences aloud and have your child walk while you speak and then execute the appropriate physical punctuation at the end of the sentence. Reverse the process, explaining that sometimes you will intentionally do a wrong move and your child has to correct you.

This is evident, for example, when students:

■ write a short report on a topic in social studies using information from at least two different sources

- demonstrate the procedures for caring for a classroom pet using props or other visual aids as well as oral explanation

- revise early drafts of a report to make the information clearer to the audience

Step by step

 Together with your child, identify an electronic game at which he is especially skilled or an electronic device (such as a VCR or home computer) he has mastered. Ask your child to share his expertise with other household members by writing out step-by-step instructions, including basic information (such as the rules of the game or how to turn on the device) as well as personal tips (such as game-winning strategies or advice on how to conduct an Internet search). Have your child create a draft of his instructions and review them with a household member who is inexperienced with the game or device. Do the instructions cover all of the important steps? Is each step explained clearly? Ask your child to revise his instructions, based on the feedback he receives. His final draft should include complete, properly punctuated sentences, correct spelling, and legible writing. Post the instructions near the game or household device, so all household members can use them.

- use the vocabulary from their content area reading appropriately and with correct spelling

- produce brief summaries of chapters from text books, clearly indicating the most significant information and the reason for its importance.

Standard 2—Language for Literary Response and Expression

Listening and Reading

1. Listening and reading for literary response involves comprehending, interpreting, and critiquing imaginative texts in every medium, drawing on personal experiences and knowledge to understand the text, and recognizing the social, historical and cultural features of the text.

Students:

■ read a variety of literature of different genres: picture books; poems; articles and stories from children's magazines; fables, myths and legends; songs, plays and media productions; and works of fiction and nonfiction intended for young readers

Charting genres

✍ *EXAMPLES OF DIFFERENT LITERARY GENRES* *At home or in a library, have your child examine a sample of each genre mentioned in the Standard and take notes on each genre's distinguishing characteristics. Have him create a chart that identifies the features of each. Explanations on the chart should be in cursive and legible, with proper spelling, punctuation, and grammar. Using the information in the chart, have your child answer, if he was to become a writer, which genre would he pursue and why?*

■ recognize some features that distinguish the genres and use those features to aid comprehension

Have your child select a topic of interest—perhaps dinosaurs, computer games, a favorite sport, or music group. Ask her to use the topic as inspiration for a short piece of poetry, drama, fiction, or nonfiction. Afterward, use the same topic, but a different literary form. In both cases, ask your child to make sure that spelling and grammar are correct, that adjectives and adverbs are used correctly and effectively, and punctuation (including parentheses, commas, apostrophes, and quotation marks) is used properly. Discuss the advantages and disadvantages of each literary form. (For example, poetry might be more evocative overall, but it's easier to give factual information in a nonfiction response.)

■ understand the literary elements of setting, character, plot, theme, and point of view and compare those features to other works and to their own lives

Together, divide horizontally lined paper into five vertical columns. Write one of the five elements in the Standard in each column. Fill in the grid with your child whenever he completes a book, movie, or videotape. You may wish to help your child with the elements by asking questions such as "What was the main setting for this story?" "Can you summarize the action of the story in one sentence?" "Who were the main characters in the story?" "What caused the action in the story to take place?" "What was the result or outcome of the action in the story?" or, "How did the story end?" Make sure each grid entry is legibly written, using correct spelling and punctuation.

■ use inference and deduction to understand the text

CHILDREN'S BOOK THAT IS NEW TO YOUR CHILD Read a book aloud that is new to your child that has detailed information about a character. Make sure your child does not look at any accompanying illustrations while you read. Afterward, have your child try to act and dress like the character,

recalling information about what the character did or said or looked like. Have your child describe why she represented the character in this way, using specific references to the story.

- read aloud accurately and fluently, using phonics and context cues to determine pronunciation and meaning

Switch-aroo

CHILDREN'S BOOKS Have your child read aloud and when she comes across an unfamiliar word, look together at the surrounding word clues. Repeat the sentence aloud, saying "blank" at the unknown word and then continue on. Ask your child what other word might work in the sentence so it makes sense. For instance, "Jose's mother is proud of him because he is (responsible). He always completes his chores on Saturday before he goes to the park." Ask your child to look for clues in the sentence that suggest a meaning for the unknown word. For example, Jose's mother is "proud," so being "responsible" must be a good thing. Jose shows he is responsible by doing work before he goes off to have fun. Based on these clues, your child can conclude that a responsible person like Jose is "someone who does what he is supposed to do." Other words that describe Jose, based on what this passage tells us, are dutiful, reliable, dependable, and trustworthy. Help your child understand whether the word or definition she selected is close to the meaning of the original unknown word (responsible). Ask your child to use the newly understood word in another sentence to enhance comprehension.

- evaluate literary merit.

Kid's view

 Tell your child that she can see her own opinions online. Have your child visit www.Amazon.com, www.bn.com, or another book-selling site that encourages visitors to post reviews. Search for a book that she has read. On the page displaying the book, select the option of writing a review. Have your child compose her own review, as described in the Standard, and then post in on the website.

This is evident, for example, when students:

- **read a picture book to the class and point out how the pictures add meaning to the story**

- **recite a favorite poem from a class anthology and tell why they chose that poem**

- **keep a reading inventory to show all the types of literature they are reading**

- **retell a familiar fairy tale or fable to the class**

- **choose books to read individually or with others.**

Speaking and Writing

2. Speaking and writing for literary response involves presenting interpretations, analyses, and reactions to the content and language of a text. Speaking and writing for literary expression involves producing imaginative texts that use language and text structures that are inventive and often multilayered.

Students:

- **present personal responses to literature that make reference to the plot, characters, ideas, vocabulary, and text structure**

Visual take

LARGE BOX, CARDBOARD, TAPE, AND SCISSORS FOR A DIORAMA Ask your child to describe his favorite book, referring specifically to its plot, characters, ideas, and vocabulary. Together with your child, create a diorama (a box with stand-up cardboard, drawn figures, and an illustrated background) that conveys his responses visually and addresses the Standard. For instance, the scene might focus on your child's favorite character engaged in what your child thinks is the most interesting part of the story.

- explain the meaning of literary works with some attention to meanings beyond the literal level .

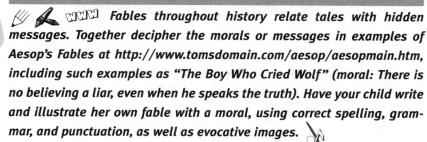

Tales that teach

Fables throughout history relate tales with hidden messages. Together decipher the morals or messages in examples of Aesop's Fables at http://www.tomsdomain.com/aesop/aesopmain.htm, including such examples as "The Boy Who Cried Wolf" (moral: There is no believing a liar, even when he speaks the truth). Have your child write and illustrate her own fable with a moral, using correct spelling, grammar, and punctuation, as well as evocative images.

- create their own stories, poems, and songs using the elements of the literature they have read and appropriate vocabulary

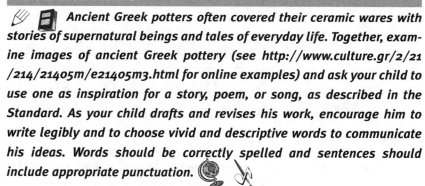

It's all Greek to me

Ancient Greek potters often covered their ceramic wares with stories of supernatural beings and tales of everyday life. Together, examine images of ancient Greek pottery (see http://www.culture.gr/2/21/214/21405m/e21405m3.html for online examples) and ask your child to use one as inspiration for a story, poem, or song, as described in the Standard. As your child drafts and revises his work, encourage him to write legibly and to choose vivid and descriptive words to communicate his ideas. Words should be correctly spelled and sentences should include appropriate punctuation.

- observe the conventions of grammar and usage, spelling, and punctuation.

Spell it

Have your child play the online game to see how she does with spelling at "Spellaroo" http://www.funbrain.com/tour/sr.html.

This is evident, for example, when students:

- perform dramatic readings or recitations of stories, poems, or plays

- write a review of a book to recommend it to their classmates

- create their own picture books or fables to keep in the classroom library

- write new endings or sequels to familiar stories

- pretend to be a character in a historical story and write letters to their class-mates about the character's life.

Standard 3—Language for Critical Analysis and Evaluation

Listening and Reading

1. **Listening and reading to analyze and evaluate experiences, ideas, information, and issues requires using evaluative criteria from a variety of perspectives and recognizing the difference in evaluations based on different sets of criteria.**

Students:

- read and form opinions about a variety of literary and informational texts and presentations, as well as persuasive texts such as advertisements, commercials, and letters to the editor

Fad diets

 With your child, examine newspaper and magazine advertisements for diets and weight-loss foods. Decipher which claims seem likely and which do not (such as losing 10 pounds in 2 days). How does the fact that the advertiser's claims are printed in a newspaper or magazine affect what you might believe about them? Would you be more or less likely to believe the claims if they were printed in a scientific or medical journal? How about if they were confirmed by a "real person"

(as opposed to a paid actor) on TV? What if you heard the claims from a friend? Based on your conclusions, discuss the methods advertisers use to persuade customers to buy other categories of products (toys, clothes, sneakers, etc.).

■ make decisions about the quality and dependability of texts and experiences based on some criteria, such as the attractiveness of the illustrations and appeal of the characters in a picture book, or the logic and believability of the claims made in an advertisement

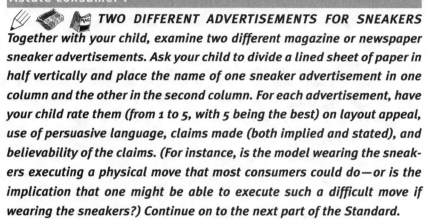

Astute consumer I

✐ 🖼 📕 TWO DIFFERENT ADVERTISEMENTS FOR SNEAKERS Together with your child, examine two different magazine or newspaper sneaker advertisements. Ask your child to divide a lined sheet of paper in half vertically and place the name of one sneaker advertisement in one column and the other in the second column. For each advertisement, have your child rate them (from 1 to 5, with 5 being the best) on layout appeal, use of persuasive language, claims made (both implied and stated), and believability of the claims. (For instance, is the model wearing the sneakers executing a physical move that most consumers could do—or is the implication that one might be able to execute such a difficult move if wearing the sneakers?) Continue on to the next part of the Standard.

■ recognize that the criteria that one uses to analyze and evaluate anything depend on one's point of view and purpose for the analysis

Astute consumer II

✐ Now, have your child divide another sheet of lined paper in half vertically and then horizontally, to make four quadrants. Write the name of each sneaker brand at the top of one of the horizontal columns. In each of the two quadrants at the top of the page, ask your child to write "My concerns" and list some of the things he looks for when thinking about new sneakers: Do they look good? Can I play well in them? Are they comfortable? Ask your child to rate each of the ads from 1 to 5 according to how well it answers (or doesn't answer) these questions. In the lower quadrants, ask your child to write "Parent's concerns," and have him list

New York State Learning Standards with Home Learning Activities *some of the things a parent might think about when shopping for new sneakers for a child: How expensive are they? How long will they last? How can they be kept clean? Again, rate each ad from 1 to 5 according to how well it provides the information parents need to make a decision about new sneakers. Ask your child to consider the ads from additional perspectives, including those of a shoe store owner, an animal rights activist, and a competitive athlete, and discuss what their reactions to these ads might be.*

■   evaluate their own strategies for reading and listening critically (such as recognizing bias or false claims, and understanding the difference between fact and opinion) and adjust those strategies to understand the experience more fully. .

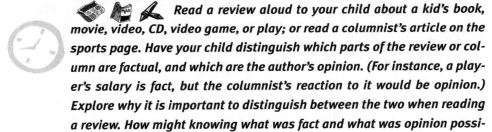

Mining fact from opinion

Read a review aloud to your child about a kid's book, movie, video, CD, video game, or play; or read a columnist's article on the sports page. Have your child distinguish which parts of the review or column are factual, and which are the author's opinion. (For instance, a player's salary is fact, but the columnist's reaction to it would be opinion.) Explore why it is important to distinguish between the two when reading a review. How might knowing what was fact and what was opinion possibly influence you?

This is evident, for example, when students:

■   listen to a book talk in class and express an opinion of the book with specific reference to the text and to some criteria for a good book

■   read several versions of a familiar fairy tale and recognize the differences in the versions

■   point out examples of false advertising in television ads for toys

■   identify the facts and opinions in a feature article in a children's magazine.

Speaking and Writing

2. **Speaking and writing for critical analysis and evaluation requires presenting opinions and judgments on experiences, ideas, information, and issues clearly, logically, and persuasively with reference to specific criteria on which the opinion or judgment is based.**

Students:

- express opinions (in such forms as oral and written reviews, letters to the editor, essays, or persuasive speeches) about events, books, issues, and experiences, supporting their opinions with some evidence

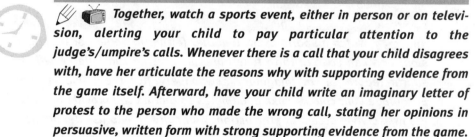

Wrong call

Together, watch a sports event, either in person or on television, alerting your child to pay particular attention to the judge's/umpire's calls. Whenever there is a call that your child disagrees with, have her articulate the reasons why with supporting evidence from the game itself. Afterward, have your child write an imaginary letter of protest to the person who made the wrong call, stating her opinions in persuasive, written form with strong supporting evidence from the game.

- present arguments for certain views or actions with reference to specific criteria that support the argument (e. g., an argument to purchase a particular piece of playground equipment might be based on the criteria of safety, appeal to children, durability, and low cost.)

Playground proposal

Have your child draft a speech to present to an imaginary city council that proposes the construction of a new, state-of-the-art playground. Encourage your child to use personal experiences and ideas to help create a full and detailed presentation that addresses the Standard

- monitor and adjust their own oral and written presentations to meet criteria for competent performance (E.g., in writing, the criteria might include development of position, organization, appropriate vocabulary, mechanics, and neatness. In speaking, the criteria might include good content, effective delivery, diction, posture, poise, and eye contact.)

Be the sportscaster

Together, watch a sporting event on television. Ask your child to pay special attention to the sportscaster. How does he or she use pacing, diction, and delivery to pull listeners into the event? After awhile, turn the volume off and ask your child to pretend to be the sportscaster, reporting the play-by-play action in a rousing and engaging manner for the television audience at home.

- use effective vocabulary and follow the rules of grammar, usage, spelling, and punctuation in persuasive writing.

Be the sports writer

Watch a sports event together (either in person or on television) and ask your child to take notes so that he can "file" a written sports report for an imaginary newspaper after the game is over. Encourage your child to take good notes so that he can provide his readers with a vivid account of the action. Your child should use details from his notes, as well as proper spelling, punctuation, and persuasive, evocative language to communicate the highlights of the game in his story.

This is evident, for example, when students:

- write a letter to the principal recommending that the school cafeteria serve pizza for lunch based on the criteria that it is nutritious and appealing to students

- give an oral report comparing several versions of the Cinderella story, pointing out similarities and differences in the versions

- in group discussion, select the most important word of a poem or story and explain its significance

- write an analysis of the effect of a major snow storm from the perspectives of a school student, a working parent, and a mail carrier

- in writing group, critique each other's writing with reference to specific criteria and revise their writing based on the group's suggestions.

Standard 4—Language for Social Interaction

Listening and Speaking

1. **Oral communication in formal and informal settings requires the ability to talk with people of different ages, genders, and cultures, to adapt presentations to different audiences, and to reflect on how talk varies in different situations.**

Students:

- listen attentively and recognize when it is appropriate for them to speak

Hiring help

Tell your child to imagine that she runs a zoo, and you are coming to interview for a job. Have your child interview you as the prospective employee, asking about your talents, interests, and experience as it relates to working in the zoo. Before the interview, discuss with your child some of the different types of jobs available at zoos, including the individuals who feed and care for the animals, the ticket takers at the gates, the veterinarians who care for the animals' health, the architects who design the habitats for the animals, and so on. Then discuss some of the characteristics of good zoo employees: individuals who love animals, individuals who are knowledgeable about each of the animals' preferred diets and habitats, individuals who are observant (to notice when animals are sick

New York Content Standards with Home Learning Activities

or need things), individuals who are strong (for moving feed bags and equipment), and so forth. Explain to your child that, during the interview, she should paraphrase your answers to each question to make sure she understands your response. At the end of the interview, ask your child which job she might place you in and why. Ask your child to cite the specific interview responses that led to her decision.

■ **take turns speaking and respond to others' ideas in conversations on familiar topics**

TV characters

 Together, view your child's favorite television show (or videotape). For this activity, each of you will pretend to be one of the characters in the show and create your own script for a new episode. Select two characters and then decide on a topic around which to build the show. (Choose something funny or outrageous, if possible, to open up the possibilities of the story line.) Improvise "in character" the dialogue and ideas for the story, revising and trying new things as you go along. Try to create a short song that the two of you can sing at the beginning and end of the show, or write new lyrics to the show's theme song that reflect the theme of your newly-created episode. When your ideas are set, have your child write out the script so you both can rehearse your lines before presenting the episode to household members and friends. During rehearsal, ask your child to focus on polishing her diction and delivery, and remind her to make eye contact with the audience during the actual performance.

■ **recognize the kind of interaction appropriate for different circumstances, such as story hour, group discussions, and one-on-one conversations.**

Volume control

Invite your child to play a game in which she will sing a favorite song, but you will change the volume! You will not alter the volume through a knob, but rather by mentioning imaginary places in which the song is being sung. Your child will need to adjust the volume of her singing to a level that is appropriate to the imaginary place you have named. When your child starts singing, call out different situations that require different volumes: in a sleeping baby's room, at a noisy construction site, in a concert arena, early in the morning when everyone is sleeping, and so forth. Listen to make sure your child adjusts her singing to an appropriate volume, and coach the singing louder or softer if necessary.

This is evident, for example, when students:

- take part in "show and tell" sessions

- participate in group discussions during "circle time"

- greet visitors to their school or classroom and respond to their questions

- bring messages to the principal's office or to another teacher.

Reading and Writing

2. Written communication for social interaction requires using written messages to establish, maintain, and enhance personal relationships with others.

Students:

- exchange friendly notes, cards, and letters with friends, relatives, and pen pals to keep in touch and to commemorate special occasions

Appreciation card

Don't wait until Valentine's Day to show your love. Have your child create an illustrated card for someone that describes in what way the person is special. Help your child create a first draft and then revise for spelling, grammar, and punctuation, and encourage your child to choose descriptive words to convey her ideas. Send the unexpected appreciation card to make someone's day.

- adjust their vocabulary and style to take into account the nature of the relationship and the knowledge and interests of the person receiving the message

Switching hats

 5 HATS OR CAPS, TAPE, BIG BAG Write the words informal conversation, debate, project *(e.g., making a model airplane, cleaning out a closet),* informational presentation, *and* imaginative presentation *on separate cards. Tape each card to the back of a hat or cap. Place the all the hats/caps in a big bag. Have your child take one of the hats out of the bag and look at the word, without letting you see what is written. Your child should then start speaking in a way appropriate to what is written as soon as she places the hat on her head (with the writing facing the back so you can't read it). It's up to you to guess which hat your child has selected. Replace the hat and repeat until you've eventually covered all five scenarios.*

- read and discuss published letters, diaries, and journals to learn the conventions of social writing.

Talk back

 Have your child read a number of letters to the editor in a children's magazine or weekly news magazine. (Help your child understand the topic and responses, if necessary.) After reading a number of letters, discuss how most letters to the editor typically fall into two responses: 1. thank you for sharing the information, or 2. your information was not accurate or was incomplete. Have your child devise a symbol for each type of letter (perhaps a "heart" for the thank you letters and a circle with an X through it for the not accurate/incomplete ones). Review the letters once again and have your child place the correct symbol next to each one. You can continue this activity in the future with new magazines.

This is evident, for example, when students:

- write thank you notes and invitations to friends

- **exchange letters with pen pals in another country**

- **write letters to relatives who live in another city.**

n.b. Because the focus of language for social interaction is on direct communication between individuals (rather than communication to a more general and perhaps unknown audience), the performance indicators for this standard are arranged to reflect the immediacy of direct communication (Listening and Speaking; Reading and Writing).

Learning Standards for Mathematics, Science, and Technology at Three Levels

Elementary Level (Revised March 1996)

Standard 1

Students will use mathematical analysis, scientific inquiry, and engineering design, as appropriate, to pose questions, seek answers, and develop solutions.

Standard 2

Students will access, generate, process, and transfer information using appropriate technologies.

Standard 3

Students will understand mathematics and become mathematically confident by communicating and reasoning mathematically, by applying mathematics in real-world settings, and by solving problems through the integrated study of number systems, geometry, algebra, data analysis, probability, and trigonometry.

Standard 4

Students will understand and apply scientific concepts, principles, and theories pertaining to the physical setting and living environment and recognize the historical development of ideas in science.

Standard 5

Students will apply technological knowledge and skills to design, construct, use, and evaluate products and systems to satisfy human and environmental needs.

Standard 6

Students will understand the relationships and common themes that connect mathematics, science, and technology and apply the themes to these and other areas of learning.

Standard 7

Students will apply the knowledge and thinking skills of mathematics, science, and technology to address real-life problems and make informed decisions.

Mathematical Analysis

1. Abstraction and symbolic representation are used to communicate mathematically.

Students:

■ use special mathematical notation and symbolism to communicate in mathematics and to compare and describe quantities, express relationships, and relate mathematics to their immediate environments.

Nutsy equations

 NOTE CARDS, NUTS Write mathematical symbols such as +, −, ÷, =, >, <, on individual note cards, reviewing what each one means with your child. Together, then translate mathematical equations into nut groups and cards. You will make up the equations and your child will select the correct math symbol card to insert within the nut groups. For the equation 3 + 4 = 7, you would place a group of 3 nuts then leave a space for a card, a group of 4 nuts, then a space for a card, and then a group of 7 nuts. To complete the equation, your child would place the + card in between the 3 nut group and 4 nut group, and the = card between the 4 and 7 group. After your child becomes adept at using the symbol cards, switch roles. Every time your child completes the equation correctly, you can eat the results!

This is evident, for example, when students:

■ describe their ages as an inequality such as $7 < r < 10$.

2. Deductive and inductive reasoning are used to reach mathematical conclusions.

Students:

■ use simple logical reasoning to develop conclusions, recognizing that patterns and relationships present in the environment assist them in reaching these conclusions.

High season attraction

Have your child describe typical weather at different times of year for your region. Then, have your child imagine working for a local tourist bureau and think about the best time of year to attract visitors and why. What will the weather be like at "high season" and what kind of activities are possible because of its predictability? Now you, playing a television travel show host, should interview your child, who will try to persuade viewers to visit the area at high season because of the predictability of the weather and its benefits.

3. Critical thinking skills are used in the solution of mathematical problems.

Students:

■ explore and solve problems generated from school, home, and community situations, using concrete objects or manipulative materials when possible.

Shoe order

Together discuss how frustrating it can be to scrounge around in the closet for the right pair of shoes. Have your child reorder the shoes in his closet according to which ones he wears the most to the least often, moving from front to back in the closet. Then ask your child to imagine that he lives in several different environments with different climates (say the Arctic Circle, rainforest, or the desert), and have your child reorder the shoes for each of these situations as well.

Scientific Inquiry

1. The central purpose of scientific inquiry is to develop explanations of natural phenomena in a continuing, creative process.

Students:

- ask "why" questions in attempts to seek greater understanding concerning objects and events they have observed and heard about.

Why do the stars shine at night?

FLASHLIGHT Stand far away from your child outside on a bright day. Turn on a flashlight and ask your child if the light is very easy to see. Go inside and repeat the experiment in a totally dark room. Based on this experience, have your child answer the riddle about why it's easier to see the stars at night.

- question the explanations they hear from others and read about, seeking clarification and comparing them with their own observations and understandings.

The big why

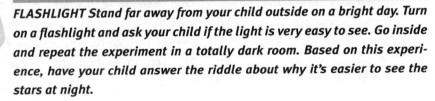 *Have your child take three minutes to list as many "why" questions as possible. (Why is the sky blue? Why do we only see stars at night?) Encourage wild imagination. Have your child think about people, places, things, time frames, foods, hobbies, sports, and so forth, flipping through a magazine for inspiration. Next, have your child choose one question to explore and explain in a report. Your child's report should include an introductory paragraph, supporting paragraphs including key details and facts, and a final paragraph summarizing his conclusions.*

- develop relationships among observations to construct descriptions of objects and events and to form their own tentative explanations of what they have observed.

This is evident, for example, when students:

- observe *a variety of objects that either sink or float when placed in a container of water.** Working in groups, they propose an explanation of why objects sink or float. After sharing and discussing their proposed explanation, they refine it and submit it for assessment. The explanation is rated on clarity and plausibility.

2. Beyond the use of reasoning and consensus, scientific inquiry involves the testing of proposed explanations involving the use of conventional techniques and procedures and usually requiring considerable ingenuity.

Students:

- develop written plans for exploring phenomena or for evaluating explanations guided by questions or proposed explanations they have helped formulate.

Is all water equal I?

 TWO PLASTIC CUPS OR CONTAINERS WITHOUT LIDS, TABLESPOON OF SALT, TAPE, WATER Review the materials listed in the activity with your child. Explain that she is going to be a salty scientist and her task will be to conduct an experiment with a sample of plain water and a sample of salt water to determine which will freeze first. Before she begins her experiment, ask your child to write out each step of the experiment, including filling both cups two-thirds full with plain water, adding the tablespoon of salt to one of the cups, using a piece of tape to identify the cup with the salt water, and then placing both cups in the freezer. In addition, her plans should include a method for monitoring the samples every ten minutes and recording observations about the status of the water in the two containers. Continue to the next part of the Standard.

- share their research plans with others and revise them based on their suggestions.

*A variety of content-specific items can be substituted for the italicized text

Is all water equal II?

Have your child review her plans with someone in the household or a friend. Is every step of the experiment explained clearly? Have any important steps been omitted? Is there anything about the experiment as written that might lead to inconclusive results or incomplete information? Help your child revise the plans for her experiment accordingly and then move to the next phase.

■ carry out their plans for exploring phenomena through direct observation and through the use of simple instruments that permit measurements of quantities (e.g., length, mass, volume, temperature, and time).

Is all water equal III?

Have your child conduct the experiment, including recording observations, and then present her results. Afterward, share with your child that salt lowers the freezing point of water. That's why the water without the salt froze first. Explain that this is why people sprinkle salt on icy sidewalks: when the ice begins to melt, the salt dissolves and the water becomes salt water. Since salt water has a lower freezing point than pure water, the ice does not form as fast.

This is evident, for example, when students:

■ are asked to develop a way of testing their explanation of *why objects sink or float when placed in a container of water.** They tell what procedures and materials they will use and indicate what results will support their explanation. Their plan is critiqued by others, they revise it, and submit it for assessment. The plan is rated on clarity, soundness in addressing the issue, and feasibility. After the teacher suggests modifications, the plan is carried out.

Students will use mathematical analysis, scientific inquiry, and engineering design, as appropriate, to pose questions, seek answers, and develop solutions.

3. The observations made while testing proposed explanations, when analyzed using conventional and invented methods, provide new insights into phenomena.

Students:

■ organize observations and measurements of objects and events through classification and the preparation of simple charts and tables.

Food favorites I

Have your child chart the favorite foods of friends and family. The chart should list each person's name and favorite food in different horizontal columns across the top of the paper. Then, there should be separate vertical rows for information about what type of food it is (beverage, snack, dessert), its flavor (sweet, salty, spicy), its temperature (hot, cold, room temperature), the amount typically eaten in a sitting (one slice, one scoop, one cup), and when it is usually consumed (for breakfast, between meals). Move to the next part of the Standard.

■ interpret organized observations and measurements, recognizing simple patterns, sequences, and relationships.

Food favorites II

Ask your child to examine his results and draw conclusions about this group's food preferences. Do the majority of people like sweets? During which meal or time of day are the most popular foods served? What do the favorites have in common and how are they different? Do most adults prefer one type of food while younger people prefer another? Based on your child's data, are there foods many people like that should be served more often? Then move on the next phase.

■ share their findings with others and actively seek their interpretations and ideas.

Food favorites III

Have your child present his findings to the polled group and ask for feedback. Does the information seem accurate to all survey participants? Does everyone agree with your child's interpretation of the data?

■ adjust their explanations and understandings of objects and events based on their findings and new ideas.

Food favorites IV

After revising his findings, have your child develop an oral and visual presentation to an imaginary food company for a new type of food, based on the findings of this activity. Ask household members or friends to be on the "board" of the food company and respond to the innovative proposal.

This is evident, for example, when students:

■ prepare tables or other representations of their observations and look for evidence which supports or refutes their explanation of *why objects sink or float when placed in a container of water.** After sharing and discussing their results with other groups, they prepare a brief research report that includes methods, findings, and conclusions. The report is rated on its clarity, care in carrying out the plan, and presentation of evidence supporting the conclusions.

Engineering Design

1. **Engineering design is an iterative process involving modeling and optimization finding the best solution within given constraints which is used to develop technological solutions to problems within given constraints.**

Students engage in the following steps in a design process:

■ describe objects, imaginary or real, that might be modeled or made differently and suggest ways in which the objects can be changed, fixed, or improved.

Creative solutions I

Encourage your child to think of a wild invention that would solve a common problem, like non-drip ice cream, self-cleaning plates, stay-soft reusable gum, and the like. Ask your child to brainstorm ways to make the invention and then move to the next step of the Standard.

■ investigate prior solutions and ideas from books, magazines, family, friends, neighbors, and community members.

Creative solutions II

Have your child investigate any possible prior solutions and also gain inspiration from the ideas listed in the Standard. Then move to Part III.

■ generate ideas for possible solutions, individually and through group activity; apply age-appropriate mathematics and science skills; evaluate the ideas and determine the best solution; and explain reasons for the choices.

Creative solutions III

Now ask your child to sketch ideas for her invention, using the components listed in the Standard. Finally end with Part IV.

■ plan and build, under supervision, a model of the solution using familiar materials, processes, and hand tools.

Creative solutions IV

APPROPRIATE MODEL MATERIALS Have your child build a model of her invention, or if this is too complicated, make detailed scale drawings with notations of materials, size, quantity, and so forth. Finally, have your child write an imaginary "press release" that will be put out by the company manufacturing this highly innovative new product. The press release should describe the purpose of the invention and provide details about the invention's benefits. The press release should be legibly written, with complete sentences, using correct punctuation and grammar. How will the press release convince the news media that this fresh product is the best thing since sliced bread?

- discuss how best to test the solution; perform the test under teacher supervision; record and portray results through numerical and graphic means; discuss orally why things worked or didn't work; and summarize results in writing, suggesting ways to make the solution better.

This is evident, for example, when students:

- read a story called Humpty's Big Day wherein the readers visit the place where Humpty Dumpty had his accident, and are asked to design and model a way to get to the top of the wall and down again safely.

- generate, draw, and model ideas for a space station that includes a pleasant living and working environment.

- design and model footwear that they could use to walk on a cold, sandy surface.

Standard 2—Information Systems

Information Systems

1. Information technology is used to retrieve, process, and communicate information and as a tool to enhance learning.

Students:

- use a variety of equipment and software packages to enter, process, display, and communicate information in different forms using text, tables, pictures, and sound.

- telecommunicate a message to a distant location with teacher help.

- access needed information from printed media, electronic data bases, and community resources.

Sports scores

 Choose a local women's or men's baseball, track, gymnastics, football, basketball, soccer, or hockey team to track throughout a season and create a chart to record the scores of each game, indicating the final score, whether the team won or lost, whether the game was home or away, and any other details your child considers relevant (weather during the game, whether a certain pitcher played, and so forth). At the end of the season, ask your child to analyze the results. Did the team win more games at home? Score more points when away? Lose more games during a particular period in the season? Based on this analysis, what could the team do to win more games next year? Discuss how else your child could apply this type of data collection and analysis.

This is evident, for example, when students:

- use the newspaper or magazine index in a library to find information on a particular topic.

- invite local experts to the school to share their expertise.

2. Knowledge of the impacts and limitations of information systems is essential to its effective and ethical use.

Students:

■ **describe the uses of information systems in homes, schools, and businesses.**

Info systems hunt

✍ *Hold a race with your child, and other household members or friends, to hunt down and identify all the information systems in your home. Set a timer for five minutes and let everyone loose with pen and paper, looking for information systems such as digital clocks, oil and gas gauges, thermometers, radios, televisions, computers, and the like. After five minutes, regroup and have players describe what type of information each system on his or her list provides. The person with the most systems noted, wins.*

■ **understand that computers are used to store personal information.**

Computer calendar

HOME COMPUTER, SOFTWARE PROGRAM WITH CALENDAR TEMPLATE Together with your child, make a list of important dates he would like to keep track of: birthdays, holidays, his Little League schedule, homework due dates, test dates, scheduled family trips, and so on. Then help your child use the calendar template or other appointment tracking system on the computer to create a personal calendar. (In Word, this is called Calendar Wizard, and you can find it by clicking on "File," then clicking on "New," and then clicking on "Other Documents.") Help your child add the dates on his list to the calendar. Have fun! Use fancy fonts for holidays and more serious fonts for important homework due dates. Show him that the calendar can be printed out and displayed, and saved on the computer for future revisions and reference.

■ **demonstrate ability to evaluate information.**

This is evident, for example, when students:

- **look for differences among species of bugs collected on the school grounds, and classify them according to preferred habitat**

Students will access, generate, process, and transfer information using appropriate technologies.

3. Information technology can have positive and negative impacts on society, depending upon how it is used.

Students:

- **describe the uses of information systems in homes and schools.**

New fangled info systems I

LIST CREATED FROM "INFO SYSTEMS HUNT" ACTIVITY Have your child review the systems discovered in the Info systems hunt activity. Help your child identify which ones have only come into most homes in the last 20 years (e.g., computers). Now continue to the next part of the Standard.

- **demonstrate ability to evaluate information critically.**

New fangled info systems II

Have your child describe how one of the new information systems is a drawback while you defend it as beneficial. For instance, you might say computers provide access to the Internet where you can get information anytime of the day or night. Your child might counter that families are spending less time together because they are finding entertainment on the Internet and not even watching television together as a group anymore.

Standard 3—Mathematics Mathematical Reasoning

1. Students use mathematical reasoning to analyze mathematical situations, make conjectures, gather evidence, and construct an argument.

Students:

■ use models, facts, and relationships to draw conclusions about mathematics and explain their thinking. .

■ use patterns and relationships to analyze mathematical situations.

■ justify their answers and solution processes.

■ **use logical reasoning to reach simple conclusions.**

This is evident, for example, when students:

■ **build geometric figures out of straws.**

■ **find patterns in sequences of numbers, such as the triangular numbers 1, 3, 6, 10, ...**

■ **explore number relationships with a calculator (e.g., 12 + 6 = 18, 11 + 7 = 18, etc.) and draw conclusions.**

Number and Numeration

2. Students use number sense and numeration to develop an understanding of the multiple uses of numbers in the real world, the use of numbers to communicate mathematically, and the use of num bers in the development of mathematical ideas.

Students:

■ **use whole numbers and fractions to identify locations, quantify groups of objects, and measure distances.**

estimate how many steps she takes a day by making a calculation for each step of her routine (the number of steps to the school bus stop, the number of steps from the school bus to the classroom, and so forth) and then by adding all of these steps together.

■ use concrete materials to model numbers and number relationships for whole numbers and common fractions, including decimal fractions.

Fractional morsel

TOAST, BUTTER Cut a piece of toast in half and then divide one half in half again. You will now have $\frac{1}{2}$ and $\frac{1}{4}$ and $\frac{1}{4}$. Cut one of the quarters in half to produce $\frac{1}{2}$, $\frac{1}{4}$, and two $\frac{1}{8}$ pieces in total. Ask your child how many different combinations she can create using these fractions: $\frac{1}{2}$ plus $\frac{1}{8}$ would give her $\frac{5}{8}$; $\frac{1}{4}$ plus $\frac{1}{2}$ would produce $\frac{3}{4}$; and so on. When you have exhausted the number of possibilities, butter your fractions and eat them!

■ relate counting to grouping and to place-value.

■ recognize the order of whole numbers and commonly used fractions and decimals.

Family line

LONG SHEET OF PAPER, Together, create a visual timeline of your family. On a long sheet of paper draw a straight line and then place dots at even intervals to represent different years, starting from your own childhood on the far left to your child's present on the right-hand side. Together, fill in events such as births, graduations, vacations, the arrival of family pets, important sports competitions, dance, music, or theatrical recitals, and so forth. Help your child identify the correct place on the timeline for each event and neatly print a label describing each occasion. Encourage your child to add a small drawing next to each entry to enliven the family timeline.

■ demonstrate the concept of percent through problems related to actual situations.

Vegetable pie

✍ **VEGETABLES** *Have your child look through the kitchen for fresh, frozen, and canned vegetables, writing their names on a list. Have your child draw a large circle on a new sheet of paper and write the vegetable names from the list, evenly spaced, around the circle's circumference. Next, have your child ask everyone in the household which of the listed vegetables is his or her favorite. Have your child divide the circle (or pie) into slices that visually illustrate the percentage of votes each vegetable received. For instance, the slice for carrots would be twice the size of the slice for brussels sprouts if two people love carrots and only one loves brussels sprouts. Have your child make a recommendation for which vegetables should be served at dinner based on the results of his pie chart.*

This is evident, for example, when students:

■ count out 15 small cubes and exchange ten of the cubes for a rod ten cubes long.

■ use the number line to show the position of 1/4.

■ figure the tax on $4.00 knowing that taxes are 7 cents per $1.00.

Students will understand mathematics and become mathematically confident by communicating and reasoning mathematically, by applying mathematics in real-world settings, and by solving problems through the integrated study of number systems, geometry, algebra, data analysis, probability, and trigonometry.

Operations

3. Students use mathematical operations and relation ships among them to understand mathematics.

Students:

■ add, subtract, multiply, and divide whole numbers.

■ develop strategies for selecting the appropriate computational and operational method in problem-solving situations.

Payment options

 While waiting on line during your next shopping trip, ask your child to help find the right bills and coins in your wallet to pay the cashier. Discuss different choices you might have, such as 5 one-dollar bills versus 1 five-dollar bill, or 5 nickels versus 1 quarter. Play "store" at home by choosing various groceries from your cupboard and asking your child to select the correct amount of coins and bills to pay for each.

■ know single digit addition, subtraction, multiplication, and division facts.

Two steps forward

 PAIR OF DIE, SHEETS OF PAPER Place 50 sheets of paper one after the other to create a meandering path through your home or yard. Have your child roll a pair of die, and add up the two numbers, moving ahead that many squares. On the next throw, have your child subtract the smaller number from the larger one, and use the answer to move ahead on the squares. For the third round, have your child multiply the two numbers and move ahead the corresponding number of squares. Repeat the rounds— addition, subtraction, multiplication—until reaching the final square. Keep track of how many rounds it takes to reach the end. Now, you take a turn (but have your child do the mathematical calculations). At the end, whoever reached the final square in the least number of rounds wins!

■ understand the commutative and associative properties.

Explain that a mathematical operation obeys the <u>commutative property</u> when the order of the two numbers does not matter. (For example, with multiplication [a × b = b × a].) The <u>associative property</u> states that the grouping of numbers is not relevant, given a, b, and c are real numbers (For example, a x [b x c] = [a x b] x c). Ask if either addition or division also obey both the commutative and associative properties. (Only addition does.)

This is evident, for example, when students:

■ use the fact that multiplication is commutative (e.g., 2 × 7 = 7 × 2), to assist them with their memorizing of the basic facts.

■ solve multiple-step problems that require at least two different operations.

■ progress from base ten blocks to concrete models and then to paper and pencil algorithms.

Modeling / Multiple Representation

4. Students use mathematical modeling/multiple representation to provide a means of presenting, interpreting, communicating, and connecting mathematical information and relationships.

Students:

■ use concrete materials to model spatial relationships.

Right-angle detective

CARDBOARD OR THICK PAPER Have your child find a "portable" right angle, such as the corner of a piece of thick paper or the cardboard from the back of a writing pad. Have your child use the right angle to check if

the walls and floor in different rooms at home truly make exact right angles. With the naked eye they may appear to be so, but the shifting of the foundation and warping of wood may have made the angles change over time.

■ construct tables, charts, and graphs to display and analyze real-world data.

Who's first

✐ *Have your child collect data during the Little League season. Encourage your child to create a chart that tracks the scores for each team in the league, along with significant statistics (number of home runs, number of strikeouts, etc.). As the season progresses, ask your child to predict which team will finish first, based on the accumulated data. Encourage your child to revise her prediction if new data warrants.*

■ use multiple representations (simulations, manipulative materials, pictures, and diagrams) as tools to explain the operation of everyday procedures.

Talking math

✐ *MILK CONTAINER Have your child look at the number of servings written on the label of a milk carton. Have her describe in words, and then write down on paper, a mathematical expression to find how many days the milk carton will last if he drinks three servings a day (# of servings/carton divided by 3 servings/day = x days). For example, if the container had 6 servings, the expression would be: 6 servings/carton divided by 3 servings/day = 2 days. Have your child practice these sorts of equations by helping you estimate how much of a product to buy and how long a product will last when shopping for the household for a week.*

■ use variables such as height, weight, and hand size to predict changes over time.

■ use physical materials, pictures, and diagrams to explain mathematical ideas and processes and to demonstrate geometric concepts.

Graph map

✐ **GRAPH PAPER** *On graph paper, have your child draw an floor plan of your home in dark pencil so that all the rooms are represented. Next, on the graph paper, have your child chart a course, from the front door to the part of the home that is farthest away, taking an interesting course, rather than the quickest route. You then should try to use the map to end up in the location where your child wants you to be. You can reverse roles, and hide a small treasure in the final location that your child will receive after reading the map correctly.*

This is evident, for example, when students:

- build a 3 x 3 x 3 cube out of blocks.

- use square tiles to model various rectangles with an area of 24 square units.

- read a bar graph of population trends and write an explanation of the information it contains.

Measurement

5. **Students use measurement in both metric and English measure to provide a major link between the abstractions of mathematics and the real world in order to describe and compare objects and data.**

Students:

- understand that measurement is approximate, never exact.

A raisin in every bite

NEW BOX OF CEREAL WITH RAISINS *Have your child look at an unopened box of cereal with a picture on front of a bowl of cereal that includes raisins. Tell your child to count how many raisins appear in the picture. Now look at the label on the package and find out how many servings the*

box contains. From these numbers, have your child estimate how many raisins are in the entire box (# raisins per bowl x # servings in box = total estimated number of raisins). Have your child verify his estimated results by counting the actual number of raisins at every breakfast serving, and adding up the results when the box is empty.

■ select appropriate standard and nonstandard measurement tools in measurement activities.

The first foot

GLUE, LONG GRAIN RICE Before 1324, there was no standard measurement of feet and inches. Sometimes people used the widths of their thumbs as a unit of measurement, but that was unreliable because each person's thumb is a different width. King Edward II of England decreed that three barelycorns (each about the size of long grain rice), laid end to end, equaled one inch. Ask your child how many barelycorns were needed to make a foot (36). Now place your child's foot on a piece of paper. Draw a straight, vertical line that parallels its length, from the tip of the big toe to the back of the heel. Then have your child place glue over the line and carefully add grains of rice end to end to see her foot measurement in King Edward's time.

■ understand the attributes of area, length, capacity, weight, volume, time, temperature, and angle.

Jogging rate

WATCH OR TIMER Ask your child to help solve the puzzle: How can we determine how far you can run in five minutes, by only allowing you to run for one minute? As a clue, you can say that the watch or timer, and multiplication, will help. Have your child actually conduct the experiment, running a distance (up and down the block, for example) for one minute, and then multiplying the distance by five.

■ estimate and find measures such as length, perimeter, area, and volume using both nonstandard and standard units.

SMALL OBJECT COLLECTION, THICK PAPER, SCISSORS, CARD-BOARD, TAPE Have your child imagine being an industrial designer commissioned to develop a box for kids to hold collectibles, such as stamps, marbles, trading cards, etc. Have your child gather a collection of small items from her room. Tell your child to measure them carefully and then sketch on thick, plain paper the size of one side of a square box she will construct to hold the items. Have your child cut out the paper model, place it on cardboard, and then trace along its perimeter. Repeat 6 times, to make the sides of the box. Tell your child to cut out the sides, and then decorate with markers and added materials (glitter, buttons, yarns, and so forth.) Tape the four sides and the bottom of the box together. Help your child hinge the top side by only securing one edge with tape. Have your child place her collection in the box to make sure it fits and add any additional decoration.

■ collect and display data.

■ use statistical methods such as graphs, tables, and charts to interpret data.

This is evident, for example, when students:

■ measure with paper clips or finger width.

■ estimate, then calculate, how much paint would be needed to cover one wall.

■ create a chart to display the results of a survey conducted among the classes in the school, or graph the amounts of survey responses by grade level.

Uncertainty

6. Students use ideas of uncertainty to illustrate that mathematics involves more than exactness when dealing with everyday situations.

Students:

- make estimates to compare to actual results of both formal and informal measurement.

- make estimates to compare to actual results of computations.

- recognize situations where only an estimate is required.

What's enough ?

At the supermarket or fruit stand, ask your child how many oranges, bananas, or apples you will need to buy for the household for a week. Is 75 pieces too many? Are 3 too few? Why? If everyone in the family ate one piece of fruit a day, how many pieces of fruit would you need for the weekend?

- develop a wide variety of estimation skills and strategies.

- determine the reasonableness of results.

- predict experimental probabilities.

Worth a shot

WASTEPAPER BASKET, BALLED PIECE OF PAPER Gather friends or household members and have your child set up a wastepaper basket across the room, with each person trying to toss a balled up piece of paper into it five times. Tell your child to record and calculate the odds of making a basket for each player.

- make predictions using unbiased random samples.

- determine probabilities of simple events.

This is evident, for example, when students:

- **estimate the length of the room before measuring.**

- **predict the average number of red candies in a bag before opening a group of bags, counting the candies, and then averaging the number that were red.**

- **determine the probability of picking an even numbered slip from a hat containing slips of paper numbered 1, 2, 3, 4, 5, and 6.**

Students will understand mathematics and become mathematically confident by communicating and reasoning mathematically, by applying mathematics in real-world settings, and by solving problems through the integrated study of number systems, geometry, algebra, data analysis, probability, and trigonometry.

Patterns / Functions

7. **Students use patterns and functions to develop mathematical power, appreciate the true beauty of mathematics, and construct generalizations that describe patterns simply and efficiently.**

Students:

- **recognize, describe, extend, and create a wide variety of patterns.**

Once and again

TEXTILES WITH PATTERNS Have your child look for repeated color or image patterns on the borders of rugs, scarves, pillowcases, towels, and other textiles. Ask your child to describe each pattern in detail and recreate it with colored markers or crayons on blank white paper. Afterward, have your child design a new textile pattern on paper, using an unusual combination of colors and images. Have your child name the pattern and decide, if it were a rug, in which room you would place it at home.

- represent and describe mathematical relationships.

- explore and express relationships using variables and open sentences.

- solve for an unknown using manipulative materials.

- use a variety of manipulative materials and technologies to explore patterns.

- interpret graphs.

Which graph?

 Together, look in the newspaper for circle graphs and those using columns. Discuss how the examples are similar and how are they different. Which type of graph would be best to describe the weather over the course of a week? And which type might be useful in quickly showing how many people in the neighborhood want a new park?

- explore and develop relationships among two- and three-dimensional geometric shapes.

Geometric view

Together, make a list of as many two- and three-dimensional geometric shapes as you can think of, including circles, cubes, cylinders, rectangles, etc. Then, choose one room in your house and look for as many examples of each geometric shape as you can find. If you are in the kitchen, a can of soup would count as a cylinder, an orange would count as a sphere, the tiles on the floor would count as squares, and so on. When your hunt is complete, count the total for each shape to see which is most common in that room.

- discover patterns in nature, art, music, and literature.

Visual patterns

 WWW *LARGE ROUND METAL OR PLASTIC CONTAINERS, TAPE, SCISSORS Together, explore the geometric pottery designs adorning the distinctive pottery of each Pueblo people at http://www.umass.edu /arthist/pots/main.html. Have your child describe the different patterns on the ceramic examples by potters from Acoma, Zuni, Hopi, and other*

Pueblos of the southwest. Today each artist sustains the unique design tradition of his or her Pueblo. Next, help your child cover a large round metal tin or plastic container with construction paper, taping it in place and cutting off any excess. Then ask your child to develop a visual pattern on the container, incorporating geometric shapes drawn in ink. You should try the activity as well, working within the same style as your child so that you develop a family style, as is typically the case in the Pueblo tradition.

This is evident, for example, when students:

■ represent three more than a number is equal to nine as $n + 3 = 9$.

■ draw leaves, simple wallpaper patterns, or write number sequences to illustrate recurring patterns.

■ write generalizations or conclusions from display data in charts or graphs.

Standard 4—Science

Physical Setting

1. The Earth and celestial phenomena can be described by principles of relative motion and perspective.

Students:

■ describe patterns of daily, monthly, and seasonal changes in their environment.

Trendy Weather

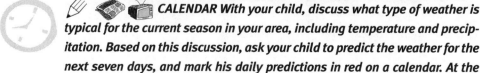
CALENDAR With your child, discuss what type of weather is typical for the current season in your area, including temperature and precipitation. Based on this discussion, ask your child to predict the weather for the next seven days, and mark his daily predictions in red on a calendar. At the

end of every day, have your child write the actual weather for the day on the calendar in black, and compare how his original predictions matched the results. (You can check temperature predictions by watching the nightly newscast or reading a report in the newspaper the next day.) For the next week, repeat the activity, adding the predictions of the local weather person as well, and then comparing your child's predictions and the weather person's with the actual results. Use a national weather map in a newspaper to show your child the factors meteorologists consider when predicting your local weather.

This is evident, for example, when students:

■ **conduct a long-term weather investigation, such as running a weather station or collecting weather data.**

■ **keep a journal of the phases of the moon over a one-month period. This information is collected for several different one-month periods and compared.**

2. Many of the phenomena that we observe on Earth involve interactions among components of air, water, and land.

Students:

■ **describe the relationships among air, water, and land on Earth.**

The foggiest idea

✍ WWW 🖊 Have your child explore types, location, and formation of fog and clouds at http://usatoday.com/weather/wcloudo.htm. Ask her to write and illustrate the adventure of a single droplet of water as it travels from clouds to the Earth. Your child's account should feature clear, grammatically correct sentences, and paragraphs that successfully develop a central idea, using supporting facts and details. 📖

This is evident, for example, when students:

- observe a puddle of water outdoors after a rainstorm. On a return visit after the puddle has disappeared, students describe where the water came from and possible locations for it now.

- assemble rock and mineral collections based on characteristics such as erosional features or crystal size features.

3. Matter is made up of particles whose properties determine the observable characteristics of matter and its reactivity.

Students:

- observe and describe properties of materials using appropriate tools.

It's in the bag I!

MEDIUM-SIZED CLEAR PLASTIC BAG, WATER Have your child fill a medium-sized clear plastic bag about one-third of the way with water. Ask him to describe the property of the water. (It's a liquid, as opposed to a solid or gas.) Now have your child blow air into the bag and seal it tightly. Have your child identify the property of the air that's in the bag (gas) before moving to the next step of the Standard.

- describe chemical and physical changes, including changes in states of matter.

It's in the bag II!

Have your child place the sealed bag in the sun and observe it every 5 minutes. What physical changes can your child describe? (Vapor—water droplets—form inside the bag.) Your child should be able to articulate that heated water creates a gas. You can have your child make similar observations when you boil water, watching carefully from a distance as the steam (gas) rises from the pot!

This is evident, for example, when students:

- compare the appearance of materials when seen with and without the aid of a magnifying glass.

- investigate simple physical and chemical reactions and the chemistry of household products, e.g., freezing, melting, and evaporating; a comparison of new and rusty nails; the role of baking soda in cooking.

4. Energy exists in many forms, and when these forms change energy is conserved.

Students:

- describe a variety of forms of energy (e.g., heat, chemical, light) and the changes that occur in objects when they interact with those forms of energy.

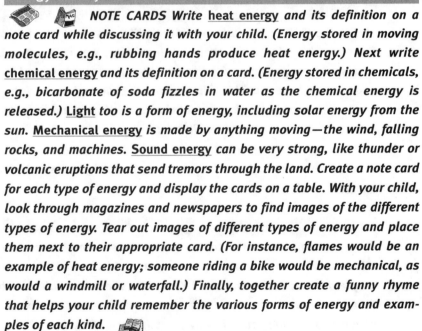

Energy variety

NOTE CARDS Write <u>heat energy</u> and its definition on a note card while discussing it with your child. (Energy stored in moving molecules, e.g., rubbing hands produce heat energy.) Next write <u>chemical energy</u> and its definition on a card. (Energy stored in chemicals, e.g., bicarbonate of soda fizzles in water as the chemical energy is released.) <u>Light</u> too is a form of energy, including solar energy from the sun. <u>Mechanical energy</u> is made by anything moving—the wind, falling rocks, and machines. <u>Sound energy</u> can be very strong, like thunder or volcanic eruptions that send tremors through the land. Create a note card for each type of energy and display the cards on a table. With your child, look through magazines and newspapers to find images of the different types of energy. Tear out images of different types of energy and place them next to their appropriate card. (For instance, flames would be an example of heat energy; someone riding a bike would be mechanical, as would a windmill or waterfall.) Finally, together create a funny rhyme that helps your child remember the various forms of energy and examples of each kind.

- observe the way one form of energy can be transformed into another form of energy present in common situations (e.g., mechanical to heat energy, mechanical to electrical energy, chemical to heat energy).

After completing the "Energy variety" activity, explain to your child that energy can change from one form to another, but it never disappears. Explore examples around the house of energy changing and have your child identify its form at each state. For example, turning on a light (mechanical to heat and light), hammering a nail into wood (mechanical to sound), removing a nail from wood and touching the warm nail (mechanical to heat), turning on a radio (mechanical to sound), and so forth. Together, conduct your usual morning routine (dressing, preparing breakfast, eating, brushing teeth, and so forth) and mention each form of energy as you go.

This is evident, for example, when students:

■ investigate the interactions of liquids and powders that result in chemical reactions (e.g., vinegar and baking soda) compared to interactions that do not (e.g., water and sugar).

■ in order to demonstrate the transformation of chemical to electrical energy, construct electrical cells from objects, such as lemons or potatoes, using pennies and aluminum foil inserted in slits at each end of fruits or vegetables; the penny and aluminum are attached by wires to a milliammeter. Students can compare the success of a variety of these electrical cells.

5. Energy and matter interact through forces that result in changes in motion.

Students:

■ describe the effects of common forces (pushes and pulls) on objects, such as those caused by gravity, magnetism, and mechanical forces.

JAR CAP OR SIMILAR SIZED OBJECT, ITEMS THAT CREATE AIR MOVEMENT SUCH AS A HAIR DRYER, PAPER FAN, BALLOON, OR TIRE PUMP Have your child place a jar cap, or similar sized and weighted object, on the floor. Experiment with sliding it across the floor by using different methods

and amounts of force: blowing with her mouth, using a hair dryer at different settings, fanning with paper, letting the air out of a balloon, or even using a bicycle tire pump. Hold an "air-force" competition with two people using the same method of propulsion and marking off how far each different force pushed the cap.

■ **describe how forces can operate across distances.**

This is evident, for example, when students:

■ **investigate simple machines and use them to perform tasks.**

Students will understand and apply scientific concepts, principles, and theories pertaining to the physical setting and living environment and recognize the historical development of ideas in science.

The Living Environment

1. Living things are both similar to and different from each other and nonliving things.

Students:

■ **describe the characteristics of and variations between living and nonliving things.**

Eagle-eye detective

The next time you run an errand in the neighborhood with your child, have her list all the nonliving and living components she can find. Can your child expand this list by adding things that are not visible during the day or at a casual glance (small insects, nocturnal animals and birds, living and nonliving things found underground, etc.)?

■ **describe the life processes common to all living things.**

Have your child select his favorite animal and find pictures of it living within its natural environment in magazines (such as National Geographic), books, online, and so forth. Your child also should learn what type of food it eats. Now ask your child to design a special animal shelter for this type of animal that will take care of any that are lost or ill. How will your child meet the basic needs of the animals in terms of food, water, and shelter, recreating its natural lifestyle as much as possible? Help your child sketch out the plans and label the building design, as well as title the shelter with an appealing and descriptive name.

This is evident, for example, when students:

- grow a plant or observe a pet, investigating what it requires to stay alive, including evaluating the relative importance and necessity of each item.

- investigate differences in personal body characteristics, such as temperature, pulse, heart rate, blood pressure, and reaction time.

2. Organisms inherit genetic information in a variety of ways that result in continuity of structure and function between parents and offspring.

Students:

- recognize that traits of living things are both inherited and acquired or learned.

Animal babies and parents

GLUE Cut out separate pictures of adult and baby animals (sheep and lambs, cats and kittens, cows and calves, etc.) from nature magazines, such as National Geographic. Place all the adult pictures on a table. Ask your child to sift through the pictures of the baby animals and match them to the correct adult. Discuss what visual clues in the pictures helped make the connection. (For instance, the lamb's wool is similar to the sheep's wool, or the bunny's ears were the same shape as those of the rabbit.) Together, paste the cutouts on paper and write an illustrated baby and parent animal book. Make sure your child's handwriting is clear and legible, and that singular and plural nouns are used correctly, along with singular possessive pronouns (for example, my/mine, his/her, hers, your/yours, etc.). All sentences should be complete and correctly punctuated, and all words should be spelled correctly.

■ recognize that for humans and other living things there is genetic continuity between generations.

You look just like your . . .

FAMILY PHOTOGRAPHS With your child, investigate a family photograph album representing numerous generations and identify the physical traits that family members share (such as height, curly hair, shape of eyes, etc.). Have your child try to identify which characteristics came from which side of the family. Ask your child to predict which traits his children might have, given the strength of particular family characteristics you've observed.

This is evident, for example, when students:

■ interact with a classroom pet, observe its behaviors, and record what they are able to teach the animal, such as navigation of a maze or performance of tricks, compared to that which remains constant, such as eye color, or number of digits on an appendage.

■ use breeding records and photographs of racing horses or pedigreed animals to recognize that variations exist from generation to generation but "like begets like."

3. Individual organisms and species change over time.

Students:

■ describe how the structures of plants and animals complement the environment of the plant or animal.

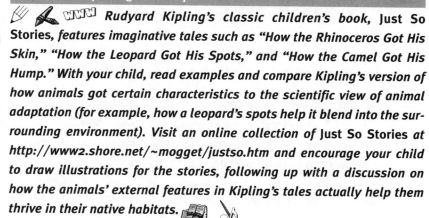

How the leopard got his spots

Rudyard Kipling's classic children's book, Just So Stories, *features imaginative tales such as "How the Rhinoceros Got His Skin," "How the Leopard Got His Spots," and "How the Camel Got His Hump." With your child, read examples and compare Kipling's version of how animals got certain characteristics to the scientific view of animal adaptation (for example, how a leopard's spots help it blend into the surrounding environment). Visit an online collection of* Just So Stories *at http://www2.shore.net/~mogget/justso.htm and encourage your child to draw illustrations for the stories, following up with a discussion on how the animals' external features in Kipling's tales actually help them thrive in their native habitats.*

- observe that differences within a species may give individuals an advantage in surviving and reproducing.

Tortoise evolution

The Galapagos Islands in South America host both domed and saddlebacked giant tortoises. Have your child discover how each type of turtle evolved because of where and how it obtains food at http://www.chias.org/www/edu/cse/wdn3x.html. Have your child write an imaginary dialogue between the two types of tortoises, discussing their similarities and differences. Your child should write in complete, correctly punctuated sentences, use past, present, and future tenses properly, and capitalize geographical names, proper nouns, and other appropriate words.

This is evident, for example, when students:

- relate physical characteristics of organisms to habitat characteristics (e.g., long hair and fur color change for mammals living in cold climates).

- visit a farm or a zoo and make a written or pictorial comparison of members of a litter and identify characteristics that may provide an advantage.

4. The continuity of life is sustained through reproduction and development.

Students:

■ describe the major stages in the life cycles of selected plants and animals.

A bug's life

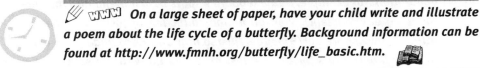 *On a large sheet of paper, have your child write and illustrate a poem about the life cycle of a butterfly. Background information can be found at http://www.fmnh.org/butterfly/life_basic.htm.*

■ describe evidence of growth, repair, and maintenance, such as nails, hair, and bone, and the healing of cuts and bruises.

Fingernail race

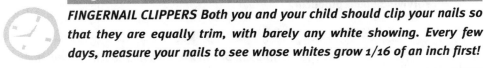 *FINGERNAIL CLIPPERS Both you and your child should clip your nails so that they are equally trim, with barely any white showing. Every few days, measure your nails to see whose whites grow 1/16 of an inch first!*

This is evident, for example, when students:

■ grow bean plants or butterflies; record and describe stages of development.

5. Organisms maintain a dynamic equilibrium that sustains life.

Students:

■ describe basic life functions of common living specimens (guppy, mealworm, gerbil).

Creature Chef

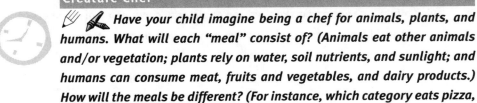 *Have your child imagine being a chef for animals, plants, and humans. What will each "meal" consist of? (Animals eat other animals and/or vegetation; plants rely on water, soil nutrients, and sunlight; and humans can consume meat, fruits and vegetables, and dairy products.) How will the meals be different? (For instance, which category eats pizza,*

and which would eat grass?) What might they share in common? (Water.)
Together, create a menu for a make-believe restaurant with a variety of
dishes to appeal to animals, plants, and humans, labeling each dish
appropriately.

- describe some survival behaviors of common living specimens.

- describe the factors that help promote good health and growth in humans.

This is evident, for example, when students:

- observe a single organism over a period of weeks and describe such life functions as moving, eating, resting, and eliminating.

- observe and demonstrate reflexes such as pupil dilation and contraction and relate such reflexes to improved survival.

- analyze the extent to which diet and exercise habits meet cardiovascular, energy, and nutrient requirements.

6. Plants and animals depend on each other and their physical environment.

Students:
- describe how plants and animals, including humans, depend upon each other and the nonliving environment.

We're all connected

 3 PLATES, SCISSORS, STRING Have your child search through magazines for pictures of foods eaten by <u>herbivores</u> (plant-eating animals), <u>carnivores</u> (meat-eating animals), and <u>omnivores</u> (plant- and animal-eating animals). Have her sort the pictures by the three categories and place them on three separate plates. Cut out pictures of animals from magazines that fit each category and place them next to their respective plate. (Don't forget to place a photograph or drawing of yourselves by the correct plate.) Finally, have your child use string to create a "food web," demonstrating who eats from each plate.

- describe the relationship of the sun as an energy source for living and non-living cycles.

This is evident, for example, when students:

- investigate how humans depend on their environment (neighborhood), by observing, recording, and discussing the interactions that occur in carrying out their everyday lives.

- observe the effects of sunlight on growth for a garden vegetable.

7. Human decisions and activities have had a profound impact on the physical and living environment.

Students:

- identify ways in which humans have changed their environment and the effects of those changes.

This is evident, for example, when students:

- give examples of how inventions and innovations have changed the environment; describe benefits and burdens of those changes.

Standard 5—Technology

Engineering Design

1. Engineering design is an iterative process involving modeling and optimization used to develop technological solutions to problems within given constraints.

Students:

■ describe objects, imaginary or real, that might be modeled or made differently and suggest ways in which the objects can be changed, fixed, or improved.

■ investigate prior solutions and ideas from books, magazines, family, friends, neighbors, and community members.

■ generate ideas for possible solutions, individually and through group activity; apply age-appropriate mathematics and science skills; evaluate the ideas and determine the best solution; and explain reasons for the choices.

■ plan and build, under supervision, a model of the solution using familiar materials, processes, and hand tools.

■ discuss how best to test the solution; perform the test under teacher supervision; record and portray results through numerical and graphic means; discuss orally why things worked or didn't work; and summarize results in writing, suggesting ways to make the solution better.

This is evident, for example, when students:

■ read a story called Humpty's Big Day wherein the readers visit the place where Humpty Dumpty had his accident, and are asked to design and model a way to get to the top of the wall and down again safely.

■ generate and draw ideas for a space station that includes a pleasant living and working environment.

■ design and model footwear that they could use to walk on a cold, sandy surface.

Tools, Resources,
and Technological Processes

2. Technological tools, materials, and other resources should be selected on the basis of safety, cost, availability, appropriateness, and environmental impact; technological processes change energy, information, and material resources into more useful forms.

Students:

■ explore, use, and process a variety of materials and energy sources to design and construct things.

Sunlit colors

 LARGE SHEETS OF LIGHT-COLORED TISSUE PAPER, BLACK CONSTRUCTION PAPER, SCISSORS, GLUE Together, explore the art of Medieval stained glass windows at http://my.bawue.de/~wmwerner/ essling/english/glaso1.html. Next, create your own simple version together to see how the sun can enliven your windows. First, have your child sketch a large rectangle, square, circle, or other geometric shape on paper. When satisfied with the shape, recreate it on a large sheet of light-colored tissue paper. Next, cut out black strips (about 1/2 inch thick) from the black construction paper. They can be straight or curved. Have your child arrange the strips on the tissue paper to create interesting shapes. Help your child carefully glue the black strips down, snipping off any portion that might run over the edges of the tissue paper design. Repeat the process with other colors of tissue paper and new designs. Tape your stained glass designs to a windowpane that receives direct sunlight and enjoy the colorful glow!

■ understand the importance of safety, cost, ease of use, and availability in selecting tools and resources for a specific purpose.

- develop basic skill in the use of hand tools.

- use simple manufacturing processes (e.g., assembly, multiple stages of production, quality control) to produce a product.

Assembly-line sandwiches

SANDWICH INGREDIENTS Set up an "assembly line" to "manufacture" sandwiches with your child and various household members or friends. One person should take the bread out of the bag and put it on a plate, then pass the plate to the second worker who spreads on mustard, the next puts on cheese, the following person puts on tomato, and so forth. Divide the sandwiches into quarters so that everyone gets to "test" at least four different "final products" for quality control. Are all the "goods" of equal quality? As assembly workers enjoy the results during the "lunch break," have your child (as the company "manager") critique the various stages of the process they all just completed. What changes might your child suggest to make the assembly-line process even better next time?

- use appropriate graphic and electronic tools and techniques to process information.

An "ax" to grind

GRAPH PAPER Explain that on graphs, an <u>axis</u> is the main line around which parts are arranged regularly. Together with your child, create a bar graph to track the amount of pocket change you have at the end of each day for one week. Draw one horizontal and one vertical line on graph paper so that they intersect in the lower left-hand corner of the page. Label the horizontal axis to track the days of the week and label the vertical axis to track the amount of change you have in your pocket at the end of the day, using evenly-spaced increments of 10¢. Each evening, place your pocket change on a flat surface and let your child count it and record the total on the bar graph. Put the change aside each evening and total it up at the end of the week. Ask your child to calculate the total and determine if there is enough change to convert to dollar bills.

This is evident, for example, when students:

- explore and use materials, joining them with the use of adhesives and mechanical fasteners to make a cardboard marionette with moving parts.

- explore materials and use forming processes to heat and bend plastic into a shape that can hold napkins.

- explore energy sources by making a simple motor that uses electrical energy to produce continuous mechanical motion.

- develop skill with a variety of hand tools and use them to make or fix things.

- process information electronically such as using a video system to advertise a product or service.

- process information graphically such as taking photos and developing and printing the pictures.

Students will apply technological knowledge and skills to design, construct, use, and evaluate products and systems to satisfy human and environmental needs.

Computer Technology

3. Computers, as tools for design, modeling, information processing, communication, and system control, have greatly increased human productivity and knowledge.

Students:

- identify and describe the function of the major components of a computer system.

- use the computer as a tool for generating and drawing ideas.

- control computerized devices and systems through programming.

ALARM CLOCKS Have your child program the alarm clocks for everyone in the household, according to the time each person needs to rise. If radio alarms are available, have your child also program in the sleeper's favorite station to hear upon waking.

■ model and simulate the design of a complex environment by giving direct commands.

This is evident, for example, when students:

■ control the operation of a toy or household appliance by programming it to perform a task.

■ execute a computer program, such as SimCity, Theme Park, or The Factory to model and simulate an environment.

■ model and simulate a system using construction modeling software, such as The Incredible Machine.

Technological Systems

4. Technological systems are designed to achieve specific results and produce outputs, such as products, structures, services, energy, or other systems.

Students:

■ identify familiar examples of technological systems that are used to satisfy human needs and wants, and select them on the basis of safety, cost, and function.

 🖊️ 🌐 *Together, imagine being a home design team commissioned by a wealthy client to build a state-of-the-art, technological dream home. Draw a quick, simple floor plan for the house on large plain paper. Next,*

think about what cool technological gadgets you will place in each room (video equipment for the bedroom, sound system for the living room, gym equipment for the "play room," coffee maker for the kitchen, electric tooth-brushes for the bathroom, and so forth). Go online and browse for products for each room. Compare the quality, features, and prices of each type of product and then write on the floor plan the names of the ones you recommend your client buy. After you have filled up the house with your list, have your child create small sketches next to the names of each product so that your client will understand what will be in the state-of-the-art home.

- assemble and operate simple technological systems, including those with interconnecting mechanisms to achieve different kinds of movement.

- understand that larger systems are made up of smaller component sub systems.

This is evident, for example, when students:

- assemble and operate a system made up from a battery, switch, and doorbell connected in a series circuit.

- assemble a system with interconnecting mechanisms, such as a jack-in-the-box that pops up from a box with a hinged lid.

- model a community-based transportation system which includes subsystems such as roadways, rails, vehicles, and traffic controls.

History and Evolution of Technology

5. Technology has been the driving force in the evolution of society from an agricultural to an industrial to an information base

Students:

- identify technological developments that have significantly accelerated human progress.

Riding the rails

Together, explore how rail transit changed the western United States at http://4museums.4anything.com/network-frame/0, 1855,5034-64587,00.html. Afterward, ask your child to identify a contemporary mode of traveling across the country (airplanes) and then to design a new transportation invention for the future. How will your child's technological invention compare to past and present forms in terms of speed, comfort, and design? Finally, have your child write a short story or lyrics for a song about the way her transportation invention will change life in the future. You child's work should offer examples of how transportation inventions directly impact human progress and society.

This is evident, for example, when students:

- construct a model of an historical or future-oriented technological device or system and describe how it has contributed or might contribute to human progress.

- make a technological timeline in the form of a hanging mobile of technological devices.

- model a variety of timekeeping devices that reflect historical and modern methods of keeping time.

- make a display contrasting early devices or tools with their modern counterparts.

- Impacts of Technology

6. Technology can have positive and negative impacts on individuals, society, and the environment and humans have the capability and responsibility to constrain or promote technological development.

Students:

■ describe how technology can have positive and negative effects on the environment and on the way people live and work.

Secondhand art

WWW *FOUND MATERIALS, GLUE, LARGE BOOT BOX As you throw things into the trash, discuss with your child how modern technology provides humans with an ever-expanding variety of products, but also creates increasing amounts of garbage. Together, explore the way concerned individuals are addressing the issue through recycling at http://www.environmentaldefense.org/issues/Recycling.html. Also learn amazing statistics about the common items we toss and which ones are recyclable by clicking on images in the virtual trash can at http://www.environmentaldefense.org/clickable_gcan/index.html. Next see how students used recycled goods to create the amusing "Trashasaurus Rex" sculpture at http://users.hsonline.net/kidatart/. Help your child collect interesting tossed items, such as broken watches and toys, gluing them onto the surface of his own "recycled box." Have your child store special items relating to meaningful experiences in the box, so that looking at them again later will "recycle" good memories.*

This is evident, for example, when students:

■ handmake an item and then participate in a line production experience where a quantity of the item is mass produced; compare the benefits and disadvantages of mass production and craft production.

■ describe through example, how familiar technologies (including computers) can have positive and negative impacts on the environment and on the way people live and work.

■ identify the pros and cons of several possible packaging materials for a student-made product.

Students will apply technological knowledge and skills to design, construct, use, and evaluate products and systems to satisfy human and environmental needs.

Management of Technology

7. Project management is essential to ensuring that technological endeavors are profitable and that products and systems are of high quality and built safely, on schedule, and within budget.

Students:

- participate in small group projects and in structured group tasks requiring planning, financing, production, quality control, and follow-up.

> **One and all**
>
> *Tour the website of artist husband and wife team Christo and Jeanne-Claude at http://www.christojeanneclaude.net/christo/xtojc/xtojc. html. Looking at the photographs, try to list all the types of people who are involved in helping these monumental environmental art projects come into existence. There are city officials, lawyers, landscapers, engineers, builders, public relations personnel, and local citizens who help with the final installations. Have your child sketch out ideas for a monumental art project that would both physically encompass a portion of your local community, as well as bring many people into the process of creation.*

- speculate on and model possible technological solutions that can improve the safety and quality of the school or community environment.

This is evident, for example, when students:

- help a group to plan and implement a school project or activity, such as a school picnic or a fund-raising event.

- plan as a group, division of tasks and construction steps needed to build a simple model of a structure or vehicle.

- redesign the work area in their classroom with an eye toward improving safety.

Systems Thinking

1. **Through systems thinking, people can recognize the commonalities that exist among all systems and how parts of a system interrelate and combine to perform specific functions.**

Students:

■ observe and describe interactions among components of simple systems.

■ identify common things that can be considered to be systems (e.g., a plant population, a subway system, human beings).

System tunes

First define <u>system</u> to your child—anything that is a regularly interacting or interdependent group of items forming a unified whole. Then, together create a list of as many systems as you can think of, including those in the Standard as well as animal, water, electrical, solar systems, and others. For each system on your list, try to think of a song that somehow relates. "Twinkle, Twinkle Little Star" or "Moon River" could relate to solar system. "Midnight Train to Georgia" could be for railroad system, "How Much is that Doggie in the Window" for animal system, "My Bonnie Lies Over the Ocean" for water system, and so on. If you run out of ideas, invent your own lyrics so that you represent each system.

Models

2. Models are simplified representations of objects, structures, or systems used in analysis, explanation, interpretation, or design.

Students:

■ analyze, construct, and operate models in order to discover attributes of the real thing.

■ discover that a model of something is different from the real thing but can be used to study the real thing.

■ use different types of models, such as graphs, sketches, diagrams, and maps, to represent various aspects of the real world. .

You be the architect!

WWW *STIFF PAPER, SCISSORS, TAPE Share that the contemporary architect I.M. Pei designed a famous pyramid-shaped entrance to the huge Louvre Museum in Paris (seen at http://www.mit.edu/people/bei /www/Pei/Louvre1.jpg). Thousands of years ago, powerful ancient Egyptians were buried in pyramid-shaped tombs (see images of Giza at http://www.ancientegypt.co.uk/pyramids/home.html, or click on the pyramids for close up views at http://www.pbs.org/wgbh/nova/pyra-mid/explore/). Have your child use stiff paper, scissors, markers, and tape to invent a new three-dimensional building, which can take the shape of any geometric solid. Have your child describe what the building will be used for. Will it be for something public, like a museum, light-house, or library, or for private use, like a home?*

This is evident, for example, when students:

■ compare toy cars with real automobiles in terms of size and function.

■ model structures with building blocks.

■ design and construct a working model of the human circulatory system to explore how varying pumping pressure might affect blood flow.

- describe the limitations of model cars, planes, or houses.

- use model vehicles or structures to illustrate how the real object functions.

- use a road map to determine distances between towns and cities.

Students will understand the relationships and common themes that connect mathematics, science, and technology and apply the themes to these and other areasof learning.

Magnitude and Scale

3. The grouping of magnitudes of size, time,frequency, and pressures or other units of measurement into a series of relative order provides a useful way to deal with the immense range and the changes in scale that affect the behavior and design of systems.

Students:

- provide examples of natural and manufactured things that belong to the same category yet have very different sizes, weights, ages, speeds, and other measurements.

- identify the biggest and the smallest values as well as the average value of a system when given information about its characteristics and behavior.

On average

Have your child write down the age of everyone (including pets) in your household. Ask your child to arrange the list according to everyone's age, from youngest to oldest. Next, have your child figure out the average age of the household by adding up all the ages and then dividing the total by the number of ages written down. (For instance, cat, 1 year old + brother, 2 years old + sister, 5 years old + self, 7 years old + mother, 34 years old + father, 35 years old = 84 years. Now 84 years ÷ by 6 members in household = 14 years old/average.)

This is evident, for example, when students:

- compare the weight of small and large animals.

- compare the speed of bicycles, cars, and planes.

- compare the life spans of insects and trees.

- collect and analyze data related to the height of the students in their class, identifying the tallest, the shortest, and the average height.

- compare the annual temperature range of their locality.

Equilibrium and Stability

4. **Equilibrium is a state of stability due either to a lack of changes (static equilibrium) or a balance between opposing forces (dynamic equilibrium).**

Students:

- cite examples of systems in which some features stay the same while other features change.

Baseball system

Ask your child to think of a baseball game as a "system" of interacting components. Have your child draw a large circle to fill up a large piece of plain paper. Tell your child to make a small symbol representing each component of the game (players, umpires, spectators, maintenance staff, and so forth). Discuss how each component executes the same job from game to game. Have your child write these down next to the symbols, for instance, players hit, catch, or throw balls; umpires rule on a play; spectators watch and cheer. Now have your child use a different colored pen and write in next to the appropriate symbol features of the game that can change from game to game (players hit differently, umpires make different amounts or types of calls, fans are more or less enthusiastic about a particular game, and so on). Afterward, your child should be able to articulate that her diagram charts the changing and invariable aspects of a system, which can be applied to any natural or human-made system.

■ distinguish between reasons for stability—from lack of changes to changes that counterbalance one another to changes within cycles.

This is evident, for example, when students:

■ record their body temperatures in different weather conditions and observe that the temperature of a healthy human being stays almost constant even though the external temperature changes.

■ identify the reasons for the changing amount of fresh water in a reservoir and determine how a constant supply is maintained.

Patterns of Change

5. Identifying patterns of change is necessary for making predictions about future behavior and conditions.

Students:

■ use simple instruments to measure such quantities as distance, size, and weight and look for patterns in the data. .

Measure up

RULER, TOYS Together with your child, make a list of your child's favorite toys and try to guess their length and width in inches. Then, using a ruler, measure each toy and write its actual measurements next to your guesses. How close were you? For more practice, try an online game "Measure it!," which uses both inches and centimeters, at http://www.funbrain.com/measure/index.html.

■ analyze data by making tables and graphs and looking for patterns of change.

This is evident, for example, when students:

- compare shoe size with the height of people to determine if there is a trend.

- collect data on the speed of balls rolling down ramps of different slopes and determine the relationship between speed and steepness of the ramp.

- take data they have collected and generate tables and graphs to begin the search for patterns of change.

Optimization

6. In order to arrive at the best solution that meets criteria within constraints, it is often necessary to make trade-offs.

Students:

- determine the criteria and constraints of a simple decision making problem.

- use simple quantitative methods, such as ratios, to compare costs to benefits of a decision problem.

Unit cost

✍ *Raid the kitchen for a whole variety of unit cost activities. Ask your child to make a list of the condiments in your kitchen: mustard, ketchup, salad dressing, jelly, etc. Your child should record the price of each condiment. (If the price label is missing, tell your child the probable cost.) Then ask your child to record how many servings are in each container, either by copying this information from the label or by making an estimate. Then ask your child to divide the total cost of the condiment by the number of servings in the container, and ask your child which is the most expensive per serving, and which is the least expensive.*

This is evident, for example, when students:

- describe the criteria (e.g., size, color, model) and constraints (e.g., budget) used to select the best bicycle to buy.

- **compare the cost of cereal to number of servings to figure out the best buy.**

Students will understand the relationships and common themes that connect mathematics, science, and technology and apply the themes to these and other areas of learning.

Standard 7—Interdisciplinary:Problem Solving:

Connections

1. **The knowledge and skills of mathematics, science, and technology are used together to make informed decisions and solve problems, especially those rela ting to issues of science/technology/society, consumer decision making, design, and inquiry into phenomena.**

Students:

- analyze science/technology/society problems and issues that affect their home, school, orcommunity, and carry out a remedial course of action. .

Get involved

Together, explore all the different ways for individuals to participate in and add to society. Brainstorm specific ways to become involved in civic improvement (neighborhood associations, community or school boards), political activities (local canvassing or fund raising), and community service (volunteering). Select one activity you can do together to contribute to your local area.

- make informed consumer decisions by applying knowledge about the attributes of particular products and making cost/benefit tradeoffs to arrive at an optimal choice.

- design solutions to problems involving a familiar and real context, investigate related science concepts to inform the solution, and use mathematics to model, quantify, measure, and compute.

Solar-powered pedals

Together, explore a brief history of solar thermal energy at http://solstice.crest.org/renewables/re-kiosk/solar/solar-thermal/history/index.shtml. Then follow the incredible journey at http://library .thinkquest.org/3684/ about high school students who created a solar-powered bicycle and entered the Solar BikeRayce USA on May 26, 1996. Have your child sketch designs for her own solar-powered sports vehicle, using information she has learned about tapping the energy of the sun for speed.

- observe phenomena and evaluate them scientifically and mathematically by conducting a fair test of the effect of variables and using mathematical knowledge and technological tools to collect, analyze, and present data and conclusions.

This is evident, for example, when students:

- develop and implement a plan to reduce water or energy consumption in their home.

- choose paper towels based on tests of absorption quality, strength, and cost per sheet.

- design a wheeled vehicle, sketch and develop plans, test different wheel and axle designs to reduce friction, chart results, and produce a working model with correct measurements.

- collect leaves of similar size from different varieties of trees, and compare the ratios of length to width in order to determine whether the ratios are the same for all species.

Strategies

2. Solving interdisciplinary problems involves a variety of skills and strategies, including effective work habits; gathering and processing information; generating and analyzing ideas; realizing ideas;making connections among the common themes of mathmatics, science, and technology; and presenting results.

Students participate in an extended, culminating mathematics, science, and technology project. The project would require students to:

- **work effectively**

- **gather and process information**

- **generate and analyze ideas**

- **observe common themes**

- **realize ideas**

- **present results**

This is evident, for example, when students, addressing the issue of solid waste at the school in an interdisciplinary science/technology/society project:

- **use the newspaper index to find out about how solid waste is handled in their community, and interview the custodial staff to collect data about how much solid waste is generated in the**

- **school, and they make and use tables and graphs to look for patterns of change. Students work together to reach consensus on the need for recycling and on choosing a material to recycle—in this case, paper.**

- **investigate the types of paper that could be recycled, measure the amount (weight, volume) of this type of paper in their school during a one-week period, and calculate the cost. Students investigate the processes involved in changing used paper into a useable product and how and why those changes work as they do.**

- **using simple mixers, wire screens, and lint, leaves, rags, etc., students recycle used paper into useable sheets and evaluate the quality of the product. They present their results using charts, graphs, illustrations, and photographs to the principal and custodial staff.**

Students will apply the knowledge and thinking skills of mathematics, science, and technology to address real-life problems and make informed decisions.

Skills and Strategies for Interdisciplinary Problem Solving

- **Working Effectively:** Contributing to the work of a brainstorming group, laboratory partnership, cooperative learning group, orproject team; planning procedures; identify and managing responsibilities of team members; and staying on task, whether workingalone or as part of a group.

- **Gathering and Processing Information:** Accessing information from printed media, electronic data bases, and community resources and using the information to develop a definition of the problem and to research possible solutions.

- **Generating and Analyzing Ideas:** Developing ideas for proposed solutions, investigating ideas, collecting data, and showing relationships and patterns in the data.

- **Common Themes:** Observing examples of common unifying themes, applying them to the problem, and using them to better understand the dimensions of the problem.

- **Realizing Ideas:** Constructing components or models, arriving at a solution, and evaluating the result.

- **Presenting Results:** Using a variety of media to present the solution and to communicate the results.

Learning Standards for Social Studies at Three Levels

Elementary Level (June 1996)

Standard 1: History of the United States and New York

Students will use a variety of intellectual skills to demonstrate their understanding of major ideas, eras, themes, developments, and turning points in the history of the United States and New York.

Standard 2: World History

Students will use a variety of intellectual skills to demonstrate their understanding of major ideas, eras, themes, developments, and turning points in world history and examine the broad sweep of history from a variety of perspectives.

Standard 3: Geography

Students will use a variety of intellectual skills to demonstrate their understanding of the geography of the interdependent world in which we live—local, national, and global—including the distribution of people, places, and environments over the Earth's surface.

Standard 4: Economics

Students will use a variety of intellectual skills to demonstrate their understanding of how the United States and other societies develop economic systems and associated institutions to allocate scarce resources, how major decision-making units function in the United States and other national economies, and how an economy solves the scarcity problem through market and non-market mechanisms.

Standard 5: Civics, Citizenship, and Government

Students will use a variety of intellectual skills to demonstrate their understanding of the necessity for establishing governments; the governmental system of the United States and other nations; the United States Constitution; the basic civic values of American constitutional democracy; and the roles, rights, and responsibilities of citizenship, including avenues of participation.

Standard 1—History of the United States and New York

1. The study of New York State and United States history requires an analysis of the development of American culture, its diversity and multicultural context, and the ways people are unified by many values, practices, and traditions.

Students:

- know the roots of American culture, its development from many different traditions, and the ways many people from a variety of groups and backgrounds played a role in creating it

Multicultural "American" meal

HAMBURGER, BUN, KETCHUP, FRENCH FRIES, AND CHOCOLATE MILK OR DRAWING OF THIS MEAL; NOTE CARDS Have your child draw the following on separate note cards: a tomato, a potato, and a chocolate bar. On the back of each card, without your child seeing, write the words "the Americas." Next have your child sketch two more cards: wheat (draw either a bread loaf or wheat stalk) and cow. On the back of these, also without letting your child see, write the words "Western Europe." Turn all the cards so the illustrations are face up and place them on the table. Then together cook a meal with the ingredients listed in the materials. (Alternatively, sketch this meal on paper.) Before digging in, ask your child whether this meal appears typically "American" (as opposed say to Chinese, Mexican, or Italian). Discuss how this seemingly "American" meal would not have been possible without cross-cultural trade starting in the 16th century. When Europeans came to the Americas they introduced, among other things, cattle and wheat. (Imagine no one had ever had a hamburger or sandwich here before!) European sailors brought back tomatoes (Imagine Italian food had previously been made without tomatoes!) as well as chocolate, and potatoes. (Corn, peppers, peanuts, turkey, and tobacco also originated in the Americas.) Have your child match the illustrated card to the correct food on the plate and then identify where the ingredient originated, the Americas or Western Europe, turning over the card for verification.

- understand the basic ideals of American democracy as explained in the Declaration of Independence and the Constitution and other important documents

Declaration theater

✍ **WWW** *Together read "The Declaration of Independence" at http://lcweb2.loc.gov/const/declar.html. You can explore some of the earlier drafts and people involved in its writing at the online exhibition, "Declaring Independence: Drafting the Documents" at http://lcweb.loc. gov/exhibits/declara/declara1.html. You also will find relevant biographies of historical personalities in the colonies at http://web.uccs .edu/~history/index/colonial.html#afroam. Use these resources to write a skit together in which household members (or your child's friends) play key players in the historical event. Encourage the actors to use appropriate expression and pacing during their performance.*

■ explain those values, practices, and traditions that unite all Americans.

American values

📺 **WWW** *Together, watch the movie* To Kill a Mockingbird, *a moving tale about Atticus Finch, a lawyer and single parent in a small southern town during the Great Depression, who defends a black man accused of assaulting a white woman. The film, based on the Pulitzer Prize winning novel by Harper Lee, is a powerful way to explore the American ideals of democracy, respect, and consideration. Helpful background information and ideas for how to use the movie as a learning tool appear at http://www.teachwithmovies.org/guides/to-kill-a-mocking-bird.html. Your child should be able to articulate how the movie's themes relate broad American values.*

This is evident, for example, when students:

■ read stories about the early days of American society and discuss the way of life of those times

■ discuss how basic ideals of American democracy are shown in such speeches as Lincoln's Gettysburg Address and Martin Luther King's "I Have a Dream" speech

■ explain ways that families long ago expressed and transmitted their beliefs and values through oral traditions, literature, songs, art, religion, community celebrations, mementos, food, and language (Taken from National Standards for History for Grades K-4)

- compare the characters and events described in historical fiction with primary sources such as historic sites themselves; artifacts of the time found in museums and at state historic sites; journals, diaries, and photographs of the historical figures in stories; and news articles and other records from the period in order to judge the historical accuracy and determine the variety of perspectives included in the story. (Adapted from National Standards for History for Grades K-4).

2. Important ideas, social and cultural values, beliefs, and traditions from New York State and United States history illustrate the connections and interactions of people and events across time and from a variety of perspectives.

Students:

- gather and organize information about the traditions transmitted by various groups living in their neighborhood and community

What's in a name?

With your child, find streets, buildings, parks, and other public monuments in your neighborhood named for individuals who helped develop your community. Are any current traditions practiced today tied to these individuals or their heritage? Use the local library or historical society for your investigations, and then have your child create a drawn "walking" tour of the neighborhood, with a brief, legible description next to each stop that represents what you have discovered.

- recognize how traditions and practices were passed from one generation to the next

Past to the present

Ask your child to describe what makes his favorite toy most special. Then fully describe your own favorite plaything from childhood. Discuss if the examples share anything in common. How are they different—in terms of function, materials, technology, and so forth? (You might notice, for instance, that plastic has replaced wood, or electronic and computer technology exists now where it might not have in your toy.) Finally, have your child describe and illustrate a toy for the next generation. Discuss how your child's imaginary toy of the future is similar to toys of the past and present.

■ distinguish between near and distant past and interpret simple timelines.

Family timeline I

FAMILY PHOTOGRAPH ALBUM Create a timeline of the household with your child. First, for every member, write down on scrap paper the dates of important events (births, graduations, weddings, trips, arrival of pets, and so forth). Look through a family photograph album for inspiration. Together, transfer your notes onto a timeline created on a long sheet of plain paper. Place the events in the correct order, starting with the earliest one to the far left and working your way to the present at the end of the paper on the right. Have your child draw small illustrations for each event/person. Display the timeline and encourage other family members to add their own illustrations for events.

This is evident, for example, when students:

■ conduct interviews with family members, collect family memorabilia such as letters, diaries, stories, photographs, and keepsakes; classify information by type of activity: social, political, economic, cultural, or religious; discuss how traditions and practices were passed from one generation to the next; determine the extent to which the traditions and practices are shared by other members of the class

■ study the history and traditions of their neighborhoods and local communities. Consider the school and school community by describing who attends school (diversity, demographics); the histories of their schools and school communities (then and now); what was taught; and rights, rules, and responsibilities (then and now).

■ research the neighborhood or local community, considering location and the significance of its location; its demographics (e.g., ethnicity, languages, religions, levels of education, age groups); the history of why it was settled, when and by whom; economic patterns and changes in employment; social and cultural life; and government and politics

■ create personal and family timelines to distinguish between near and distant past and identify family origins; interpret simple timelines by recognizing correct chronological order of major events such as Native American settlement of North America, Columbus's voyage in 1492, the American Revolution, writing the Constitution, the presidency of Abraham Lincoln, World War I, and the beginning of space exploration.

Students will use a variety of intellectual skills to demonstrate their understanding of major ideas, eras, themes, developments, and turning points in the history of the United States and New York.

3. Study about the major social, political, economic, cultural, and religious developments in New York State and United States history involves learning about the important roles and contributions of individuals and groups.

Students:

■ gather and organize information about the important accomplishments of individuals and groups, including Native American Indians, living in their neighborhoods and communities

Native Americans then and now

WWW *The Iroquois, who call themselves the Haudenosaunee (People of the Longhouse), inhabited the land now part of upstate New York long before European contact. Together, learn about the people's past and current lives, as well as the original Native American sport of lacrosse at http://www.peace4turtleisland.org/. Additional information is available at http://lucy.ukc.ac.uk/EthnoAtlas/Hmar/Cult_dir/Culture.7849. With your child, investigate which native peoples first inhabited your area. Are there local sites that carry Native American names? If possible, attend public Native American festivals together. Your child should understand that many*

native people today uphold ancient customs but also are very much like everyone else. They are doctors, lawyers, teachers, students, artists, and so forth. Native children eat the same foods, wear the same sneakers, watch the same television shows, and listen to the same music as your child.

■ classify information by type of activity: social, political, economic, technological, scientific, cultural, or religious

I spy

First, discuss the following categories with your child: social (related to community life), political (related to the government), economic (related to money), cultural (related to the arts, materials, beliefs, and customs of a people). Now, as you walk or drive through the neighborhood, play a game with your child in which you identify items you see that reflect a certain type of activity. For instance, you might say, "I spy a mosque (or church or synagogue)." Your child then names one of the appropriate categories stated in the Standard—in this case "religion." You might then say, "I spy a post office," and your child would say "political," or "cultural" for movie theater, and so forth. Eventually, let your child both "spy" and categorize.

■ identify individuals who have helped to strengthen democracy in the United States and throughout the world.

Rosa Parks

WWW DIORAMA MATERIALS Read about Rosa Parks, the woman who changed the nation at http://www.grandtimes.com/rosa.html. Then read what other youngsters have said about her at http://www .leap.yale.edu/lclc/town/stand/rosa.html. Together, create a diorama of an important moment in Rosa Park's life that honors her contribution to American history.

This is evident, for example, when students:

■ listen to and participate in classroom debates and discussions of important events and people in U. S. history and New York history, and examine more than one viewpoint on some events and people

- discuss heroes, why some people are heroes, and why some individuals might be heroes to certain groups and not to others

- conduct a historical case study about an important environmental concern affecting their city's or neighborhood's water supply, housing accommodations, or transportation system, and examine competing views on the issues

- investigate the importance of scientific and technological inventions such as the compass, steam engine, internal combustion engine, and computer chip.

4. The skills of historical analysis include the ability to: explain the significance of historical evidence; weigh the importance, reliability, and validity of evidence; understand the concept of multiple causation; understand the importance of changing and competing interpretations of different historical developments.

Students:

- consider different interpretations of key events and/or issues in history and understand the differences in these accounts

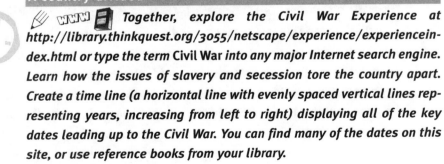

A country divided

Together, explore the Civil War Experience at http://library.thinkquest.org/3055/netscape/experience/experienceindex.html or type the term Civil War into any major Internet search engine. Learn how the issues of slavery and secession tore the country apart. Create a time line (a horizontal line with evenly spaced vertical lines representing years, increasing from left to right) displaying all of the key dates leading up to the Civil War. You can find many of the dates on this site, or use reference books from your library.

- explore different experiences, beliefs, motives, and traditions of people living in their neighborhoods, communities, and State

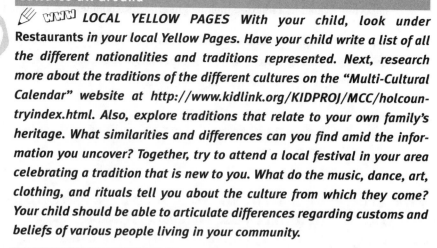

Cultures all around

✍ 🌐 *LOCAL YELLOW PAGES With your child, look under* Restaurants *in your local Yellow Pages. Have your child write a list of all the different nationalities and traditions represented. Next, research more about the traditions of the different cultures on the "Multi-Cultural Calendar" website at http://www.kidlink.org/KIDPROJ/MCC/holcountryindex.html. Also, explore traditions that relate to your own family's heritage. What similarities and differences can you find amid the information you uncover? Together, try to attend a local festival in your area celebrating a tradition that is new to you. What do the music, dance, art, clothing, and rituals tell you about the culture from which they come? Your child should be able to articulate differences regarding customs and beliefs of various people living in your community.*

■ view historic events through the eyes of those who were there, as shown in their art, writings, music, and artifacts.

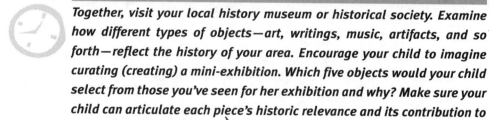

You be the curator

Together, visit your local history museum or historical society. Examine how different types of objects—art, writings, music, artifacts, and so forth—reflect the history of your area. Encourage your child to imagine curating (creating) a mini-exhibition. Which five objects would your child select from those you've seen for her exhibition and why? Make sure your child can articulate each piece's historic relevance and its contribution to the exhibition as a whole. ✍

This is evident, for example, when students:

■ read historical narratives, literature, and many kinds of documents and investigate building, tools, clothing, and artwork to explore key events and/or issues in the history of their city, community, neighborhood, state, and nation; summarize the main ideas evident in the source and identify the purpose or point of view from which the source was created; discuss how interpretations or perspectives develop and change as new information is learned. **(Based on National Standards for History Grades K-4)**

- visit historic sites, museums, libraries, and memorials to gather information about important events that affected their neighborhoods, communities, or region

- explore the literature, oral traditions, drama, art, architecture, music, dance, and other primary sources of a particular historic period.

Standard 2—World History

1. The study of world history requires an understanding of world cultures and civilizations, including an analysis of important ideas, social and cultural values, beliefs, and traditions. This study also examines the human condition and the connections and interactions of people across time and space and the ways different people view the same event or issue from a variety of perspectives.

Students:

- read historical narratives, myths, legends, biographies, and autobiographies to learn about how historical figures lived, their motivations, hopes, fears, strengths, and weaknesses

Intrepidly forward

COLLAGE MATERIALS, JUNK MAIL, PASTE, AND SCISSORS Together, watch The Autobiography of Miss Jane Pittman, a fictionalized account of one of the last surviving slaves from her childhood on a plantation, through Reconstruction, to the Civil Rights Movement of the early 1960s. Helpful background information and ideas for how to use the movie as a learning tool appear at http://www.teachwithmovies.org/guides/autobiography-of-miss-jane-pittman.html. After, have your child create a collage expressing Pittman's hopes, fears, strengths, and weaknesses. Your child should be able to articulate these aspects of the character when discussing his work.

■ explore narrative accounts of important events from world history to learn about different accounts of the past to begin to understand how interpretations and perspectives develop

Abigail and John Adams

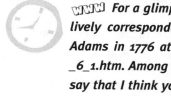

🕮 *For a glimpse of life during the American Revolution, explore the lively correspondence between Abigail Adams and her husband John Adams in 1776 at http://www.longman.awl.com/history/primarysource _6_1.htm. Among other poignant topics, Abigail Adams wrote, "I can not say that I think you very generous to the Ladies, for whilst you are proclaiming peace and good will to men, Emancipating all Nations, you insist upon retaining an absolute power over Wives." Together discuss what new insights you have about the American Revolution from reading these primary source documents. How do they "personalize" an event in history in a way that may not be possible through textbooks or history books?*

■ study about different world cultures and civilizations focusing on their accomplishments, contributions, values, beliefs, and traditions.

Asian online

🕮 *Explore a wide variety of topics about Japan and China on http://www.columbia.edu/itc/eacp/asiasite/askframe.htm. Explore the evidence of either of these cultures in your own lives. For instance, have you ever had Chinese food? (Including pasta, which was first invented by the Chinese not the Italians!) Have you ever seen folded paper artwork of oragami? Finally, read about famous Asian Americans in art, education, literature, religion and philosophy at http://www.ithaca.edu/library /htmls/humasia.html. Your child should be able to discuss the way some of these individuals have contributed to society.*

This is evident, for example, when students:

■ create a list of characteristics for the concept of civilization, focusing on the early civilizations that developed in Mesopotamia, Egypt, and the Indus Valley

- analyze pictures and maps of the civilizations of Kush and Egypt, including information about their architectural, artistic, and technological achievements

- assume the roles of citizens, merchants, foreign residents, or slaves in ancient

- Sparta or Athens, describing life in these city-states, the rights and responsibilities of a citizen in each city, and their social and political roles

- research different kinds of sources (archaeological, artistic, written) about the civilizations in the Americas before the coming of the Europeans (Taken from National Standards for World History)

- study about the major cultural achievements of an ancient civilization (e.g., West African, Japanese, Chinese, European).

2. Establishing time frames, exploring different periodizations, examining themes across time and within cultures, and focusing on important turning points in world history help organize the study of world cultures and civilizations.

Students:

- distinguish between past, present, and future time periods

History chronology

 Create separate note cards for events that occurred at different times in history. Select ones that will be familiar to your child (for example, age of the dinosaurs, invention of the telephone, computer technology, child's trip to the dentist, etc.). Then have your child put the cards in the correct order, from things that happened long ago to just yesterday. Explain that your child's life has a history, just like large world events. Ask your child to make a list of special memories or events in his life, beginning with his earliest special memory and working chronologically up to the present.

■ develop timelines that display important events and eras from world history

Family timeline II

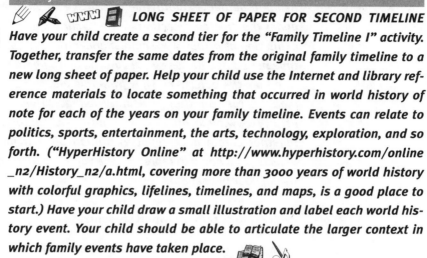 *LONG SHEET OF PAPER FOR SECOND TIMELINE Have your child create a second tier for the "Family Timeline I" activity. Together, transfer the same dates from the original family timeline to a new long sheet of paper. Help your child use the Internet and library reference materials to locate something that occurred in world history of note for each of the years on your family timeline. Events can relate to politics, sports, entertainment, the arts, technology, exploration, and so forth. ("HyperHistory Online" at http://www.hyperhistory.com/online _n2/History_n2/a.html, covering more than 3000 years of world history with colorful graphics, lifelines, timelines, and maps, is a good place to start.) Have your child draw a small illustration and label each world history event. Your child should be able to articulate the larger context in which family events have taken place.*

■ measure and understand the meaning of calendar time in terms of years, decades, centuries, and millennia, using BC and AD as reference points

Art time

 Together, explore the websites for some of the finest art museums throughout the world, using the list of sites provided by The Art Museum Network at http://www.amn.org/#. Encourage your child to examine art from as many different centuries as she can find. Print out pictures of images and objects that are especially interesting to your child, and note when each piece was made and its country of origin. Have your child place the images in chronological order on a counter, table, or the floor. Which pieces were made fairly close together in date (such as decades apart), and which ones are centuries or even millennia apart?

■ compare important events and accomplishments from different time periods in world history.

WWW PERSONAL OBJECTS REPRESENTING PEOPLE IN YOUR HOUSE-HOLD Together, explore the interactive, illustrated timeline of Africa under the "history" section in the "Smithsonian African Voices Virtual" exhibition at http://www.mnh.si.edu/africanvoices/. Select a particular time period and discuss what can you learn about traditional African culture from the objects on view from this era. Next, research similar information for another culture, using "HyperHistory Online" at http://www.hyperhistory.com/online_n2/History_n2/a.html. Finally, together curate a personal exhibition of your family, using symbolic objects from home to represent the values, beliefs, activities, and identities of your household.

This is evident, for example, when students:

■ **arrange the events in a historical narrative, biography, or autobiography in correct chronological order**

■ **group important historic events in world history according to clearly defined time periods (periodization). For example, periods might include early civilizations, rise of empires, age of exploration, the twentieth century**

■ **create, as part of a class, a mural-sized, illustrated timeline of important achievements, inventions, and accomplishments of nineteenth century Europe and America (Adapted from National Standards for World History)**

■ **identify key turning points and important events in world history and explain their significance**

■ **create personal and family timelines to distinguish between near and distant past and interpret simple timelines that show a progression of events in world history; create a picture timeline tracing developments in world history, such as the appearance of the wheel, making simple tools out of iron (Hittites), building the pyramids, building Roman aqueducts, inventing paper in China, astronomical discoveries in the Muslim world, metallurgy advances in West Africa, and the invention of the steam engine in England. (Adapted from National Standards for History for Grades K-4)**

Students will use a variety of intellectual skills to demonstrate their understanding of major ideas, eras, themes, developments, and turning points in world history and examine the broad sweep of history from a variety of perspectives.

3. Study of the major social, political, cultural, and religious developments in world history involves learning about the important roles and contributions of individuals and groups.

Students:

■ understand the roles and contributions of individuals and groups to social, political, economic, cultural, scientific, technological, and religious practices and activities

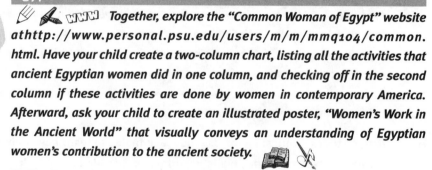

Egyptian women's world

✐ ✎ 🌐 *Together, explore the "Common Woman of Egypt" website at http://www.personal.psu.edu/users/m/m/mmq104/common. html. Have your child create a two-column chart, listing all the activities that ancient Egyptian women did in one column, and checking off in the second column if these activities are done by women in contemporary America. Afterward, ask your child to create an illustrated poster, "Women's Work in the Ancient World" that visually conveys an understanding of Egyptian women's contribution to the ancient society.*

■ gather and present information about important developments from world history

A day without print

🌐 *Together, explore the "Printing: History and Development" website at http://www.digitalcentury.com/encyclo/update/print.html. Discuss the impact of each technological development on society—who could read and write and who had access to books. Finally, have your child imagine what might happen if all printing disappeared for a day. What would it be like to go through a day without books, signs, adver-*

tisements, instruction manuals, product information, labels, and so forth? How would this affect communication, travel, entertainment, school, jobs, eating, shopping, advertising, and so forth?

- understand how the terms social, political, economic, and cultural can be used to describe human activities or practices.

Categorized day

 ✐ ▨ Discuss the following categories with your child, having him write each at the top of one of four vertical columns on a piece of paper: social (relating to community life), political (relating to the government), economic (relating to money), cultural (relating to the arts, materials, beliefs, and customs of a people). Together with your child, review today's newspaper, identify the category that applies to each story, and ask your child to note the topic of each story on the appropriate list. For example, your child would write the word "election" in the political column in response to a campaign story, or he would write "volunteers" in the social column for a story about a group of citizens involved in disaster relief. As you categorize the newspaper stories together, discuss which aspects of your daily lives would fall into each of these categories.

This is evident, for example, when students:

- read historical stories, myths, legends, and fables to learn how individuals have solved problems, made important contributions, and influenced the lives of others

- listen to historical narratives about the history of children and families in different cultures throughout the world to learn about different family structures; children's, women's, and men's roles; daily life; religious or spiritual beliefs and practices; customs and traditions

- read biographies about famous historical figures, focusing on their personal lives, goals, and accomplishments and the effects of their achievements on the lives of others

- write historical narratives in the form of letters, diary accounts, or news reports from the point of view of a child who lived during a particular historic time period and who witnessed an important event or development

■ listen to and participate in classroom debates and discussions of important myths, legends, people, and events in world history; determine admirable traits and identify examples of courage.

4. The skills of historical analysis include the ability to investigate differing and competing interpretations of the theories of history, hypothesize about why interpretations change over time, explain the importance of historical evidence, and understand the concepts of change and continuity over time.

Students:

■ consider different interpretations of key events and developments in world history and understand the differences in these accounts

Earliest history

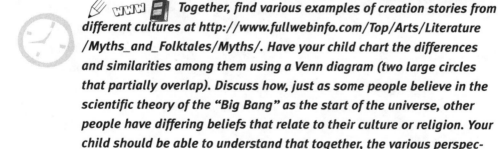 *Together, find various examples of creation stories from different cultures at http://www.fullwebinfo.com/Top/Arts/Literature /Myths_and_Folktales/Myths/. Have your child chart the differences and similarities among them using a Venn diagram (two large circles that partially overlap). Discuss how, just as some people believe in the scientific theory of the "Big Bang" as the start of the universe, other people have differing beliefs that relate to their culture or religion. Your child should be able to understand that together, the various perspectives provide a fascinating kaleidoscopic view on the possible beginnings of the world.*

■ explore the lifestyles, beliefs, traditions, rules and laws, and social/cultural needs and wants of people during different periods in history and in different parts of the world

Hispanic profiles

✍️ 🌐 *Together, read profiles from each of the categories listed in the "Famous Hispanics in the World and History" website at http://coloquio.com/famosos.html. Have your child select two of the profiles and together, conduct additional research on these two individuals, taking notes as you learn important details about their lives. Based on your research, conduct an imaginary dialogue between these individuals with each of you playing one of the roles. Be sure your child uses details from her research during this dialogue.*

■ view historic events through the eyes of those who were there, as shown in their art, writings, music, and artifacts.

Expanded Truth

🌐 *Together, examine the "Selected Civil War Photographs" website at http://memory.loc.gov/ammem/cwphome.html. The American Civil War was the first war documented by photography, which had just been invented. People who saw the images were horrified, believing them to be fully faithful documents of the deadly battles, hardship, and destruction. In truth, although the war was terrible, some of the photographers manipulated their images, moving dead soldiers and their guns to make the pictures look more dramatic. Together, take opposite sides of the argument about whether it was right for the photographers to manipulate their images in order to enhance their impact. Did the photographers do a good thing by shocking citizens with tragic photographs, since the soldiers fighting the war faced hardships and adversity daily? Or was it dishonest for the photographers to alter the scenes they photographed?*

This is evident, for example, when students:

■ explain different perspectives on the same phenomenon by reading myths from several civilizations, recognizing the different ways those people explained the same phenomenon (e.g., how the world was created)

- listen to historical stories, biographies, or narratives to identify who was n what events occurred, where the events took place, and the outcomes or consequences

- list analytical questions to guide their investigations of historical documents, pictures, diary accounts, artifacts, and other records of the past

- construct picture timelines that show important events in their own lives, including descriptions of the events and explanations of why they were important.

Standard 3—Geography

Students will use a variety of intellectual skills to demonstrate their understanding of the geography of the interdependent world in which we live—local, national, and global—including the distribution of people, places, and environments over the Earth's surface.

1. Geography can be divided into six essential elements which can be used to analyze important historic, geographic, economic, and environmental questions and issues. These six elements include: the world in spatial terms, places and regions, physical settings (including natural resources), human systems, environment and society, and the use of geography. (Adapted from The National Geography Standards 1994: Geography for Life)

Students:

- study about how people live, work, and utilize natural resources

Closet detective

Have your child imagine that he has been sent by a newspaper from another planet to write a story about daily life in your community. What can your child, as the investigative reporter, determine about people's

lives from all the items in your closets? What do the articles reveal about dress customs, work, recreation, and use of natural or manufactured resources? Have your child write an article for an imaginary newspaper about his discoveries. His article should feature a headline, an introductory paragraph presenting the central idea of the story, a supporting paragraph (or paragraphs) that includes details of his discoveries, and a concluding paragraph summarizing his ideas. Sentences should be complete, with correct grammar and punctuation, and words should be spelled correctly and used appropriately.

■ draw maps and diagrams that serve as representations of places, physical features, and objects .

Room map

COMPASS Have your child select a favorite room at home and draw a simple map, using a compass to indicate North, South, East, and West, and including symbols for particular objects (e.g., bed, closets, bookshelves.) Give the map to another household member and see if he or she can identify which room it is without being told.

■ locate places within the local community, State, and nation; locate the Earth's continents in relation to each other and to principal parallels and meridians. (Adapted from National Geography Standards, 1994)

Where did we begin?

Trace all the locations where your family has lived from as far back as you can remember through the generations on the interactive world map at "Maps.com: Online World Atlas" at http://www.maps.com/explore/atlas/physical/. The site allows you to click on any part of the world for more refined maps.

■ identify and compare the physical, human, and cultural characteristics of different regions and people (Adapted from National Geography Standards, 1994)

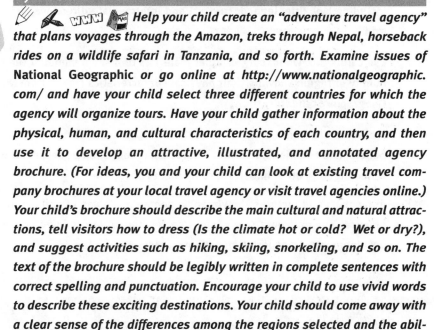 *Help your child create an "adventure travel agency" that plans voyages through the Amazon, treks through Nepal, horseback rides on a wildlife safari in Tanzania, and so forth. Examine issues of National Geographic or go online at http://www.nationalgeographic. com/ and have your child select three different countries for which the agency will organize tours. Have your child gather information about the physical, human, and cultural characteristics of each country, and then use it to develop an attractive, illustrated, and annotated agency brochure. (For ideas, you and your child can look at existing travel company brochures at your local travel agency or visit travel agencies online.) Your child's brochure should describe the main cultural and natural attractions, tell visitors how to dress (Is the climate hot or cold? Wet or dry?), and suggest activities such as hiking, skiing, snorkeling, and so on. The text of the brochure should be legibly written in complete sentences with correct spelling and punctuation. Encourage your child to use vivid words to describe these exciting destinations. Your child should come away with a clear sense of the differences among the regions selected and the ability to articulate this both in writing and art.*

■   **investigate how people depend on and modify the physical environment.**

 Walk or drive around your neighborhood and have your child identify and describe the human and physical characteristics that help distinguish your locale. Is it noisy or quiet? Crowded or spacious? Is it mostly grass and trees or sidewalks and buildings? Is there something (a building, mountain, or river) that she feels particularly captures the characteristics of your home area?

This is evident, for example, when students:

■   **draw simple maps of their communities or regions showing the major landmarks, industries, residential areas, business districts, transportation networks, health and educational facilities, and recreation areas**

- examine different kinds of maps to identify and define their components, including key, title, legend, cardinal and intermediate directions, scale, and grid

- use cardboard, wood, clay, or other materials to make a model of their community or region showing their physical characteristics (Taken from National Geography Standards, 1994)

- read about children living in other cultures to learn about their customs, beliefs, and traditions; natural resource use; food; shelter; socialization and schooling; and other important components of culture

- draw maps and pictures showing how people make use of and modify their physical environments (e.g., land use for agriculture, mining, residential developments, transportation networks, recreation).

2. Geography requires the development and application of the skills of asking and answering geographic questions; analyzing theories of geography; and acquiring, organizing, and analyzing geographic information. (Adapted from: The National Geography Standards, 1994: Geography for Life)

Students:

- ask geographic questions about where places are located; why they are located where they are; what is important about their locations; and how their locations are related to the location of other people and places (Adapted from National Geography Standards, 1994).

Family locations

 Have your child examine an atlas to find the latitude and longitude of your town, as well as the place you and your parents (your child's grandparents) grew up.

- gather and organize geographic information from a variety of sources and display in a number of ways

Athletic geography

Together with your child, identify three favorite athletes who were born outside of the United States. (In addition to baseball, basketball, hockey, football, and soccer players, don't forget marathon runners, tennis players, and participants in the Olympic competitions.) Help your child research the geographic location of each athlete's country of origin using a world map or the "Online World Atlas" site at http://www.maps.com/explore/atlas/physical/. Have your child create a mini exhibition about each athlete's country, using charts, maps, posters, and so forth.

◼ analyze geographic information by making relationships, interpreting trends and relationships, and analyzing geographic data. (Adapted from National Geography Standards, 1994)

Hot and cold lands

On a globe or a map of the world, have your child locate the equator. Ask, "If places along the equator are the warmest on earth, then which areas on the map would likely be the coldest?" As a hint, you might mention which areas are the farthest away from this warm zone (North and South Poles). If your child believes the South Pole would be warm because it is "south," view pictures of the South Pole at http://astro.uchicago.edu/cara/vtour/pole/. Next, locate your own home's region on the map and discuss its weather in relation to the equator and poles. What other locations on the map likely experience similar temperatures to where you live?

This is evident, for example, when students:

◼ read historical narratives and talk about the importance of where places are located, try to determine why they are located where they are, and assess the relationship of location to other locations and people in the story

◼ use a map grid (e.g., latitude and longitude or an alphanumerical system) to answer questions about location and place

- use different types of map scales (linear, fractional, and word) to measure the distance between two places

- map the locations of places in the community or region, using appropriate symbols (e.g., dots or points for cities and towns; different shapes for residential and business areas; lines for transportation networks)

- present oral and written reports using maps, charts, tables, graphs, and other visual displays showing spatial relationships, locations, and other geographic information.

Standard 4—Economics

1. **The study of economics requires an understanding of major economic concepts and systems, the principles of economic decision making, and the interdependence of economies and economic systems throughout the world.**

Students:

- know some ways individuals and groups attempt to satisfy their basic needs and wants by utilizing scarce resources

Every drop counts

 GLOBE TAPE Ask your child if there is more water or land on Earth as you both examine a globe or world atlas for visual clues. Although Earth has more water than land, only about one percent of the water on the planet is usable for cooking, drinking, bathing, and growing crops. The rest is salty or frozen. Water conservation is very important. Together with your child, brainstorm ways your household can help out. (For example, turn the faucet off after wetting a toothbrush rather than letting it run while brushing; don't linger in the shower; fix leaky faucets; fill the kitchen sink with dirty dishes and soak, rather than running water

while cleaning each one individually; run only full loads in washers and dishwashers.) Encourage your child to create illustrated signs for all her ideas and then display them in the appropriate locations to remind household members to help in the conservation effort.

■ explain how people's wants exceed their limited resources and that this condition defines scarcity

Keeping stock

Explore the concept of supply and demand on your next trip to the grocery store. Together, study the inventory at your local supermarket, paying special attention to categories where a lot of merchandise is displayed—peanut butter, breakfast cereal, ice cream, bread—and categories where very little merchandise is displayed—specialized gourmet foods. Ask your child what would happen if everyone in the neighborhood stopped eating peanut butter sandwiches and started eating anchovy paste sandwiches instead. What would happen to the store's inventory of these products? If your child was the store manager, would he change the number of supplies previously ordered for each of these goods? Ask the store manager if there has ever been a situation where customer demand exceeded store supply—rock salt during a snowstorm; batteries and candles during an electrical blackout; charcoal briquettes during cookout season, etc. Now, ask your child to consider the opposite scenario: would he stop shopping at this store and shop elsewhere if it no longer sold certain products?

■ know that scarcity requires individuals to make choices and that these choices involve costs

Recycled costs

Have your child imagine running a recycled paper goods store, where the napkins, paper towels, tissue paper, and toilet paper are all environmentally safe products made out of 100 percent recycled goods. Explain that recycled goods are usually more expensive than regular commercial brands because they are more expensive to produce. Ask your child to create an attractive illustrated sign for the store window that will convince people that it's worth buying these products, even though the cost is slightly higher. The sign should clearly present information on what scarce resources (forests, for instance) are being saved by the extra money they are spending. You and your child can visit your local health food store and examine existing recycled paper goods for ideas as well.

- study about how the availability and distribution of resources is important to a nation's economic growth

- understand how societies organize their economies to answer three fundamental economic questions: What goods and services shall be produced and in what quantities ? How shall goods and services be produced?

Young entrepreneur

Ask your child to imagine setting up two types of businesses. One will sell goods and another will sell services. Brainstorm what kind of goods your child might be able to make to sell (cookies or lemonade, for example). What kind of service might your child think of offering to make money (newspaper delivery, dog walking, baby-sitting, errand running, for instance)? For each example, have your child identify who is the producer (himself) and who would be the consumer (neighbors, family, and so forth). When you run errands together, have your child note whether you are buying goods or services, and who is the consumer and who is the producer in each instance.

- For whom shall goods and services be produced?

- investigate how production, distribution, exchange, and consumption of goods and services are economic decisions with which all societies and nations must deal.

Lemonade for sale

MATERIALS FOR SETTING UP A LEMONADE STAND Use the creation of a lemonade stand to explore the issue of production and consumption. Ask your child to fully consider how the weather, location of the stand, price, and resources—such as number of lemons, glasses, and so forth—will

affect her business. After the venture, discuss what further insight your child gained about production and consumption from the experience. How might she amend the endeavor next time to make it more successful?

This is evident, for example, when students:

■ role-play a family or group situation in which group members make an economic decision about whether to purchase a new car, plan a family or group trip, or invest the money

■ discuss the differences between capital, human, and natural resources and classify pictures of each resource type in the appropriate category

■ use map symbols to locate and identify natural resources found in different regions of the United States and in other countries in the Western Hemisphere

■ identify several personal as well as family buying choices, list their associated costs and benefits, and explain how and why particular decisions are/have been made; clarify how prices and one's own values influence individual and family decision making

■ describe the characteristics of at least two of the following economic units: a family, a worker, a small business, a labor union, a large corporation, a government agency (local, state, or national); identify the kinds of economic choices each economic unit must make and explain the positive and negative results of at least one choice

■ organize information based on interviews of a laborer, a service provider, a small business owner, a banker, a business executive, an elected government official, or a government employee to identify how individuals produce and distribute goods and services, why individuals make the kinds of decisions they make, and how individuals describe the effects of their decisions on others

■ observe economic characteristics of places; draw conclusions about how people in families, schools, and communities all over the world must depend on others to help them meet their needs and wants.

Students will use a variety of intellectual skills to demonstrate their understanding of how the United States and other societies develop economic systems and associated institutions to allocate scarce resources, how major decision-making units function in the U.S. and other national economies, and how an economy solves the scarcity problem through market and nonmarket mechanisms.

2. Economics requires the development and application of the skills needed to make informed and well-reasoned economic decisions in daily and national life.

Students:

■ locate economic information, using card catalogues, computer databases, indices, and library guides

More than coins

WWW *Together explore the "Artistry of African Currency" on the online Smithsonian exhibition at http://www.si.edu/nmafa/exhibits/site/metal.htm, which examines cloth, tools, metal, jewelry, and their economic role in traditional African societies. Discuss what kind of "currency" your family sometimes uses besides coins and bills. Has your child ever bartered for something with candy, toys, or promises to do chores? Has your child ever received permission to stay up late as "payment" for a good deed? Your child should understand that "currency" in all cultures can take many forms, not just government-issued coins and bills.*

■ collect economic information from textbooks, standard references, newspapers, periodicals, and other primary and secondary sources

Sports arena I

✍ WWW Have your child imagine developing a campaign to convince the local community that it is economically wise to build a new sports arena. Call or visit a local stadium or arena, conduct research online, or write to the stadium's public relations office to obtain the following infor-

mation: What is the seating capacity of the stadium? How much money does a hot dog and soda cost? How much does parking cost? (If you are unable to obtain this information through research, invent realistic hypothetical numbers.) Next have your child tabulate the sales in the arena, on average, per game by adding up the cost per person (seat, food, drink) and multiplying it by the number of seats in the arena. (For this activity, assume every game is a sellout.) Now calculate the amount of sales from parking by assuming that only 35 percent of the arena attendees pay for parking—the others are either passengers or arrive by public transportation. Now have your child combine these two amounts and multiply them by the number of games played in the arena each season. (Again, make a rough estimate if real numbers aren't available.) Proceed to the next part of the Standard. 1 2 3

■ make hypotheses about economic issues and problems, testing, refining, and eliminating hypotheses and developing new ones when necessary

Sports arena II

Help your child make hypotheses about the amount of money that a new sports arena might bring into the area, using the information from Part I. Help your child make decisions about the seating capacity for the new arena (Should it be bigger? Smaller?), parking capacity, and special features to attract more visitors (Replace hot dogs with more expensive tacos? Sell banners and puffy fingers?). Discuss how greater attendance at the arena might benefit the surrounding community—more customers at local restaurants and gas stations, more job opportunities at the stadium, etc. Help your child keep building and refining a case for the new sports arena and proceed to the next step. 1 2 3

■ present economic information by developing charts, tables, diagrams, and simple graphs.

Sports arena III

Have your child create graphs, posters, tables, diagrams, and so forth for a visual and oral presentation to "local community leaders" (friends and household members). Your child should be able to use the information gathered to support his proposal in a confident, articulate manner.

This is evident, for example, when students:

■ collect and discuss newspaper articles about economic issues and problems affecting their community, region, or the State

■ design a display board showing how they might acquire and spend income

■ research a local industry to determine what it produces, how it makes this product, its distribution system, and how the finished product is marketed

■ analyze a set of graphs or tables showing selected imports and exports for the United States to make hypotheses about what

■ might happen if these imports or exports increase or decrease in value

■ use a variety of textbooks and news articles to identify a list of potential economic problems or issues facing the United States or other nations in the Western Hemisphere. Working in groups, brainstorm a list of possible solutions, the potential effects of these solutions, and rank order the solutions in terms of their likelihood of success.

Standard 5—Civics, Citizenship, and Government

1. **The study of civics, citizenship, and government involves learning about political systems; the purposes of government and civic life; and the differing assumptions held by people across time and place regarding power, authority, governance, and law. (Adapted from The National Standards for Civics and Government, 1994)**

Students:

■ know the meaning of key terms and concepts related to government, including democracy, power, citizenship, nation-state, and justice

Lawless havoc

Have your child tell a story about your neighborhood if all the laws were suspended one day. What might it be like in stores, restaurants, on the streets, in cars, on public transportation, and the like? Use the tale as the basis for a discussion about why there are laws that everyone must obey and consequences for violating them. Explore how certain rules in your household keep order as well. Ask your child to suggest a new law for your neighborhood or household, and discuss whether this new law would meet the criteria of existing laws—to preserve order, safety, and fairness.

■ explain the probable consequences of the absence of government and rules

■ describe the basic purposes of government and the importance of civic life

Democratic dessert

Gather household members together and offer them a choice of one of two desserts you will serve at dinner (for instance, cake or fruit). Have your child explain that to be fair, each person in the family will get a single vote, and whichever dessert gets the most votes, will win. Ask your child to oversee the voting, tabulating, and announcement of results.

- understand that social and political systems are based upon people's beliefs

- discuss how and why the world is divided into nations and what kinds of governments other nations have.

This is evident, for example, when students:

You rule

Explain the definition of a <u>monarchy</u> to your child (a nation or a state ruled completely by a single person). You can use kings and queens in fairy tales or other books your child has read as examples. Next, explain a <u>republic</u>, where citizens vote for elected officials who are responsible to them. Ask which type of system is used in the United States. Finally, have your child imagine she is going to be a leader, either a monarch or elected official. Which would she choose to be? You should take the opposite choice of your child. Now both of you should try to persuade the other that your choice is best, speaking about the advantages of your choice and disadvantages of the other person's selection.

- create a chart on newsprint listing the reasons for creating governments and the reasons why all groups and societies create rules and laws

- create a class constitution and develop class rules

- role-play a day without rules or laws

- collect and discuss newspaper cartoons dealing with rules and laws

- compile a list of different nations of the world and identify the type of government each nation has

- compare governmental structures of the United States and Canada, and selected nations of Latin America

- hold a mock trial focusing on situations that embody such concepts as fairness, justice, or equality.

2. The state and federal governments established by the Constitutions of the United States and the Stateof New York embody basic civic values (such as justice, honesty, self-discipline, due process, equality,majority rule with respect for minority rights, and respect for self, others, and property), principles, and practices and establish a system of shared and limited government. (Adapted from The National Standards for Civics and Government, 1994)

Students:

■ explain how the Constitutions of New York State and the United States and the Bill of Rights are the basis for democratic values in the United States.

■ understand the basic civil values that are the foundation of American constitutional democracy

Inalienable rights of the Synpies

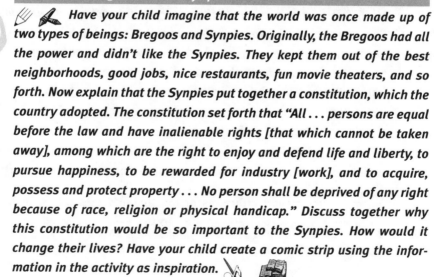

Have your child imagine that the world was once made up of two types of beings: Bregoos and Synpies. Originally, the Bregoos had all the power and didn't like the Synpies. They kept them out of the best neighborhoods, good jobs, nice restaurants, fun movie theaters, and so forth. Now explain that the Synpies put together a constitution, which the country adopted. The constitution set forth that "All . . . persons are equal before the law and have inalienable rights [that which cannot be taken away], among which are the right to enjoy and defend life and liberty, to pursue happiness, to be rewarded for industry [work], and to acquire, possess and protect property . . . No person shall be deprived of any right because of race, religion or physical handicap." Discuss together why this constitution would be so important to the Synpies. How would it change their lives? Have your child create a comic strip using the information in the activity as inspiration.

■ know what the United States Constitution is and why it is important. (Adapted from The National Standards for Civics and Government, 1994)

Founding dads

✍ 🌐 *Together explore the biographies of the delegates to the "Constitutional Convention of 1787" at http://www.nara.gov/exhall /charters/constitution/confath.html. Click on representatives from your state to learn more about these men. Together, use the information to create a skit in which your state's delegates present the United States Constitution to people at home, convincing them to support the document. When preparing and rehearsing the skit, encourage your child to use proper diction and maintain good posture. During the final performance, your child should speak clearly and audibly and make eye contact with the audience.* 📖 🎬

■ **understand that the United States Constitution and the Constitution of the State of New York are written plans for organizing the functions of government**

New York State Constitution

🌐 *Examine various articles of the New York State Constitution at http://www.harbornet.com/rights/newyork.txt. Ask what the constitution covers that is surprising to your child (possibly labor relations or transportation). Have your child articulate why it might be important for each state, rather than the federal government, to regulate certain issues. For instance, why might this be so in terms of labor relations? (Consider how the variation from state to state of type of industry, labor supply, economy, and so forth might affect state laws.)*

■ **understand the structure of New York State and local governments, including executive, legislative, and judicial branches**

Who's on first?

✍ 📰 *When you read the local newspaper, show your child photographs of elected officials—the mayor, congressman, and so forth—and discuss his or her job. Encourage your child to create a gallery of politicians by cutting out newspaper photos, labeling them with each individual's name and position, and displaying them together. Over the next few days, see if your child can begin to identify the pictures of these individuals in the paper herself and recall their role in government. Ask your child which of these offices she might want to run for personally and why. How might your child want to affect the political life of your state or community?*

■ identify their legislative and executive representatives at the local, state, and national governments. (Adapted from The National Standards for Civics and Government, 1994)

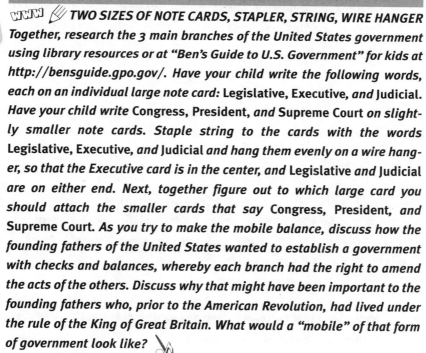

Checks and balance mobile

WWW *TWO SIZES OF NOTE CARDS, STAPLER, STRING, WIRE HANGER Together, research the 3 main branches of the United States government using library resources or at "Ben's Guide to U.S. Government" for kids at http://bensguide.gpo.gov/. Have your child write the following words, each on an individual large note card:* Legislative, Executive, *and* Judicial. *Have your child write* Congress, President, *and* Supreme Court *on slightly smaller note cards. Staple string to the cards with the words* Legislative, Executive, *and* Judicial *and hang them evenly on a wire hanger, so that the Executive card is in the center, and* Legislative *and* Judicial *are on either end. Next, together figure out to which large card you should attach the smaller cards that say* Congress, President, *and* Supreme Court. *As you try to make the mobile balance, discuss how the founding fathers of the United States wanted to establish a government with checks and balances, whereby each branch had the right to amend the acts of the others. Discuss why that might have been important to the founding fathers who, prior to the American Revolution, had lived under the rule of the King of Great Britain. What would a "mobile" of that form of government look like?*

This is evident, for example, when students:

■ create a list of basic civic values and discuss how these can best be modeled on the personal and classroom level

■ create a chart comparing the organization of local, state, and federal governments

- given a list of local, county, state, and national leaders, determine which are elected and which are appointed

- identify those branches of government responsible for making, enforcing, and interpreting local, state, and national laws

- compare and contrast New York State government with the federal government by creating charts of each level

- simulate or role-play an activity dealing with the functions of the branches of government

- create a timeline that charts events leading up to the writing of the Declaration of Independence and the United States Constitution.

Students will use a variety of intellectual skills to demonstrate their understanding of the necessity for establishing governments; the governmental system of the U.S. and other nations; the U.S. Constitution; the basic civic values of American constitutional democracy; and the roles, rights, and responsibilities of citizenship, including avenues of participation.

3. Central to civics and citizenship is an understanding of the roles of the citizen within American constitutional democracy and the scope of a citizen's rights and responsibilities.

Students:

- understand that citizenship includes an awareness of the holidays, celebrations, and symbols of our nation

Singing of America

Sing different songs that express American ideals (for example, "America the Beautiful," "The Star Spangled Banner," "This Land is Your Land," "My Country 'Tis of Thee," "You're a Grand Old Flag," "I'm a Yankee Doodle Dandy") and try having your child make up new verses to express her own feelings and ideas about the country.

- examine what it means to be a good citizen in the classroom, school, home, and community

- identify and describe the rules and responsibilities students have at home, in the classroom, and at school Get involved Together, explore all the different ways for individuals to participate in and add to society. Brainstorm specific ways to become involved in civic improvement (neighborhood associations, community or school boards), political activities (local canvassing or fund raising), and community service (volunteering). Select one activity you can do together to contribute to your local area.

- examine the basic principles of the Declaration of Independence and the Constitutions of the United States and New York State

Rewriting the Constitution

✍ WWW Together read the "Constitution for the United States of America" at http://constitution.by.net/. Then both you and your child should separately rewrite the Preamble, an Article, or one of the Amendments in your own words. Read one another's versions and make suggestions on how to revise and clarify them. Share your renditions with other members of the household. 📖

- understand that effective, informed citizenship is a duty of each citizen, demonstrated by jury service, voting, and community service

You elect

✍ ✎ Have your child nominate a model citizen, as outlined in the Standard, for a "Model Citizen Hall of Fame." The person can be a sports, entertainment, or historical figure, or a person who lives in your community. Have your child create a poster for the person that would convince others to vote for him or her. Other members of the household can participate in this activity as well, and then you can "vote" as a group on whether to induct these individuals into your family's "Model Citizen Hall of Fame." 📖 ✍

- identify basic rights that students have and those that they will acquire as they age.

www *Together, visit "Youth Summits" at http://www.civicmind .com/summits.»htm, a website listing engaging projects across the country in which students explore the political and legal issues that affect them. Investigate how many of the groups are addressing problems of violence. In particular, have your child read a description of one event at http://www.abanet.org/publiced/youth/tab18.html and identify which Constitutional right the student was defending (freedom of speech).*

This is evident, for example, when students:

- interview or survey adults in the community to identify some ways they participate in political action, voluntary activities, or community service

- draft a classroom charter, a constitution, or a set of laws that defines a code of conduct

- discuss and agree on a classroom charter and compare it to the United Nations Convention on the Rights of the Child

- use dramatic play with puppets to investigate the consequences of breaking a rule (e.g., a child arrives home late for dinner)

- make pages for a big book for each holiday

- understand the significance of and recite the Pledge of Allegiance

- discuss the colors of the American flag and make personal flags as symbols of themselves

- examine the flags of other nations

- undertake a mock trial based on themes from classroom books.

4. The study of civics and citizenship requires the abi lity to probe ideas and assumptions, ask and answer analytical questions, take a skeptical attitude toward questionable arguments, evaluate evidence, formulate rational conclusions, and develop and refine participatory skills.

Students:

■ show a willingness to consider other points of view before drawing conclusions or making judgments

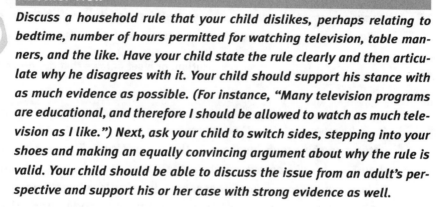

Another view

Discuss a household rule that your child dislikes, perhaps relating to bedtime, number of hours permitted for watching television, table manners, and the like. Have your child state the rule clearly and then articulate why he disagrees with it. Your child should support his stance with as much evidence as possible. (For instance, "Many television programs are educational, and therefore I should be allowed to watch as much television as I like.") Next, ask your child to switch sides, stepping into your shoes and making an equally convincing argument about why the rule is valid. Your child should be able to discuss the issue from an adult's perspective and support his or her case with strong evidence as well.

■ participate in activities that focus on a classroom, school, or community issue or problem

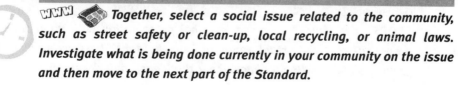

Problem busting I

Together, select a social issue related to the community, such as street safety or clean-up, local recycling, or animal laws. Investigate what is being done currently in your community on the issue and then move to the next part of the Standard.

■ suggest alternative solutions or courses of action to hypothetical or historic problems

Problem busting II

After reviewing what is or has been done in your community related to your child's topic, have your child brainstorm alternative measures. Go for broke, thinking of outrageous solutions with a wild imagination. Have your child write them down on paper. At this stage it does not matter if the ideas are feasible or not. Help your child understand that problems are rarely solved by first taking into account the inherent limitations of solutions. Then move to the next step.

■ evaluate the consequences for each alternative solution or course of action

Problem busting III

Discuss each of the scenarios your child suggested, having your child write the pros and cons next to each possible solution, and then move on.

■ prioritize the solutions based on established criteria

Problem busting IV

Now, have your child either present or imagine presenting these alternatives to the group involved in the issue. How will your child order them? What will be the criteria—their cost, time factors, feasibility? Before moving to the final phase, have your child rehearse her presentation, being aware of diction, presentation style, and physical gestures.

■ propose an action plan to address the issue of how to solve the problem.

Problem busting V

PROPS Have your child make her final presentation with appropriate props, either to the actual group, or household members acting as the group. Ask for gentle feedback about the ideas, their development, and your child's delivery.

This is evident, for example, when students:

■ brainstorm a list of alternative solutions for a real classroom or school problem

- write letters to the local paper suggesting preferred alternatives in a local issue

- develop a historic walking tour of the neighborhood or community

- role-play the main characters involved in an actual community controversy, attempting to generate alternatives in their roles

- create a school newspaper or school-wide gallery showing student and faculty works of art

- debate topics important to students

- hold a mock trial including witnesses, attorneys, jurors and a judge.